AKWESASNE
Divided by more than the St. Lawrence River

Ernest R. Rugenstein PhD

AKWESASNE
Divided by more than the St. Lawrence River

A FICTION4ALL PAPERBACK

© Copyright 2019
Ernest R. Rugenstien PhD

The right of Ernest R. Rugenstein to be identified as author and channel of this work has been asserted by him in accordance with the Copyright, Designs and Patents Act 1988.

All Rights Reserved

No reproduction, copy or transmission of the publication may be made without written permission.

No paragraph of this publication may be reproduced, copied or transmitted save with the written permission of the publisher, or in accordance with the provisions of the Copyright Act 1956 (as amended).

Any person who does any unauthorised act in relation to this publication may be liable to criminal prosecution and civil claims for damages.

ISBN: 978-1-78695-240-0

This Edition
Published 2019
Fiction4All
www.fiction4all.com

Cover Design:

Table of Contents

AKWESASNE 1

Ernest R. Rugenstein PhD 3

AKWESASNE 3

BOOK DEDICATION 9

PREFACE 11

ACKNOWLEDGMENTS 15

INTRODUCTION: 17

CHAPTER 1 21

   Understanding the Politics and Institutions at Akwesasne 21

   Akwesasne Governmental Institutions 23

   The United States and Akwesasne 27

   Canada & Akwesasne 29

   State and Provincial Institutions and Jurisdictions 32

   The Complex Structure of Authorities and Control 34

CHAPTER 2 36

   The Past at Akwesasne 36

   Prologue of Troubles: The Garrow Trial 36

   Mrs. P.L. (Annie) Garrow 42

CHAPTER 3 68

   The Activism of the 60's, 70's and the 1980's .. 68

   Warriors 83

Smuggling 85

CHAPTER 4 97
The Gnashing of Nations 97
Clashing at the Casino 101
Referendum and the Results 118

CHAPTER 5 132
Cops, Culture, and Conflicts 132
The Ferociousness of Borderlands 142
Conflicts and Convictions 151
May Day 157

CHAPTER 6 165
Ganienkeh, Oka, Warriors, and the Governor. 165
A Change or A Coup? 191
Oka and the Warriors 199
Epilogue of the Troubles 207

CHAPTER 7 211
A System Analysis of Cultures and the Uprising 211
A Look at the Internal System 212
The External Pressure on the System 221
A System Analysis of the Uprising 228
CONCLUSION: 237
An Event that Changed the Course of History 237

APPENDIX 1: RESEARCH 241
Document Research 241

Uprising Resources 241
Sovereignty and Gambling Resources 246
Resources on the American Indian Movement 258
APPENDIX 2: OTHER SOURCES 264
BIBLIOGRAPHY 266

List of Figures
Figure 1: Map of Akwesasne and Surrounding Area
Figure 2: Jurisdictional Map of Akwesasne
Figure 3: Reservation of the St. Regis Indians 1890
Figure 4: Ontario Hydro Blueprint 1958
Figure 5: Akwesasne Cigarette Smuggling Routes
Figure 6: Map of Akwesasne Roads
Figure 7: Conflict between NYSP and Mohawks
Figure 8: Anti-Gambling Roadblock
Figure 9: NYSP Examine Bullet Marks

BOOK DEDICATION

This book is dedicated to Esther M. Bonaparte. The picture on the front cover is her christening day photograph. She was born October 24, 1914, to Agnes Cree and Frank Cook of Akwesasne. The picture is exemplary of the dichotomy she grew up with. She is dressed in her Roman Catholic christening gown and swaddled on a Native cradleboard. It shows her growing up in "Mohawk" culture and living in an English world. At one point in her life, she married a white man but never was seen equal to whites.

She was a member of the St. Lucy's Catholic Church in Syracuse, NY and a member of the Kateri Tekawitha Circle. Additionally, she was a founding member of the North American Indian Club of Syracuse

On October 9, 2005, Esther Margaret Bonaparte passed away at the age of 90 years old. Her children include Joyce (the late Richard) Kelso of Ogdensburg, Honora Anne Bonaparte, Gary (Jessica) Bonaparte of Syracuse, Sheree Peachy (Richard Skidders) Bonaparte, Tami Bonaparte of Akwesasne and daughter in-law, Helen Falcone. Loving grandmother of Keli, Rick, Arron, Jason, Erich, Cheavee, Tasha, Tara, Ahtkwiroton, Stephanie, Ietsistohkwaroroks, Matthew, Ciele, Konwahontsiawi, Karonhiotha, Adam, Zoo, DonJon, Iaonhawinon, Tehrenhniserakhas, Taylor, Ienonkwatsheriiostha, Colton, Cheya, Sako. Ella,

Marcey, Elcey, Jasper, Maverick, Darryl, and Havoc; and 23 great-grandchildren. She is survived by many nieces, nephews, relatives, and friends. Predeceased by her husband, Hubert Bonaparte and former husband, William Brenno; two sons, Allen and John Bonaparte; one grandson, Daryl Bonaparte; one granddaughter, Katsi-bear; five sisters, Louise Bigtree, Theresa Cree, Mae Syron, Harriett Sielawa and Ann Barnes; one brother, and Tom Cook.

One last important note, Esther was an avid New York Yankee Fan!

PREFACE

As I was preparing to write my dissertation there were two areas I was interested in. One was the minority population of Germans living in Poland after World War Two, the other was the Mohawks of Akwesasne and their interaction with the federal governments that surround them. The thrust of this book is one close to my heart. It comes from a combination of being a Cultural Historian, the fact that my wife and her extended family are Mohawk with many still living at Akwesasne, and finally my affinity for those cultures being oppressed by more powerful cultures.

I have always loved history even at a young age and I think it's because I like stories. Many times, I encounter students that will tell me, "they don't like history," or that it's "boring." I tell them that history is just that, a story. As in any account of any story, there are main characters, plots and sub-plots, and in most cases the perception of good and bad. The history of the division at Akwesasne is such a story. I have a deep interest in the history of different cultures. In particular, the minority culture that is enveloped within a major culture.

In 1989-1990 my family and I were living outside Ogdensburg, NY. The conflicts occurring at Akwesasne consumed the interest of everyone in the North Country. Roads had to be blocked and detours were needed to get from Massena to Malone, NY. My wife's extended family, being from Akwesasne gave me a unique insight into the impact of the event. The occurrences were discussed at the time with family members who often spoke about the effect it had on families on and off the reservation. Part of my family was involved also. My sister used to charter tours with *Peter Pan Bus Lines* from Rochester, NY to the *Mohawk Bingo Palace* at Akwesasne. We visited with my sister and brother-in-law at Flanders Inn in Massena, NY. This is where the excursion group would stay each night and then be shuttled each day to the reservation. My sister told me how she would advertise, charter the bus and would get the group together. The Reservation was the closest gambling opportunities at the time. People would come to Akwesasne from Rochester and Syracuse, NY and Ottawa, Ontario as well as other locations in the region. At times gun fire would erupt and busses were fired upon. Not everyone on both sides of the reservation embraced the new gambling on the one US side. Being connected to these events in so many different ways, the fact that different cultures were involved, and the historic significance of the event all piqued my historical curiosity.

The separation of the Mohawks of Akwesasne begins in a practical way beginning in the Nineteenth Century. Their reservation was "legally" divided after the War of 1812 because of the Jay Treaty. The Mohawks still suffer from being divided by two national governments and three provincial/state governments. Tribal governmental systems are imposed on either side of the border by the paternalistic United States and Canadian governments. This imposition has divided the Mohawks of Akwesasne by more than just the St. Lawrence River but by borders imposed upon them.

This book is a reflection of what occurred in 1989 -1990 at Akwesasne and the history that propelled those events. It starts with Mrs. Annie Garrow walking down the road about two miles from her house on the south shore of the St. Lawrence River to Hogansburg, NY. A trip she had made many times. She was carrying some baskets to sell. Her walk never took her off the reservation, she didn't have to cross the river. But she crossed a border that was imposed upon the Mohawks. It would lead to a US Supreme court and start a situation that eventually leads to the 1989-1990 uprising the Mohawks found themselves in.

Some have said that this was just a Mohawk Civil War, others have said that it was a squabble amongst the Mohawks over who was making money and who was controlling it. The book proposes that a system that was imposed on the Mohawks failed. If the Natives had their traditional government or at the very least a unified government that governed the entire territory, I predict this would never have escalated to the point of destruction and death. However, with the territory divided, two different governments and five administrative districts enforcing laws, the outcome was violence.

In general, no race, creed. or color has been more oppressed or had genocide committed against them as the Native American of the Americas. From the 15th century to the 18th century 95% of the Native population was exterminated. Scholarly estimates of Native American population loss are as high as 100 million. Where did they go? They didn't move, they were killed by disease (at times intentionally spread), enslaved and worked to death by the European invaders, or just killed as one would kill a bothersome coy-dog. The Natives that were left were coerced into leaving their land. This was typically accomplished through promises in treaties, none of which were eventually kept. In the case of Akwesasne, treaties imposed a border that wasn't there.

Are there different interpretations of the cause of the uprising in 1989 -1990, of course? However, as Robert A. Rosentstone tells us in his book, *History of Film, Film on History*, "No matter how much research we do, no matter how many archives we visit, no matter how objective we try to be, the past will never come to us in a single version of the truth." That is certainly true of this uprising at Akwesasne. The research that went into deciphering the history of the 1989-1990 uprising and placing it in a chronological order can be found in the appendix.

ACKNOWLEDGMENTS

This work's genesis is my doctoral dissertation *Clash of Cultures: Uprising at* Akwesasne. There are a number of individuals I want to thank for their critique of my dissertation and therefore the creation of this book. My wife and partner Keli (Keli Rugenstein, Ph.D.) is the first I would like to thank. She has read and reread this manuscript numerous times and put up with my late nights as I wrote both the dissertation and the reworking of it into this document. Without her support, I doubt I would have been able to finish.

I would further like to thank those who were instrumental in the creation of this work, offering input and suggestions. They include Professor Dan S. White, Ph.D. of the University at Albany, SUNY, Patricia West-McKay Ph.D. who is Co-Director of the Center for Applied Historical Research at the University at Albany, SUNY and who is also Director of the Martin van Buren National Historic Site of the National Park Service. Dr. Arlene Sacks, Ed.D., Chair of my Doctoral Committee and Director of the Graduate Programs at the Florida campus Of *Union Institute and University* (*The Union Institute*), was similarly a contributor to the book.

Others who have read over the manuscript and have offered feedback include Charles (Chaz) Kader and Doug George-Kanentiio both from Akwesasne. A thank you goes out to Stephen R. Walker Designs for his help with my book cover. Finally, I want to thank my sons Don and Ernest

Kristoph who gave up time with their Dad so that he could do research and write.

INTRODUCTION:

What Uprising, Where? Akwesasne?

During 1989 and 1990 there was an uprising at Akwesasne (the St. Regis Indian Reservation) near Massena, New York and Cornwall, Ontario. The event was marked by violence and death, with large amounts of property and infrastructure destroyed or damaged, and families and friends torn apart. Others who were involved went to prison, were fined, or went into self-imposed exile to escape the pressures of the aftermath.

(Figure 1. Map of Akwesasne and the Surrounding Area. Page 122)

The reservation sits on both sides of the St. Lawrence River. Approximately two-thirds of the reservation lies on the US side of the border and one-third on the Canadian side.[1] Akwesasne is located in part of two counties of New York State and two Canadian provinces and interacts with five different jurisdictional governments. The indigenous Mohawk culture is surrounded by and interacts with five larger cultures: the French

---

[1] James Bell, *Implementation of Promoting Safe and Stable Families by American Indian Tribes Final Report – Volume II Case Study Reports* (Arlington, VA: James Bell Associates, Inc., 2004), 153. The Canadian side of the reservation extends for 7,400 acres and on the American side of the border the reservation covers 14,648 acres.

Canadian, the English Canadian, northern New York (along the St. Lawrence River) and the cultures of both federal governments. Akwesasne has two independent, elected tribal councils that govern the Canadian and American sides respectively.

There are two generally accepted theories why the uprising occurred. One theory is that the problems of 1989 and 1990 were a continuation of an ongoing feud between the Mohawks and the US and Canadian federal governments. This feud centered upon the issue of Mohawk sovereignty, the right of free and easy access across the border, control of their land, and the ability not to be charged duties or taxes for crossing the border.[2] Other sharp controversies arose from time to time, but these were the issues that caused the most friction. However, there are a few differences between the uprising at Akwesasne and the other government interactions of the past. In this uprising, traditional friends and cohorts were split down non-traditional party lines. Not only were there splits among historic allies; previously opposing sides on all other issues formed an alliance on this one. The major differences in the 1989 through 1990 uprising were the loss of lives at Akwesasne, and later at Kanesatake, (near Oka),

---

[2] "Sovereignty is the claim to be the ultimate political authority, subject to no higher power as regards the making and enforcing of political decisions . . . Sovereignty should not be confused with freedom of action: sovereign actors may find themselves exercising freedom of decision within circumstances that are highly constrained by relations of unequal power." *The Concise Oxford Dictionary of Politics*, s.v. "Sovereignty."

Canada and the lawlessness and violence that occurred.

The other accepted theory for the violence at Akwesasne is it was a civil war over the issue of gambling, much like the US Civil War involved the issue of slavery. The situation was exacerbated by the response of the state, provincial, and federal governments involved, and their initial reluctance to get ensnared in the situation.

There is a yet an unexplored theory for the conflict and violence. The historical record indicates increasing conflict between the various cultures at Akwesasne since the 1950s. This intensified in 1989 and reached a peak in mid-1990. During 1989, the Canadian government, the provinces of Ontario and Québec, the US federal government, and New York State ignored requests from the elected Canadian and American tribal governments for assistance. Despite this, the elected tribal governments were still encumbered by the rules and regulations of their respective federal governments and jurisdictional considerations. The external cultural and jurisdictional restraints prevented the tribal governments to combine to settle the problems that developed at Akwesasne during this time.

By 1990, the various governments realized the seriousness of the situation but the one authority that had the greatest ability to act, New York State, did not do so until after the loss of life. The weight of this prolonged cultural conflict on Mohawk society was evidenced by the destruction of infrastructure and the blockading of roads and death. When examining the events at Akwesasne psychologically, the situational stress of the situation caused people to act out and became violent. As the stress and anxiety increased people acted violently. This scenario created stress resulted in the Mohawks acting out in a predictable manner, striking out at others. As the various systems involved broke down, stress and anxiety increased through all of the systems.

CHAPTER 1

Understanding the Politics and Institutions at Akwesasne

To understand the situation at Akwesasne, it is important to review and understand the various jurisdictions and institutions that are encountered on the reservation. These institutions include various governmental, police and investigative agencies with their associated federal, provincial or state and tribal jurisdictions. Examining the Government at Akwesasne, includes an assessment of the Longhouse/ Traditionalist government, the Canadian Mohawk government, the American Mohawk government, and the Warriors. Additionally, there is a need to investigate the relationship between the United States federal government and Akwesasne and between the Canadian federal government and Akwesasne.

Akwesasne is surrounded and divided by two federal jurisdictions: The United States and Canada. Additionally, the reservation must contend with the governments of New York State and the provinces of Ontario and Québec.[3] Residents of the reservation have three area codes: 613 that covers Southeast Ontario, 514 covering Southwest Québec, and 518 covering Northeast New York. Each serves a different portion of the reservation. This division

---

[3] Michael T. Kaufman, "To the Mohawk Nation, Boundaries Do Not Exist," *The New York Times*, April 13, 1984.

is echoed by zip codes; the American side's zip code is 13655 and the Canadian side is H0M 1A0. The population of this multi-jurisdictional community is about 13,000 people.[4] Because of this unique situation, school students are also affected. Some children from the US side of the border go to Canadian schools, and all or some Canadian children go to US Head Start programs.[5]

There are three competing self-governments on the reservation loyal followings; the Canadian Mohawk Council of Akwesasne, the St. Regis Mohawk Tribal Council, and the Longhouse Mohawk Nation. Traditionalists from both sides of the reservation follow the rituals and traditions of the Longhouse government however the federal, state, and provincial governments do not officially recognize the Longhouse government. The St. Regis Mohawk Tribal Council oversees "funding programs from Washington and Albany" and interacts with the US side of the reservation.[6] The Mohawk Council of Akwesasne connects with Ottawa for Canadian programs and agendas. Each recognized council has its band (membership) lists for its community. Technically, residents of the reservation cannot vote for both councils, however, there is nothing to stop a resident from one side of

---

[4] Russel Roundpoint, "Akwesasne, Ca.," Mohawk Council of Akwesasne, http://www.akwesasne.ca/ (accessed September 10, 2007).

[5] Kaufman, "To the Mohawk Nation, Boundaries Do Not Exist."

[6] Ibid.

the reservation from moving from one voting roll to the other.[7]

Akwesasne Governmental Institutions

The Traditionalists of Akwesasne are called the Mohawk Nation and choose their leaders by the ancient, hereditary method of the Longhouse religion. According to Chief Mike Mitchell, of the Canadian Mohawks, the Creator in the Longhouse Religion sent a son to earth to end wars between different tribes. This Peacemaker, who was immaculately conceived near Kingston, Ontario, eventually united the Mohawks, Oneidas, Onondagas, Cayugas and Senecas - who all speak Iroquoian languages, into the Five Nations Confederacy. A clan system crossing tribal divisions was established to keep the fighting nations together.[8] The electoral system of the confederacy was based on the clans also. The clan mothers were the oldest women in the clan and they designated and dropped chiefs after conferring with other women of the tribe.[9]

Eventually, the US and Canadian governments suppressed the traditional tribal governmental system and imposed elected systems of government on both sides of the border. In the 1980s, the Mohawks began withdrawing children from outside schools.[10] Those who maintained their traditional

---

[7] Ibid.
[8] Ian Austen, "Tribal Ways Rip Indian Family Apart on Reserve," *The Globe and Mail*, June 23, 1980.
[9] Ibid.
[10] Ibid.

governmental loyalties did not serve in the armed forces or pay taxes.[11]

The Mohawk Council of Akwesasne (MCA) is the tribal government elected by the residents. In its official capacity, it interacts with the federal government and the governments of the provinces of Ontario and Québec. Much of the council's time is consumed with jurisdictional problems and protecting the rights of its residents. The council regulates justice, economics, environment, and governance in its jurisdiction. The MCA is politically obligated to specific areas of community work and to "portfolio committees to achieve community goals."[12]

The council consists of twelve district chiefs and a grand chief elected every four years. The twelve district chiefs represent the districts of TsiSnaihne (Snye), Kanarakon (St. Regis), and Kawehnoke (Cornwall Island). The electoral process includes the three districts electing the Grand Chief and the four other Chiefs. Additionally, the MCA has ten departments that cover services such as education, police, and health for the residents of the community.[13]

---

[11] Alan Richman, "15 Traditionalists Serving 3-Year Terms," *New York Times*, August 31, 1979.

[12] Russel Roundpoint, "Akwesasne, Ca.," Mohawk Council of Akwesasne, http://www.akwesasne.ca/ (accessed September 10, 2007). Committees are centered on specific issues and concerns but are not standing committees.

[13] *Ibid.*, Akwesasne Mohawk Board of Education, Akwesasne Mohawk Police Services, Department of Central Resource Services, Department of Community and Social Services, Department of Economic Development, Department of Environment,

The St. Regis Mohawk Tribal Council at Akwesasne is the legally elected and federally sanctioned government of the Mohawks in the US. Only the United States and the New York State engage with the tribal council chiefs during intergovernmental relations. This is also true of inter-tribal organizations and tribal relationships. The council consists of three chiefs, three sub-chiefs, and a tribal clerk. Elections occur every year on the first Saturday of June, when one chief and sub-chief are elected. The tribal clerk is elected every three years.[14]

The tribal council chiefs set tribal policies and make major decisions for the tribe. They manage the day-to-day operation of the government, and ensure that the services and various programs, offered to the residents of the reservation, are of good quality. The chiefs approve contracts and grants, settle land disputes on the reservation, and help residents with different problems interact with the tribal government. The tribal clerk, certifies and regulates tribal membership, records meetings of the council, and assists residents in making wills and other documentation.[15]

The Mohawk Warrior Society, although not part of Akwesasne government, is included because

---

Department of Health, Department of Housing, Department of Justice, Department of Technical Services.

[14] Chief Lorraine M. White, Chief James W. Ransom and Chief Barbara A. Lazore, "Saint Regis Mohawk Tribe: Helping Build a Better Tomorrow," Saint Regis Mohawk Tribe, http://srmt-nsn.gov/gov.htm (accessed September, 14 2007).
[15] Ibid.

of the position it was accorded by New York State during the uprising at Akwesasne. The society had its beginnings in the late 1960s at the Kahnewake and Akwesasne reservations. It was organized by young people in the community to revive the language, teaching, and culture in Mohawk territories. They were community based and oriented. The Warriors general plan was to protect Mohawk territory and reclaim lost land using the Great Law of Peace as their guide. They employed different tactics to achieve their goals, such as, setting up obstructions and barriers across the road to keep Canadian and US officials off reservations. To purify their reservations and lands, they would expel whites, and when they could, they would reoccupy ancient Mohawk territory.[16]

In the 1970s and 1980s the Warriors became involved in the cigarette trade that generated money for them and the traditional governments. By the end of the 1980s the two-separated over casino gambling on the reservations; this blurred the boundary between different factions on the reservations.[17] However, by 1992 the Warrior Society, Traditionalists, and the Tribalists agreed on the concept of self-governing and moved in that direction.[18]

---

[16] Alfred Taiaiake and Lana Lowe, "Warrior Societies in Contemporary Indigenous Communities," in A Background Paper Prepared for the Ipperwash Inquiry, (University of Victoria, 2005), 10-13.

[17] Ibid., 20.

[18] CP, "Akwesasne Mohawks Finally Bury the Hatchet," *Toronto Star*, January 9, 1992.

The United States and Akwesasne

Beginning in 1789, the US War Department was responsible for trade with the Indians and controlled the removal of Indians from their lands to the west and their internment on reservations. Ostensibly, they were to protect the Indians from exploitation, but according to congress the War Department's ability to administer the situation was unsatisfactory. The Bureau of Indian Affairs (BIA) was created in 1824 as part of the US War Department. The new agency was not any better at administering and protecting Indian rights and eventually only administered land issues.[19] In 1928, the *Meriam Report* found that most Indians received lands that were typically poor for agriculture and that the fertile lands ended up in the possession of non-Indians. The report illuminated how the allotment policies that had been practiced so far had not worked.[20] Finally, in 1949, the BIA was transferred to the US Department of the Interior.

During the 1950s the BIA's services grew to include agricultural extension, land acquisition, range management, and forestry. However, in the 1960s by congressional legislation, the BIA began to devolve. Education and health was shifted from

---

[19] The Columbia Electronic Encyclopedia © 2000–2007 Pearson Education, s.v. "Bureau of Indian Affairs," http://www.infoplease.com/ce6/history/A0825102.html (accessed September 5, 2007).

[20] Kevin K. Washburn, "Tribal Self-Determination at the Crossroads," *The Wilson Quarterly* 31, (Spring 2006):1-23.

the BIA to the Department of Health and Human Services. In the 1970s, the policy of eventual termination and assimilation of Indian tribes was rescinded and a new policy of self-determination began.[21] "Congress passed a series of laws, including the *Indian Self-Determination Act, the Indian Child Welfare Act*, and the *Health Care Improvement Act*, which aimed to improve the quality of reservation life without destroying tribal government."[22] Since then, the US and the BIA's interaction with the tribes have been in flux from "respecting tribal sovereignty to extinguishing it."[23]

The US Border Patrol (USBP) is another federal agency that interacts with the Indians of Akwesasne and has jurisdiction over the entire border. Congress passed the Labor Appropriation Act of 1924 on May 28, 1924 and established the US Border Patrol (USBP). The purpose was to secure the borders between Custom Houses. The USBP jurisdiction was increased to patrol the seacoast in 1925. In 1952, congressional legislation codified laws that allowed Border Patrol agents to search any type of transportation for illegal immigrants or contraband in the United States including the St. Lawrence River, which divides the two portions of Akwesasne. These problems of illegal immigrants and contraband increased, and in

---

[21] C.L. Henson, "From War to Self-Determination: A History of the Bureau of Indian Affairs," American Studies Resources Centre, Liverpool John Moores University, http://www.americansc.org.uk/Online/indians.htm (accessed July 10, 2007).
[22] Ibid.
[23] Ibid.

the 1980s, USBP increases the size of the force and used more technology, such as night-vision scopes and modern computer processing.[24]

Canada & Akwesasne

The Canadian government, through the Ministry of Indian Affairs and Northern Development, known as Indian and Northern Affairs Canada (INAC), administers Indian affairs in Canada. The INAC has two distinct offices to administer: Indian and Inuit Affairs, and Northern Affairs. The authority stems from the *Department of Indian Affairs and Northern Development Act,* in conjunction with the *Indian Act*, as well as territorial acts and legal obligations found in section 91(24) of the Commission Act (1867).[25] INAC is mandated to meet the Canadian government's political, legal, and treaty obligations to Indians, Inuit, and Northern communities. To satisfy these responsibilities, INAC has to work together with other federal and provincial ministries, agencies, and territories.[26]

---

[24] US Customs & Border Protection, "US Customs and Border Protection: Securing America's Borders," US Customs & Border Protection,

http://www.customs.gov/xp/cgov/border_security/border_patrol/border_patrol_ohs/history.xml (accessed June 8, 2007).

[25] Ministry, Indian and Northern Affairs, "Mandate, Roles and Responsibilities," Minister of Public Works and Government Services Canada, http://www.ainc-inac.gc.ca/ai/mrr-eng.asp#ft1a (accessed October 1, 2007).

[26] Ibid.

A basic function of INAC is to support aboriginal peoples in building communities that are economically, socially, and physically healthy and dynamic. The department ensures that self-government agreements and land claims are negotiated correctly. INAC also is charged with providing services such as housing, infrastructure, and education to the communities, which are to be equivalent to the services enjoyed by the balance of the residents of Canada. "INAC is also responsible for ensuring the honorable fulfillment of the Crown's obligations in lands, revenues and trusts, as well as for matters relating to First Nations governance."[27]

The Constitutional Act (1982) protects the political and civil rights of Indians and the Inuit in Canada. The act gives the federal government sole jurisdiction over Indians and Indian lands other than provincially patrolled roads. Additionally, the act identifies and approves already established treaty and Indian rights. The first part of *The Constitutional Act* is *The Charter of Rights and Freedoms* guarantees that no other provisions or legislature will hinder or obstruct any aboriginal rights or any rights that are gained from settlements from land claims.[28] The Charter guarantees, "Certain rights and freedoms shall not be construed so as to abrogate or derogate from any aboriginal peoples of Canada."[29] This includes any rights or freedoms specified by the *Royal Proclamation of*

---

[27] Ibid.

[28] Ibid.

[29] Canada, *The Constitution Act (*1982), Part I §25.

October 7, 1763. Also guaranteed are any freedoms or "rights that now exist by way of land claims agreements or may be so acquired. Notwithstanding any other provision of this Act, the aboriginal and treaty rights referred to in this subsection are guaranteed equally to male and female persons."[30] Additionally, there are provisions that if a Constitutional Convention was called, representation from the aboriginal groups would be included in any discussions.[31]

Royal Canadian Mounted Police (RCMP) is the federal agency that is concerned with Indians and other indigenous peoples. In 1920, the federal government consolidated existing police services and created the RCMP, which enforces federal law in all the provinces and territories. Two other agencies, the Preventive Service and the National Review, were absorbed into the RCMP in 1932 and created the RCMP Marine Section. Additionally, the RCMP works with Indians to strengthen their communities and to work cooperatively with their organizations. This includes the development and evaluation of "practical and culturally sensitive policing services that are acceptable to Aboriginal peoples."[32] Programs include the RCMP Aboriginal Youth Training Program (AYTP),

---

[30] Ibid., Part II §35.

[31] Ibid., Part IV.1 §37.1.

[32] Royal Canadian Mounted Police, "Royal Canadian Mounted Police: Historical Highlights," Minister of Public Works and Government Services Canada, http://www.rcmp-grc.gc.ca/history/highlights_e.htm#Expansion (accessed June 8, 2007).

RCMP Community Suicide Intervention Program, the Commissioner's National Aboriginal Advisory Committee (CNAAC), Community Justice Forums (CJF), and the RCMP First Nations Community Policing Service (FNCPS). The federal government introduced the First Nations Policing Policy in June 1991, which gave Indian communities the opportunity to participate in provincial and federal governments in developing dedicated policing services in their communities.[33]

State and Provincial Institutions and Jurisdictions

The Ontario and Québec provincial and the New York State governments interact with Akwesasne in a law enforcement capacity. Each is charged with the safety and protection of the citizenry of their respective jurisdictions. Although each government is staffed and authorized differently, their jurisdiction includes the entire territory of their respective state or province.

Since their beginnings in 1917, the New York State Police have had jurisdiction throughout the entire state. Divided into 11 troops, they guarantee that New York highways are safe and secure. Part of their responsibilities includes responding to cell phone 911 emergencies, providing driver education, and promoting public relations at schools, civic organizations, government organizations, and citizen groups. They apprehend criminals and murderers. They interdict drug traffickers, seize

---

[33] Ibid.

drugs and other contraband, and expropriate their assets. The New York State Police discharge the Governor's instructions and dictates throughout the state.[34]

The Ontario Provincial Police (OPP) had their beginning in 1909 and were restructured in 1921. They operate in six regions and provide services for 2.3 million people throughout the province. They provide police jurisdiction to the rural areas of Ontario, and police municipalities. The OPP is a partner in the First Nations Police Services (FNPS) that promotes a constabulary for Indian reservations.[35] First introduced by the federal government, the FNPS encourages building and maintaining close relationships with Indian and Aboriginal community leaders. The FNPS promotes open dialogue and works to enhance the OPP's understanding of cultural differences. Additionally, FNPS provides opportunities for Indians to join the OPP.[36]

The Sûreté du Québec, the provincial police of Québec, was created on February 1, 1870 and is divided into 10 different districts. They have jurisdiction over the province of Québec and are

---

[34] New York State Police, "Overview: New York State Police," New York State Police, http://www.troopers.state.ny.us/ (accessed June 5, 2007).

[35] Ontario Provincial Police, "A Brief History of the O.P.P.," Government of Ontario, Canada, http://www.opp.ca/Recruitment/opp_000580.html (accessed June 6, 2007).

[36] Ontario Provincial Police, *Ontario Provincial Police: Provincial Business Plan 2005*, (Orilla, Ontario: Ontario Provincial Police, 2005).

charged with keeping the peace and public order. The Sûreté du Québec promotes the human rights of the people and protects their property. Additionally, they provide assistance to rural and municipal police forces.

The Complex Structure of Authorities and Control

The jurisdiction of the Mohawks at Akwesasne has a complex structure of authorities and control. This small enclave, located in northern New York, southeastern Ontario and southwestern Québec, contends with five external governmental jurisdictions. The federal jurisdictions impose different governmental systems on their respective sides of the border and upon the people of Akwesasne. The Mohawks are encumbered with different forms of government, rules of legislation, and elections. Additionally, there is the situation of a Native constabulary and how this is actualized. Neither side of the US-Canada border is coordinates with the other.

Although the federal governments have primary jurisdiction over their portion of Akwesasne, the second level of government, state or provincial, that interacts on a daily basis through police patrols. The New York State Police, the Ontario Provincial Police, and the Sûreté du Québec have jurisdiction over their portion of the reserve and control criminal investigation, road patrols, and interdiction of contraband. The New York State Police have jurisdiction over the communities of Racquette Point, Roosevelton, Frogtown, and Hogansburg.

The Ontario Provincial Police has jurisdiction over Cornwall Island, and the Sûreté du Québec covers St. Regis Village and Snye, Québec.[37] Although these agencies could coordinate with each other, they typically do not. Even though the Mohawks of Akwesasne consider themselves culturally and historically one entity they are jurisdictionally divided. (See Figure 2. Page 123 Jurisdictional Map of Akwesasne)

---

[37] Elizabeth C. Petros, "Mohawks Forming Auxiliary Police Force," *The Post-Standard*, November 22, 1989.

CHAPTER 2

The Past at Akwesasne

Prologue of Troubles: The Garrow Trial

The history of the Mohawks at Akwesasne originates when two families from Kahnawake settled there around 1754.[38] Other Mohawks, from what is now called the Mohawk Valley, migrated north at about the same time. In 1759, Abenakis, fleeing the French and Indian War (the Seven Years War), took refuge at Akwesasne along with a number of Onondagas from the Oswegatchie mission (in Ogdensburg, New York).[39] After the war, many of the Abernakis left and return home. Those who remained became part of the base of the present-day reservation.[40]

---

[38] French missionaries converted some of the Mohawks to Catholicism. The idea was "grouping the Iroquois neophytes on the banks of the St. Lawrence, to guard them from the persecution and temptation to which they were subject amid the pagan influences of their own villages. In 1667, the missionary prevailed upon seven communities to take up their residence at Laprarie, opposite Montreal." *The Catholic Encyclopedia*, vol. III. (New York: Robert Appleton Company, 1908), s.v. "Akwesasne"

[39] "A confederation of Algonquin tribes, comprising the Penobscots, Passamaquoddies, Norridgewocks, and others, formerly occupying what is now Maine, and southern New Brunswick." Thomas Campbell, "Abenakis," Robert Appleton Company, http://www.newadvent.org/cathen/01039b.htm (accessed November 12, 2008).

[40] St. Regis Mohawk Tribe, "Tribal History," St. Regis Mohawk Tribe, http://srmt-nsn.gov/his.htm (accessed February 25, 2007).

During the French and Indian War, the Mohawks of Kahnawake and Akwesasne fought on the French side, while the rest of their Iroquoian brothers fought on the side of the English. This split led to numerous problems and at the end of the war the Mohawks of Kahnawake and Akwesasne found themselves ostracized from the other Iroquois. The French wanted to consolidate their position and created the Seven Nations of Canada that included both Kahnawake and Akwesasne.

With the Revolutionary War, affections were altered again. The Seven Nation Confederacy of Canada and the Mohawks of the Six Nations Confederacy supported the British while the Mohawks of Kahnawake and Akwesasne supported the colonists. After the war, the Mohawks of the Six Nations Confederacy, led by Joseph Brant, resettled in Canada. *The Treaty of Paris* (1783) ended the war and set the boundary between the US and Canada at the 45th parallel. This new border affected Akwesasne by dividing it between the US and Canada, and that began the problems that persist today.

The Mohawks of Akwesasne/St. Regis participated in, or were affected by, five treaties between the beginning of the eighteenth century and the beginning of the nineteenth century. On October 22, 1784, at Ft. Stanwix, New York, the Mohawks, as part of the Iroquois Nation, signed the *Treaty with the Six Nations*. This was a peace treaty in which the US made peace with the Senecas, Mohawks, Onondagas, and Cayugas, and received them into US protection upon a number of conditions, including the US taking Indian hostages, and giving goods to, "be delivered to the said Six Nations for their use and comfort."[41] The treaty set the borders of the Iroquois in western New York. This was supplemented by the treaty of January 9, 1789, at Ft. Harmar, Ohio. The treaty reinforced the *Treaty with the Six Nations*; however, it did deal with the "adjudication of crime" and did not return land to the Senecas.[42]

The *Treaty with the Six Nations of 1794,* also known as the *Treaty of Konondaigua* (Canandaigua, NY) or the *Pickering Treaty,* was an important peace treaty. It covered all of the Six Nations, especially the Senecas, but the Mohawks were scarcely represented. The treaty guaranteed tranquility, reciprocal peace, non-disturbance, dealt with lands that were previously ceded or reserved, and an annuity that was expected from the US government.[43] However, the *Treaty with the Seven Nations of Canada and the Iroquois of Akwesasne and Kahnawaka* of May 31, 1796, between New York State and the US government, affected the Mohawks much more. For an initial sum and subsequent annual payment, the Seven Nations, Akwesasne and Kahnawaka, relinquished ownership of their land to New York State. Akwesasne's reserve was described in the treaty as

---

[41] "Treaty with the Six Nations," October 22, 1784, *Indian Affairs: Laws and Treaties, vol. II* (1904): 5,6.

[42] D'Arcy McNickle, *The History and Culture of Iroquois Diplomacy: An Interdisciplinary Guide to the Treaties of the Six Nations and Their League*, eds. Francis Jennings, William N. Fenton, Mary A. Druke and David R. Miller (Syracuse, NY: Syracuse University Press, 1995), 201. Mohawks did not ratify this treaty.

[43] Ibid., 203.

a "tract equal to six miles square, reserved in the sale made by the commissioners of the land-office of the said state, to Alexander Macomb, to be applied to the use of the Indians of the village of St. Regis."[44] The reservation, included mills, built on the Salmon and Grass Rivers, and adjacent hay fields required to keep the mills supplied.

In Albany, New York, on March 29, 1797, the *Treaty with the Mohawks* was signed between the Mohawk nation residing in Upper Canada, and the state of New York and the US government. The treaty stated that the Mohawks would relinquish their lands to the State of New York. New York paid the Mohawks a total of one thousand dollars, for the use of their national land. It was paid by the deputies and distributed to the various people of the nation according to use. The deputies were paid a total of five hundred dollars to cover their expenses. Additionally, "during the time they [deputies] have attended this treaty: and [paid by the State] the sum of one hundred dollars, for their expenses in returning, and for conveying the said sum of one thousand dollars, to where the said nation resides."[45]

Two treaties and a special explanatory article during this period affected the Mohawks of Akwesasne, although they were not with the Mohawks. These were the *Jay Treaty: Treaty of Amity, Commerce, and Navigation* (1794), the *Explanatory Article to Article 3 of the Jay Treaty*

---

[44] "Treaty with the Seven Nations of Canada," January 31, 1797, *Indian Affairs: Laws and Treaties, vol. II* (1904): 45, 46.

[45] "Treaty with the Mohawk," April 27, 1798, *Indian Affairs: Laws and Treaties, vol. II* (1904): 50, 51.

(1796), and the *Treaty of Ghent* (1814). The *Jay Treaty* helped to normalize relations between Great Britain and the young US. After the Revolutionary War and the *Treaty of Paris* (1783), the British did not leave US territory and they pressed US seaman into service for the British Navy. Additionally, they seized US ships and disrupted commerce. The treaty helped to normalize relations, stopped the seizure of ships, and released the seaman from service. It also guaranteed that the Indians had easy access across the US-Canadian border. The treaty agreed that it "shall at all times be free to His Majesty's subjects, and to the citizens of the United States, and also to the Indians dwelling on either side of the said boundary line."[46] It allowed people to freely to pass back and forth by water, land, or inland navigation "into the respective territories and countries of the two parties, on the continent of America, (the country within the limits of the Hudson's Bay Company only excepted) and to navigate all the lakes, rivers and waters thereof, and freely to carry on trade and commerce with each other."[47]

This portion of the treaty was further explained and reinforced by the *Explanatory Article to Article 3 of the Jay Treaty* (1796). This article explicitly stated that there could not be conditions in any treaty concluded after this by either Great Britain or

---

[46] "The Jay Treaty," November 19, 1794, *Treaties and Other International Acts of the United States of America: Documents 1-40: 1776-1818, vol. 2,* ed. Hunter Miller (Washington: Government Printing Office, 1931).
[47] Ibid.

the US "with any other State or Nation, or with any Indian tribe, can be understood to derogate in any manner from the rights of free intercourse and commerce secured by the aforesaid third Article of the treaty of Amity, commerce and navigation."[48] *The Jay Treaty* and this article are quoted often, not only by the Mohawks, but also by the other Iroquois and Indian tribes, to legitimize the crossing of the border.

The other treaty that affected the Mohawks and reinforced their rights was the *Treaty of Ghent* (1814). The *Treaty of Ghent,* which ended the War of 1812, restored all the Indian rights that had questioned since the beginning of the war. The various Indian tribes allied with either the US or Great Britain, and the warring powers doubted the loyalty of the other side's allies. The treaty states that "the Tribes or Nations of Indians with whom they may be at war at the time of such Ratification, and forthwith to restore to such Tribes or Nations respectively all the possessions, rights, and privileges which they may have enjoyed or been entitled to in one thousand eight hundred and eleven previous to such hostilities."[49] The treaty codified

---

[48] P. Bond and Timothy Pickering, "Explanatory Article to Article 3 of the Jay Treaty, Signed at Philadelphia," May 5, 1796, *Treaties and Other International Acts of the United States of America: Documents 1-40: 1776-1818, vol. 2,* ed. Hunter Miller (Washington: Government Printing Office, 1931).

[49] "Treaty of Ghent, 1814," *Treaties and Other International Acts of the United States of America: Documents 1-40: 1776-1818, vol. 2*, ed. Hunter Miller (Washington: Government Printing Office, 1931).

the rights the "tribes and nations" would regain and the conditions to keep them. (See Figure 3. Reservation of the St. Regis Indians. St. Lawrence & Franklin Counties, NY 1890. Page 124)

To assess the effects of the treaties and articles that have affected the Mohawks of Akwesasne and the US government, we will examine the trial *United States v. Mrs. P.L. Garrow (NO. 4018)* March 1, 1937.[50] The case underscores the finer points of the legislative enactments and includes case law. Garrow's argument presented the Indian understanding of the various treaties and legislative enactments. The US government's argument demonstrated their interpretation of the law and statutes.

Mrs. P.L. (Annie) Garrow

Mrs. P.L. (Annie) Garrow was a "full-blooded Mohawk" who lived on the Canadian side of Akwesasne near the international boundary.[51] She entered the US portion of the reservation at Hogansburg, New York with twenty-four ash splint baskets that were dyed different colors. Officials detained her and charged her a duty according to the 1930 Tariff Act, paragraph 411. She protested the action, claiming her right by the *Jay Treaty,* to bring

---

[50] United States v. Mrs. P.L. Garrow, No. 4081, *Indian Affairs: Laws and Treaties, Part V: Important Court Decisions on Tribal Rights and Property, vol. V*, ed. Charles J. Kappler (Washington: Government Printing Office, 1941).

[51] Ibid.

her possessions across the border duty-free.[52] In the strict interpretation of the treaty, what she said was valid. The *Explanatory Article to Article 3 of the Jay Treaty* has even greater specificity since it states that the provision of Article 3 cannot be changed or altered by any subsequent treaties or agreements. If the treaty had been honored, Garrow would have been within her rights. She appealed to the *United States Court of Customs and Patent Appeals* who decided the case in her favor, based on a previous

---

[52] United States v. Mrs. P.L. Garrow, No. 4018, 71 *Treasury Decisions* 421, (U.S. Supreme Court, 1937).

case decision, *McCandless v. United States, 25 F. (2d) 71*.[53]

However, Customs as part of the US federal government, and to some extent the Canadian government, saw it differently than the court. The US Supreme Court reviewed the case and the relevant treaties, laws, and statutes and reversed the

---

[53] United States v. Mrs. P.L. Garrow, No. 4018, *Indian Affairs: Laws and Treaties, Part V: Important Court Decisions on Tribal Rights and Property*, vol. *V*, ed. Charles J. Kappler (Washington: Government Printing Office, 1941). 773;

"The trial court relied strongly upon *McCandless* v. *United States, supra*, decided March 9, 1928. In that case, which involved a writ of habeas corpus, a full-blooded Indian of the Iroquois tribe, born in Canada, crossed the border line from Canada and was arrested on complaint of the Commissioner of Immigration for an alleged violation of law in entering the United States without complying with the immigration laws. He was ordered deported, whereupon he sued out a writ of habeas corpus. The United States District Court granted the writ and discharged the petitioner. The Circuit Court, speaking through Buffington, Circuit Judge, affirmed the order of discharge, holding that the general acts of Congress did not apply to members of the Indian tribes. Article III of the Jay Treaty was brought into question and was discussed at length. The court held that the declaration of the War of 1812 did not end the treaty rights secured to the Indians through the said Jay Treaty, so long as they remained neutral. Finally, the court held that the rights granted by said article III were permanent, and were, at most, only suspended during the existence of the War of 1812. Therefore, it was held that the petitioner might pass and repass freely, under and by virtue of the provisions of said article III. This case was not appealed to the Supreme Court. This may have been occasioned by the fact that on April 2, 1928, an act of Congress was approved which provided that the Immigration Act of 1924 should not apply to Indians crossing the international border." Ibid., 775.

findings of the *United States Customs Court, T.D.* 4820.

The government's appeal before the Supreme Court stated that the *United States Court of Customs and Patent Appeals* was erroneous, as specified in the following brief:

> (1) Article 3 of the Jay Treaty of 1794 was annulled by the War of 1812
>
> (2) Alternatively, if Article 3 of the Jay Treaty was not abrogated by the War of 1812, it is, nevertheless, in conflict with a subsequent statute. It is well settled that when a Treaty and a Statute are in conflict, that which is later in date prevails.
>
> (3) Assuming, for the sake of argument, that Article 3 was not abrogated but is still in force and effect, the importation is not within the purview of the language of said Article 3.[54]

Garrow and her counsel contested the appeal, stating that Article 3 of the *Jay Treaty* (1794), as it applied to Indians, was self-executing and still in effect. Further, they argued that, "an act to regulate the collection of duties on imports and tonnage, approved March 2, 1799, (1 Stat. 627)" supported Article 3 of the *Jay Treaty*.[55] Garrow's counsel quoted section 105 to support their case:

> ... That no duty shall be levied or collected on the importation of peltries brought into the territories of the United

---

[54] Ibid., 773.
[55] Ibid., 775.

States, nor on the proper goods and effects of whatever nature, of Indians passing, or repassing the boundary line aforesaid, unless the same be goods in bales or other large packages unusual among Indians, which shall not be considered as goods belonging bona fide to Indians, nor be entitled to the exemption from duty aforesaid.[56]

However, the 1799 statute was unnecessary in guaranteeing Indian rights to travel across the border because there was more recent legislation that affected her case. The War of 1812 abrogated any agreements between the two nations. By 1814, the war was grinding to an end, and the US was looking for a diplomatic way out. However, the *Treaty of Ghent* (1815), which ended the war, returned all the rights that had been in place in 1811. Garrow et. al. pointed to subsequent legislation from 1816-1894 that allowed Indians to

---

[56] Ibid.

move freely across the border.[57] The various statutes during this period, usually included the phrase: ". . . peltries and other usual goods and effects of Indians passing or repassing the boundary line of the United States, under such regulations as the Secretary of the Treasury may prescribe: *provided*, That this exemption shall not apply to goods in bales or other packages unusual among

---

[57] "An act to regulate the duties on imports and tonnage, of April 27, 1816 S. L.,

Vol. 3, Chap. CVII. An act in alteration of the several acts imposing duties on imports of May 19, 1828, S. L., Vol. 4, Chap LV. An act to alter and amend the several acts imposing duties on imports, of July 14, 1832. S. L., Vol. 4, Chap. CCXXVII.

An act to provide revenue from imports, and to change and modify existing laws

imposing duties on imports, and for other purposes, of August 30, 1842. S. L.,

Vol. 5, Chap. CCLXX. An act reducing the duty on imports, and for other purposes, of July 30, 1846. S. L., Vol. 9, Chap. LXXIV. An act to provide for the payment of outstanding Treasury notes, to authorize a loan, to regulate and fix the duties on imports, and for other purposes, of March 2, 1861. S. L., Vol. 12, Chap. LXVIII. An act to provide increased revenue from imports, to pay interest on the public debt, and for other purposes, of August 5, 1861. S. L., Vol. 12, Chap. XLV. An act to increase the duties on tea, coffee, and sugar, of December 24, 1861. S. L., Vol. 12, Chap. II. An act to increase duties on imports, and for other purposes, of June 30, 1864. S. L., Vol. 13, Chap CLXXI.

An act to reduce internal taxes, and for other purposes, of July 14, 1870. S. L.,

Vol. 16, Chap CCLV. An act to reduce duties on imports, and to reduce internal taxes, and for other purposes, of June 6, 1872. S. L., Vol. 17, Chap. CCCXV. The tariff act of October 1, 1890, S. L., Vol. 26, Chap, 1244, The tariff revision of August 27, 1894, paragraph 582, S. L., Vol. 28, Chap. 349." Ibid., 775-576.

Indians."[58] This phrase included gave credence to Garrow's claim. However, this changed in 1897, when the phrase was omitted in the tariff act of July 24, 1897 and in subsequent legislation. Garrow and her counsel argued that since the *Jay Treaty* was self-executing, the omissions did not fundamentally change their argument since the preponderance of evidence supported their contention. This was the viewpoint among most Indians; especially at Akwesasne.

Supreme Court Justice George Sutherland delivered the U.S. government's view.[59] The court agreed that not all treaties between the two parties were abrogated because of the war. He cited examples such as treaties concerning boundaries, the ability of citizens in one territory to hold, buy, and sell land in the other territory, cession, and transactions and other interaction which were completed acts. However, treaties of alliance or amity have a political component; they fall under the category of treaty that encourages fidelity and

---

[58] Ibid.

[59] George Sutherland was born in Buckinghamshire, England, 15 March 1862 and died in Stockbridge, Mass., 18 July 1942. . . "[His] appointment to the Supreme Court was by President Warren G. Harding on 5 September 1922. . . [Sutherland] was a strong conservative, [and] remained on the Court long enough to witness the demise of substantive due process, a doctrine that had become almost synonymous with his name. In his last years on the Court, his detractors castigated him as one of the Four Horsemen who repeatedly struck down New Deal social legislation."
The Oxford Companion to the Supreme Court of the United States, s.v. "George Sutherland," http://www.answers.com/topic/george-sutherland (accessed May 07, 2007).

harmony between international states.[60] This type of treaty is "absolutely annulled by war."[61]

The court decided that article 3 of the *Jay Treaty* was annulled by the War of 1812. This discharged any responsibilities or obligations between the two international states. The court differentiated between article 3 and article 9, which was still in force.[62] The court held that article 9 covered the longevity of existing rights. These are rights that are settled and absolute and "neither the owners nor their heirs or assigns are to be regarded as aliens."[63] The court, however, interpreted Article 3 as a fundamental part of the treaty that did not have any compulsory or mandatory life apart from it. Interestingly the court found the Tariff Act of March 2, 1799, was still in force and had not been abrogated during the war.

When the war ended with the *Treaty of Ghent* (1814), the court indicated that this treaty changed the Indian's rights from inalienable to conditional rights that were controlled by statute. Article 9 of the *Treaty of Ghent* states:

---

[60] United States v. Mrs. P.L. Garrow, Kappler, 777.

[61] Ibid.

[62] "It is agreed, that British Subjects who now hold Lands in the Territories of the United States, and American Citizens who now hold Lands in the Dominions of His Majesty, shall continue to hold them according to the nature and Tenure of their respective Estates and Titles therein, and may grant Sell or Devise the same to whom they please, in like manner as if they were Natives; and that neither they nor their Heirs or assigns shall, so far as may respect the said Lands, be and the legal remedies incident thereto, be regarded as Aliens."

"The Jay Treaty," *Treaties and Other International Acts*, Article 9.

[63] United States v. Mrs. P.L. Garrow, Kappler, 777.

The United States of America engage to put an end immediately after the Ratification of the present Treaty to hostilities with all the Tribes or Nations of Indians with whom they may be at war at the time of such Ratification, and forthwith to restore to such Tribes or Nations respectively all the possessions, rights, and privileges which they may have enjoyed or been entitled to in one thousand eight hundred and eleven previous to such hostilities. Provided always that such Tribes or Nations shall agree to desist from all hostilities against the United States of America, their Citizens, and Subjects upon the Ratification of the present Treaty being notified to such Tribes or Nations, and shall so desist accordingly. And His Britannic Majesty engages on his part to put an end immediately after the Ratification of the present Treaty to hostilities with all the Tribes or Nations of Indians with whom He may be at war at the time of such Ratification, and forthwith to restore to such Tribes or Nations respectively all the possessions, rights, and privileges, which they may have enjoyed or been entitled to in one thousand eight hundred and eleven previous to such hostilities. Provided always that such Tribes or Nations shall agree to desist from all hostilities against His Britannic Majesty and His Subjects upon the Ratification of the present Treaty being notified to such Tribes or Nations, and shall so desist accordingly.[64]

Although this gave the Indians their 'rights'

---

[64] "Treaty of Ghent," *Treaties and Other International Acts of the United States of America,* Article 9.

back, this was not, in the opinion of the court, a self-executing provision.[65] The treaty was a contract between the US and the tribes or nations to restore the rights prior to 1811. This treaty was not the same as article 3 of *the Jay Treaty*; this provision of the Ghent treaty was legally bestowed and could be legally removed.

The second aspect of the case was the legal status of Garrow's entrance into the US. She was a Mohawk Indian who lived at Akwesasne on the Canadian side of the border and entered the US from Canada. Although the *United States Court of Customs and Patent Appeals* decided the case in Garrow's favor, the Supreme Court, investigating Garrow's case, had a different opinion. The *United States Court of Customs and Patent Appeals* viewed Garrow's status as the US District Court had. Both decided that Garrow, a "full-blooded" Indian, stood outside the purview of the US Congress. The Supreme Court, citing the 1929 case of *Karnuth, Director of Immigration, et al.* v. *United States ex rel. Albro*, saw Garrow as an alien entering the US.[66] The court saw no difference between

---

[65] "A self-executing provision is one which supplies the rule or means by which the right given may be enforced or practiced or by which a duty enjoined may be performed."
"The Pacific Reporter with Key-Number Annotations," in National Reporter System - State Series, vol.144 Permanent Edition (St. Paul: West Publishing Co., 1915), 12.

[66] "In 1929, the case of *Karnuth, Director of Immigration, et al.* v. *United States ex rel. Albro*, came before the Supreme Court, and was decided. (279 U. S. 231.) A writ of habeas corpus had been sued out on behalf of two aliens who were detained by immigration officials, and who had entered this country from Canada. The respondent Mary Cook was a British subject, born in Scotland, who

members of an Indian tribe and immigrants as described in *Karnuth*; the judges did not differentiate between Indians and other Canadian citizens. The Indians living in Canada were wards of that government and would be described as subjects or citizens.[67]

Therefore, the Supreme Court found that Garrow had to pay the required duty under paragraph 411 of the Tariff Act of 1930. They found that the *Jay Treaty* was abrogated by the War of 1812 and the rights given back to Indians in 1814 were restored by statute. Thus, two viewpoints were documented of the situation at Akwesasne on the US side of the border. The government saw the situation as two countries with citizens who wanted to interact outside the agreed-upon immigration and trade laws. The Mohawks of Akwesasne held to the

---

came to Canada in 1924. The respondent Antonio Danelon was a native of Italy who came to Canada in 1923. These persons resided at Niagara Falls, Ontario. The latter claimed to be a Canadian citizen, by reason of his father's naturalization. Both respondents had been crossing back and forth over the boundary line, in pursuance of employment in the United States, for a considerable period before their detention. The Federal District Court sustained the action of the immigration officials, and dismissed the writ. This judgment, on appeal, was reversed by the Circuit Court of Appeals, which held that if the statute were so construed as to exclude the aliens in question, it would conflict with article III of the Jay Treaty of 1794. Certiorari was granted and the case came before the Supreme Court. That court referred to the hereinbefore quoted provisions of said article III of the Jay Treaty. The contention made by Government counsel was that the treaty provision relied on was abrogated by the War of 1812, and it was upon this point that the case was decided." United States v. Mrs. P.L. Garrow, Kappler, 777.

[67] Ibid., 778.

rights of the *Jay Treaty* and free access across the border.

Two historically significant acts that affected the Mohawks at Akwesasne indirectly but demonstrated the US government's attitude towards Indians were the *Indian Removal Act* (1830) and the *Dawes Severalty Act* (1887). The *Indian Removal Act* removed Indians from desirable farmland in several states and territories and moved them to the US territory west of the Mississippi River. While it assured the eradication of rights or privileges that they had over their ancestral land, it gave them some assurances of the continued use and possession of their new property, provided that they did not abandon it or become tribally extinct.[68] Indian possession of land had been an ongoing debate in congress and society. With the acquisition of the Louisiana Purchase (1803) a solution to the Indian "problem" seemed near at hand. The societal atmosphere was that because of progress, the Indians, as with other powerful tribes of the past would disappear. The US and Canadian governments thought that the "savage indigenous culture" would not survive the onslaught of civilization. Congress authorized President Andrew Jackson to enforce the statues of the *Indian Removal Act*. Many tribes from the Southeast, Florida, and what was known at the time as the Northwest (area around the Great Lakes) were forced to move. The tribes were mistreated and

---

[68] "Indian Removal Act of 1830," in The Cherokee Removal: A Brief History with Documents, ed. Theda Perdue and Michael D. Green (New York: St. Martin's Press, 1995).

many died during this forced migration from their ancestral homelands to areas completely foreign to them.[69]

The other act was the *Dawes Severalty Act* (1887). The act was passed to break up reservation land held by tribes into individual parcels with the idea that this would encourage the assimilation of Indians into the majority culture.[70] The Dawes Act and the "subsequent acts that extended its initial provisions was purportedly to protect Indian property rights, particularly during the land rushes of the 1890s in realty this is not what happened."[71] Each Indian family would be given a parcel of land for them to farm and after a period of time, they would pay taxes on the land, as did citizens. Land that was not allotted would revert to the federal government and sold to non-Indian homesteaders. The Dawes act, without consultation with the Indian tribes or Indians, extinguished tribal rights with the Indians and forced them into full citizenship. [72]

Both of these acts demonstrated the federal government's attitude towards Native Americans during this period. As discussed previously the Mohawks saw their rights suffer as the government

---

[69] Brian K. Landsberg, ed., "Indian Removal Act," in Major Acts of Congress, Macmillan-Thomson Gale eNotes.com, http://www.enotes.com/major-acts-congress/sep/indian-removal-act (accessed June 6, 2009).

[70] Brian K. Landsberg, ed., "Indian General Allotment Act (Dawes Act) of 1887," in Major Acts of Congress, Macmillan-Thomson Gale eNotes.com, http://www.enotes.com/major-acts-congress/sep/indian-removal-act (accessed June, 8 2009).

[71] Ibid.

[72] "An act to provide for the allotment of lands in severalty to Indians on the various reservations." Ibid.

embraced assimilation. The Garrow case is rooted in this change of attitude. Other portions of the Iroquois Confederacy were affected by these acts. After the Indian removal act's subsequent treaties some Onondaga, Seneca, and Cayuga Indians moved west to reservations in Oklahoma. In fact, many Eastern Indians went to new reservations from Wisconsin to Oklahoma.[73]

In the twentieth century, a number of federal acts of legislation passed by Congress challenged Native sovereignty. These included the *Indian Citizen Act* (1924), the *Seneca Conservation Act* (1927), *the Snell Bill* (1930), the *Indian Reorganization Act* (1934), and the *Selective Service Act* (1940).

In 1924, the *Indian Citizen Act* was passed by Congress to extend US citizenship to Indians. The government was attempting to assimilate the Native populations and be egalitarian to all those who lived within its border. However, a major portion of the Indian population rebuffed the US offer. The Iroquois saw it as an encroachment toward the demise of their sovereign rights. Their reason was that they could not be sovereign and citizens of another entity.[74] In 1927, Congress, colluding with an unscrupulous Seneca Council, passed an act that allowed New York State to regulate land on reservations through game laws. In return, the

---

[73] lee Sultzman, "Iroquois History," First Nations, http://www.tolatsga.org/iro.html (accessed June 2, 2009).

[74] Laurence M. Hauptman, The Iroquois and the New Deal (Syracuse: Syracuse University Press, 1988), 5-6.

Seneca Conservation Act allowed the Seneca reservations to sell game licenses to non-Indians.[75]

The New Deal brought a plethora of legislation affecting Iroquois sovereignty and their relationship with New York. Not all attempts to change the connection between the state and the Iroquois were passed by Congress. The *Snell Bill* of 1930 is an example of the political atmosphere. The proposed bill was an attempt by New York State to obtain civil regulatory jurisdiction over the Iroquois. It has given the state total control over reservations and imposed civil laws over the residents.[76] The *Indian Reorganization Act* of 1934 was one of the most comprehensive laws to be passed by congress. It included a number of provisions that established education and financial loan programs and "cultural encouragement of Indian higher education as well as the establishment of tribal elections, constitutions, and corporations."[77] The act seemed fair and encouraging for the evolution of Iroquois culture. The various nations of the Iroquois rejected the act. The tribes thought they were a sovereign nation that could not be regulated by a foreign nation. There were other factors that weighed into the decision to steer away from the act; a dislike of the commissioner,[78] an ingrained distrust of the US

---

[75] Ibid., 8.

[76] Seneca Nation, "Communication of Complaint," Honor Indian Treaties: Break A Treaty, Break the Law, www.honorindiantreaties.org/ (accessed January 6, 2006).

[77] Hauptman. *The Iroquois and the New Deal,* 8.

[78] Wilcomb E. Washburn, "Native Americans and the New Deal: The Office Files of John Collier, 1933–1945," Lexisnexis, http://www.lexisnexis.com/academic/2upa/Anas/NativeAmericansNew Deal.asp (accessed

government, and a suspicion of the new rules and regulations.[79]

Over a year before Pearl Harbor, in August 1940, the BIA Commissioner John Collier and Selective Service representatives met to brainstorm on how to register Indians for selective service. In September, Congress passed the *Selective Service Act,* and in October, Congress passed the *Nationalities Act.* This act granted citizenship to all Indians without impairing tribal authority. That same month over 1,785 Indians were inducted into the armed services.[80] By the attack on Pearl Harbor, December 7, 1941, nearly 5,000 Indians, still declaring their sovereignty, had enlisted in the armed services.[81] Although many Indians enlisted into the military, this did not mean they had surrendered their sovereignty. The state government was motivated to extend its control of Indian reservations and tried to expand civil law

---

October 4, 2005).

John Collier was an opponent of the assimilation policy that had governed federal-Indian programs. As a veteran social worker, he founded the American Indian Defense Association in 1923 and won respect among reformers for his policies and through writings and legislative battles he was part of during the 1920s. During the 12 years he was commissioner, federal policies changed drastically to the detriment of the Native American population.

[79] Hauptman. *The Iroquois and the New Deal,* 9.

[80] U.S. Department of Defense, "American Indian Heritage Month: American Indians in World War II," American Forces Information Service, http://www.defenselink.mil/specials/nativeamerican01/wwii.html (accessed October 3, 2005). According to Selective Service officials in January1942, 99 percent of all eligible Native Americans had registered for the draft.

[81] Ibid.

over them. The New York State Joint Legislative Committee on Indian Affairs repeatedly petitioned Congress to extend state civil jurisdiction over Indian land. The US Court of Appeals in 1942 stated in *United States v. Forness*, that New York could not extend its civil laws over the Seneca Reservations.[82] In 1950, Congress reversed its direction and passed legislation that sanctioned state courts limited civil jurisdiction. Congress limited general civil regulatory, (tax authority jurisdiction) to New York State over the Six Nations Territory and reservations.[83]

In Canada, the situation was different. In 1840, the *Act of Union* was signed by the British colonies. This placed Upper and Lower Canada under a centralized government with equal representation in the assembly. By1850, the situation had become a stalemate, and it was difficult to form a government.[84] The economy of the new union needed to be invigorated. In February 1855, Canada and the US signed the *Canadian-American Reciprocity Treaty of 1855*, which lasted until March 1866. "It provided for free trade in all natural products, free access for United States fisheries to the Atlantic coastal waters of British North America, and access to the St. Lawrence River for American vessels under the same tolls as native

---

[82] Seneca Nation, "Communication of Complaint," 21.
[83] Ibid.
[84] Alvin Finkel and Margaret Conrad, *History of the Canadian Peoples: 1867 to the Present, vol. 2,* (Toronto: Copp Clark Ltd., 1998),10,29,30.

vessels."[85] The treaty allowed Canada, a small country with a population of 3 million people, into a market of 33 to 34 million people.[86] Results were ambiguous, but it is clear that the Reciprocity Treaty did not provide, by itself, the basis for Canada's economic recovery. Its effect paled in comparison to the "really dynamic forces of railway construction in the 1850's and the American Civil War, reconstruction, and inflation of the 1860's."[87]

The Canadian government in the 1860s saw the US government's desire to expand throughout all of North America by its actions on its southern border. British troops had defended Upper and Lower Canada the last time the US attacked them during the War of 1812. When the Civil War began in America, its manifest destiny was derailed for the war's duration. However, the threat of attack was a possibility after the Civil War. The US returned to its expansionist policies, buying Alaska from the Russians in 1867 and showing an interest to acquire Rupert's Land.[88] Although the US did not bring its million-man army against them, the Canadians remained leery of US expansionism.[89]

In 1864, Canada had a failed government and the provinces were over-extended because of loan guarantees and railroad subsidies, the Canadian province made overtures to the British Maritimes to

---

[85] Lawrence H. Officer and Lawrence B. Smith, "The Canadian-American Reciprocity Treaty of 1855 to 1866." *The Journal of Economic History* 28, no. 4 (1968): 598.

[86] Ibid.

[87] Ibid., 623.

[88] Ultimately sold to Canada in 1869 by the Hudson Bay Company.

[89] Finkel and Conrad, *History of the Canadian Peoples,* 7.

form a United Province that would include the Northwest Territory. This eventually led to three conferences: Charlottetown, Prince Edward Island in September 1864, Québec City October 1864, and London in the winter of 1866-1867. In March 1867, the British Parliament passed the *British North America Act*. In addition to forming a federal dominion and addressing natural resources, the act placed Indians throughout Canada under the jurisdiction of the federal government and registered.[90]

During the early 1870s, the early Dominion of Canada was engaged in securing treaties with Indians and with configuring the provinces of Manitoba and British Columbia.[91] Beginning in 1869 and lasting through 1870, the government took steps to arrange the huge tracks of land for agricultural settlement. The controversial land titles erupted into the Riel Rebellion in the agricultural colony of Red River.[92] The only important settlement in the west, east of the Rockies, was the Red River colony. The largest number of settlers was Métis.[93] Their leader, Louis Riel, defied the

---

[90] Ibid., 29-30, 41.

[91] Bonnie Leask, Melissa Cote, Marlene Lumberjack, Blair McDaid, Eldon Henderson and Dustin Francis, "History of the Indian Act," *Saskatchewan Indian*" 08, no. 03 (1978): 4.

[92] D. Aldan McQuillan, "Creation of Indian Reserves on the Canadian Prairies 1870-1885," *Geographical Review* 70, no. 4 (1980): 379.

[93] "Prior to Canada's crystallization as a nation in west central North America, the Métis people emerged out of the relations of Indian women and European men. While the initial offspring of these Indian and European unions were individuals who possessed mixed ancestry, the gradual establishment of distinct Métis

new governor and seized Fort Garry, setting up his own provisional government. Riel forwarded Ottawa his demands that the civil and the land rights of the people be protected. He imprisoned Ontario settlers who opposed him and had Thomas Scott executed for trying to continue the resistance against the Métis.[94]

The Métis were particularly politicized because of Riel. Métis people were known as "mixed bloods" with Indian and European parentage. As the numbers of Métis grew, there was a settling of distinct Métis communities outside of Indian and European cultures and settlements. The subsequent intermarriage between Métis women and men resulted in the beginning of a new Aboriginal people.[95]

The *Dominion Lands Act* (1872) opened 160 acres of land to farmers who cleared 10 acres, built a home, and registered their settling within three years. The act was intended to encourage European settlers but not aboriginal or Métis settlers.[96] In

---

communities, outside of Indian and European cultures and settlements, as well as, the subsequent intermarriages between Métis women and Métis men, resulted in the genesis of a new Aboriginal people - the Métis." Métis National Council, "Who Are the Métis?" Métis National Council, http://www.metisnation.ca/who/index.html (accessed August 18, 2007).

[94] Finkel and Conrad, *History of the Canadian Peoples*, 37-41.

[95] D.N. Collins, R. Todd, G. Mercer, H.N. Nicholson, D.S. Wall and M. Thornton. *Aboriginal People and Other Canadians: Shaping New Relationships*, eds. Martin and Roy Todd Thornton (Ottawa: University of Ottawa Press, 2001),10,17,21,43, 146-147.

[96] Finkel and Conrad, *History of the Canadian Peoples*, 41.

1873, the Canadian government created the Royal Northwest Mounted Police in an attempt to end situations such as this and bring law and order to the area.

Additionally, the government signed a number of treaties with the Indians that began with *Treaty One* in 1871 and ended with *Treaty Seven* in 1877.[97] The purpose of these treaties was to obliterate Indian title to lands planned for the onrush of European and white immigration that began in 1873. By signing the treaties, the Indians were to receive inalienable reserves of land, clothing, and payments of cash. After consultation with chiefs, the land was to be surveyed for the desired locations of the reserves. The individual Indian bands were to be given farm implements, potatoes, grain, livestock, and seed for farming. There was also a promise of schools to provide education for the children.[98]

In 1876, the *Indian Act* was passed consolidating the federal government's policies on Indians. It tended to be a living document and was revised periodically. The philosophy of the act was that "[Indians] were still incapable of integrating into 'civilized' society and therefore needed supervision in their economic, political, and social activities."[99] With the signing of the act the political structure changed. It went from the traditional structure of Band Chiefs and councils to a regional and national hierarchy. The act also

---

[97] McQuillan, "Creation of Indian Reserves," 382; Finkel and Conrad. *History of the Canadian Peoples,* 40-41.
[98] Ibid.
[99] Ibid.

determined who was an Indian. Eventually, the Indians had restrictions placed upon them including not drinking alcohol and not practicing their native religion.[100] The treaties had a provision for hunting and fishing rights in areas that were not settled or which were not set aside for lumber or mining. All of the Indians were encouraged to take up farming, and allowed to substitute livestock (animal husbandry) in the place of farm implements (agriculture). Additionally, the federal government surveyed the land and identified portions for Indian reservations.[101]

From 1876 to 1880, the surveys of Indian land, which had been promised by the federal government, were delayed. One problem was the lack of surveyors. Because of immigration increases, surveying crews were busy preparing land for the coming European and white occupiers. Between the delays in setting up the reserves and the shortage of buffalo, the Indians were not interested in settling permanently; they wanted to follow their traditional ways. Eventually, the lack of sufficient game reduced the Indians to a state of starvation, and eventually, to dependence on the federal government for food and supplies.[102] Evidence supports that the federal government did try, in good faith, to help the Indians become self-supporting farmers. The Indian Commissioner, as early as 1873, said that the best way to get the Indians to settle down was to give them a connection to the land. Part of the solution was to

---

[100] Ibid.
[101] McQuillan, "Creation of Indian Reserves," 382.
[102] Ibid., 384.

hire farmers from Ontario to establish European style model farms where the Indians could learn the techniques for this style of farming through observation and practical experience. By 1881, there were twenty-six instructors with some of them tending herds of government cattle. These herds were broken up and given to individual Indian bands. Ranching became much more prevalent than root-crop farming.[103]

The *Indian Advancement Act* (1884) tried to give increased powers to local government and to raise money. However, it took away the same powers by appointing the local Indian Agent as chairman of the Council.[104] Agents played a key role in locating reserves and affecting the geographic distribution of Indians. It appears that most agents performed their duties fairly.[105]

The Canadian government, until the Great Depression, made changes and amendments to the *Indian Advancement Act* that impinged upon the Indians. These changes prohibited the incitement of riots of Indians and half-breeds against the Canadian government and the sale of ammunition to Indians. The act declared the Mohawk celebration known as the Potlatch, and various other traditional dances and customs, illegal. During and after the Great Depression through to the end of the Second World War, these changes and amendments decreased significantly. In the late 1940s, a Joint

---

[103] Bonnie Leask, Melissa Cote, Marlene Lumberjack, Blair McDaid, Eldon Henderson and Dustin Francis, "History of the Indian Act," *Saskatchewan Indian* 08, no. 03 (1978): 4.

[104] Ibid.

[105] McQuillan, "Creation of Indian Reserves," 387.

Committee of the Senate and House of Commons declared that all the sections of the act should be repealed or removed to encourage the transition of Indians into Canadian citizens.[106]

The Seaway Brings Devastating Changes

The building of the St. Lawrence Seaway, reaching across Northern New York and Southern Canada, impacted the Mohawks on both sides of the river. Joint international construction of the Seaway began in 1954 and the first ocean-going vessels entered the system on April 25, 1959.[107] The impact on the several reservations was enormous, both in the number of acres taken and in affecting the quality of ancestral life. One reservation that was impacted was the St. Regis Indian Reservation/Akwesasne. (See Figure 4, Ontario Hydro Blueprint for Cornwall-Massena Section of the Seaway July 1958. Page 125)

The St. Lawrence Seaway project helped make regions on both sides of the United States and Canada border economic powerhouses. It had the opposite effect on Akwesasne. The reservation lost parts of its shoreline and entire islands beneath the rising waters. The power project disrupted the spawning patterns of fish and reduced the oxygen levels in the water. The power-generating capability and the cheap utility rates attracted three

---

[106] McQuillan, "Creation of Indian Reserves," 387; Leask, "History of the Indian Act."; Finkel and Conrad, *History of the Canadian Peoples*, 235-237.

[107] Darren Bonaparte, "The History of Akwesasne: From Pre-Contact to Modern Times," Wampum Chronicles, http://wampumchronicles.com/history.html (accessed August 17, 2005).

major industrial plants (Alcoa, Reynolds Aluminum, and General Motors) to the area upriver and upwind of Akwesasne. These plants released large quantities of mercury and polychlorinated biphenyls (PCBs) into the St. Lawrence River, which contaminated the river, air, and soil with toxic chemicals and adversely affected the fishing, farming, and health of the community.[108] The project displaced and relocated six hundred and fifty families, (approximately nine thousand people), forty-seven miles of highway, and forty miles of double track railroad; it also resulted in the condemnation of approximately 100 square miles of property.[109] Other losses were Barnhart Island, the building of an international bridge across Cornwall Island, the installation of a customs house and associated complex located at the entrance to Canada and the reservation.[110] To build the Customs complex and bridge, the Canadian government condemned over 130 acres of land for the buildings, the bridge, and approach ways. This was done despite of objections to the expropriation of Akwesasne lands and the breaking of treaties.[111] What further compounded the problem was that Cornwall Island, which connected both sides of the reservation, was now cut off from the reservation on the US side. Building the Seaway caused the loss of

---

[108] Ibid.

[109] Laurence M. Hauptman, *The Iroquois Struggle for Survival: World War II to Red Power* (Syracuse: Syracuse University Press, 1986), 133.

[110] Bonaparte, "The History of Akwesasne."

[111] Hauptman, *The Iroquois Struggle for Survival*, 147.

traditional ways of Mohawk life and changed the face of their community forever.

Opposition to the Seaway and the changes it brought was bitter and in some locations, there was "open rebellion."[112] The Seaway introduced a new approach to protesting for the Mohawks. As early as August 1957, activism began in open opposition to the Seaway with the occupation of land near Ft. Hunter, New York. Although the yearlong action was unsuccessful, it foretold the direction of the future.[113] Since the building of the Canadian custom offices and the formalization of the border in the 1950s there have been, and continue to be, conflicts between the Mohawks and the US and Canadian governments.[114]

---

[112] Ibid., 136.
[113] Ibid., 149.
[114] CP, "Indians Take Trailer from Customs Site." *The Toronto Star*, May 10, 1989.

CHAPTER 3

The Activism of the 60's, 70's and the 1980's

The 1960s witnessed the change and recognition of various problems occurring in the US. We see the birth of the Civil Rights movement come into its own, with the recognition of many minority groups ignored in the past. One minority that was looking to see things change was the Indians, especially the Iroquois. The beginnings of the American Indian Movement (AIM) and "Red Power" were in the 60s, 70s, and 1980s..[115] Indians protested and demanded that treaties be upheld, that land taken unscrupulously be returned, that bones taken from graves be given back for the reinternment, and that taken artifacts be repatriated. It was also a time, when non-Indians were ejected from reservations and non-tribal police forces were asked not to enter reservations uninvited.

In 1968, after years of the Canadian government imposing tariffs and taxes on goods that the Mohawks brought across the border, over 100 Mohawks, predominantly women and children blocked the International Bridge at Cornwall with their bodies and their vehicles. They sat down and threw themselves in front of tow trucks to keep the

---

[115] Alfred Taiaiake and Lana Lowe, "Warrior Societies in Contemporary Indigenous Communities," in A Background Paper Prepared for the Ipperwash Inquiry, (University of Victoria, 2005),10-15.

bridge from being cleared. The protesters faced down both the Royal Canadian Mounted Police and the Ontario Provincial Police for what they believed in, with over forty people arrested.[116] Around the same time, the Kahnawake Singers Society began using the term 'warrior society.' It originally began as a group of young people who were committed to Mohawk[117] "teachings, language, and structure."[118] Their tactics to invoke change included barricades, roadblocks, eviction of non-Indian people from reservations, and repossessing original lands.[119] In January 1969, as a result of the bridge occupation and blockage, the State Department and Indian Affairs Bureau officials had a meeting with Canadian representatives to try to settle the disagreement between the Canadians and Mohawks. Their concern focused on the custom duties paid by Indians for purchases bought in the US and taken to Canada. US Representative J.M. Hanley (NYS), who requested the meeting, intervened on behalf of Indian representatives who were not invited.[120] The Canadian government finally relented to the Indian's demands after a series of negotiations and another sit-in in February 1969.[121] However, in March 1969 seven Mohawk Indians went on trial protesting Canadian customs and duty by blocking the international bridge.

---

[116] Hauptman, *The Iroquois Struggle for Survival*, 148-149.

[117] In original quote, the name used was Kanien´kehaka.

[118] Alfred and Lowe, "Warrior Societies," 14.

[119] Ibid.

[120] Staff, "Attempt to Settle Dispute between Mohawks and Canada over Customs Duties," *New York Times*, January 18, 1969.

[121] Hauptman, *The Iroquois Struggle for Survival*, 148-149.

Evictions of non-Indians from Iroquois reservations began in the 1970s. In September 1970, the Tuscarora nation evicted forty non-Indian families from the reservation.[122] In 1973, the Mohawk Warrior Society backed by the Longhouse, forced whites living on the Kahnawake reservation near Montreal to leave. During the eviction process, violence and riots broke out.[123] The 1970s also brought the occupation of historic Indian lands. Indians began occupying territory that they believed was theirs by treaty or because treaties were broken. This began when Mohawks, inspired by the occupation of Alcatraz Island, landed on Stanley and Loon islands in the St. Lawrence River and occupied them.[124]

An ongoing problem was the return of artifacts. In April 1970, the Iroquois went to Albany, New York to retrieve their sacred Wampum Belts from the New York State Museum. By agreement the State University of New York was made the keeper of the Wampum in 1898.[125] In March 1971, bills were introduced in the New York State Assembly to strengthen treaty rights, to recognize an 1813 law concerning free passage on freeways and toll roads, return of the Wampum Belts, and to change the 1898 law.[126] Although Governor Nelson

---

[122] Staff, "Tuscarora Indians Get Court Permit to Evict Non-Indian Families," *New York Times*, September 1, 1970.

[123] Alfred and Lowe, "Warrior Societies," 28-30.

[124] Ibid.

[125] Staff, "Iroquois Confed Leaders in Albany, NY," *New York Times*, April 17, 1970.

[126] Staff, "Series of Bills to Strengthen Treaty Rights of Reservation Indians," *New York Times*, March 11, 1971.

Rockefeller signed a bill allowing the NYS Assembly to return the five Wampum Belts in July 1971 they were not returned at that time. In March 1976, a bill was introduced for the ninth time in nine years to return the Wampum Belts. It was sponsored by Senator Joseph F. Lisa, but opposed by James H. Donovan because of a conflict at Moss Lake between Mohawks and the state. New York State, again, agreed to return the Wampum. In August 1989, the New York State Regents allowed public comment on the situation.[127] The Wampum Belts were finally returned to the Iroquois in July 1996.[128]

These events inspired Warrior societies to emerge and grow. Warrior societies were used by a number of different nations in the Iroquois confederation. In 1971, the Onondagas tried to block roadways through their land and called in the Mohawk Warrior Society to help block the road. In 1973, the Kahnawake Longhouse sanctioned this same society to evict whites from the Kahnawake reservation.[129] Riots ensued, which caused Kahnawake to send out scouts to search for land within their historic territory in New York and Vermont. On May 13, 1974, a group of Mohawks occupied an abandoned Girl Scout camp at Moss Lake, New York and claimed it as lost Mohawk

---

[127] Harold Faber, "New York Returning Wampum Belts to Onondagas," *New York Times*, August 13, 1989.

[128] Robert L. Smith, "Iroquois Treasures Returning Home under Order of Congress, Museums Are Returning Sacred Objects Belonging to Native Americans," *The Post Standard*, July 5, 1996.

[129] Alfred and Lowe, "Warrior Societies," 28-30.

territory. During the occupation, two people were accidentally shot, and many non-Indians protested the takeover. Although the Mohawks had no legal right to the land, New York negotiated a trade in 1977 for a state recreation area on Miner Lake, about 50 miles east of Akwesasne near Altona, New York in Clinton County.[130] This new location was named Ganienkeh and was occupied a year later, in 1978.[131] Events were becoming more confrontational.

On May 22, 1979, US federal workers were clearing trees on the Akwesasne Reservation land to construct a perimeter fence under a program approved by the elected chiefs. Some of the land that was cleared was owned by traditionalist Chief Loran Thompson. [132] He was upset with federal workers cutting trees for the fence and confiscated their chainsaws and other equipment, claiming that the project was illegal under tribal and NYS law. Thompson agreed to meet with tribal and elected officials the next week. Later that day eight New York State Police and three tribal police came to Thompson's house to arrest him. A struggle ensued,

---

[130] Measured from Hogansburg, NY (44.973N, -74.663W), which is on the Akwesasne/St. Regis Reservation.

[131] Gail Landsman, "Ganienkeh: Symbol and Politics in an Indian/White Conflict," *American Anthropologist* 87, no. 4 (1985): 827.

[132] "Traditionalists do not vote, pay taxes or serve in armed forces and have been withdrawing children from outside schools. They believe in absolute sovereignty of Indian people and Indian lands. Contemporary Mohawks, generally Christians, favor modern form of elective government and want benefits and accept obligations of citizenship." Alan Richman, "15 Traditionalists Serving 3-Year Terms," *New York Times*, August 31, 1979.

and a seventy-three-year-old woman was injured and taken to the hospital. Thompson was charged with resisting arrest, as well as the charge of grand larceny. Over 100 traditionalists took over the community building for eleven hours and on May 29 demanded the resignation of the tribal police, who were an all-Native arm of the Franklin County Sheriff's Department. The District Attorney of Franklin County, Joseph Ryan, authorized twenty-three warrants for the arrest of traditional Indians involved in the takeover. Over the summer, negotiations were conducted concerning Thompson and the others under indictment. Eventually 15 traditionalists ended up serving three-year terms.[133]

On August 28, 1979, the New York State Police conducted a pre-dawn raid with 50 troopers and a special-forces assault team that included three helicopters and thirty police squad cars. The police confronted 50 barricaded and armed Mohawks to serve twenty-three arrest warrants authorized by the Franklin County District Attorney. After a ten-hour siege, the police had only served two of the twenty-three arrest warrants. Later that day, the police withdrew so that state and federal mediators could meet with the Mohawks. By August 29, fifty to two hundred Mohawks remained behind barricades and "refused to concede sovereignty."[134]

---

[133] Richman, "15 Traditionalists Serving 3-Year Terms," 2; SPCL, "300 Indians Defy New York State Authority," *The Globe and Mail*, November 19, 1979.

[134] GAM, "Troopers Leave Reservation," *The Globe and Mail*, August 29, 1979; Alan Richman, "50 to 200 Upstate NYS Mohawk Indians, Traditionalists Who Refuse to Concede Sovereignty over Land to State," *New York Times*, August 29, 1979,

This event started to change how the Mohawks interacted with the state and federal governments. Many Indians living on the reserve decided that the Native system of justice was more just than the state and federal governments they had to comply with. Ed Benedict, the spokesman for the Traditionalists, stated how a number of Christian Indians supported the traditionalists in this situation. When Franklin County District Attorney Ryan was going to indict the Mohawks for the takeover in May 1979, Benedict disagreed, citing the *Canandaigua Treaty* (1794). He stated the treaty contends, "Only the US Federal Government is authorized to settle disputes between Indians and non-Indians."[135] By August 29, 1979, the road to Raquette Point was barricaded. Benedict emphasized that they would remain and be manned by armed Indian guards until the jurisdictional issues were resolved.[136] The resolution was slow in coming. Fletcher Graves of the US Department of Justice (1989) spoke on the problem at Raquette saying, "It took over a year to get things straightened out. The issue in 1979 turned on the type of government the community wanted to have and the rights of the state to call police in."[137]

By June 13, 1980, the situation had changed significantly in many ways. The Traditionalists were still camped on Thompson's property at Raquette Point, and more than just the New York

---

4; SPCL. "300 Indians Defy New York State Authority," *The Globe and Mail*, November 19, 1979.

[135] Ibid.
[136] Ibid.
[137] Rick Hornung, *One Nation under the Gun: Inside the Mohawk Civil War* (New York: Pantheon, 1991), 53.

State Police were opposed to them. The Tribalists, known previously as Contemporary or Christian Indians, accused the Traditionalists of outside influenced. The Tribalists wanted the Traditionalists to obey the elected government and settle their dispute with the state and the Tribal government. Because of the threat of violence, the New York State Police separated the two groups. The Traditionalists believed armed conflict was imminent and that the state police were going to invade their area. However, they did not invade. Governor Hugh Carey assured the Mohawks at Raquette Point that the police would not invade the Traditionalists' area. Raymond Harding, a spokesman for the governor, held separate meetings with the Tribalists, and the Traditionalists on June 16. The meetings resolved the dispute and the Tribalists backed away from the barricades.[138]

The conflict remained located on the US side of the border. The only involvement from the Canadian side of the reservation was providing food and other supplies.[139] The situation dragged on and eventually ended without violence or death. In 1981, the tribal police force on the US side was disbanded after a vote on the reservation.[140]

---

[138] Ian Austen, "Indians Meet State Envoy as Reserve Tension Eases," *The Globe and Mail*, June 17, 1980, Canada; Ian Austen, "Troopers Keep Peace in Mohawk Dispute," *The Globe and Mail*, June 16, 1980, Canada; Ward Morehouse III, "Feuding Mohawk Groups, NY Troopers in Standoff," *Christian Science Monitor*, June 24, 1980.

[139] Ibid.

[140] Matthew Cox, "In St. Regis Strife, Echoes of History," *The Post-Standard*, July 10, 1990.

This is a modern example, of Mohawks taking up arms over jurisdictional problems. It was different from blocking bridges and protesting - it was an armed defense of their territory when they were confronted by a superior and alien power. The New York State authorities, external to the reservation, assisted the Tribalists faction, which was united around and supported, the federally recognized Tribal government. On the other side, the Traditionalists, who scorned modern tribal government in favor of the Longhouse style. The external forces, alleged by the Tribalists as being involved with the Traditionalists, were agents of the American Indian Movement (AIM). The consequences of these events include state and federal law enforcement and the Warrior faction aligned with the AIM. Another consequence of this event that would have an impact on the future; the Traditionalist movement split into two different factions, the Warrior Society and the Mohawk Council of Chiefs.[141] A third consequence of this split was the growth of the Mohawk Warrior Society and its financing by the cigarette market between Akwesasne and Kahanawake.[142]

---

[141] Ibid.

[142] "Teyowisonte ... 'US Mohawks, particularly the Warrior Society, got a bad name because we were always associated with cigarette smuggling and super bingos.'" and "Through the 1970s and 1980s, the Kahnawake-based Mohawk Warrior Society expanded to the neighboring community of Akwesasne and was instrumental to the establishment of a lucrative cigarette trade that generated revenue for both the Warrior Society and the traditional governments in the Kanien'kehaka communities." And "1980s: Growth of Mohawk Warrior Society, financially supported by burgeoning cigarette trade

The New York State Police were brought onto the reservation a number of times. On May 10, 1984, they responded to a riot and the burning of an unlicensed bar. Three weeks prior to this incident there were nine alcohol-related deaths; a recent one had been a woman who was eight weeks pregnant. Two establishments, Josie's Bar and Vera's Bar, both unlicensed, were identified as sites of trouble. According to Hogansburg Fire Chief, Frank A. Lacerenza, a group of Indian women who formed a Mothers Against Drunk Driving (MADD) group, had been protesting against the unlicensed bars on May 8.[143] On May 9, two people were killed on a motorcycle after leaving Josie's Bar. On May 10th, New York State Police took the owner of Josie's, Josephine White, into custody in connection with the accident. There were about 250 to 300 protesters surrounding the building as the State Police took White away. The police did not disperse the crowd and around 9 PM about 50 men pushed through the front of the crowd, broke into the bar, and started it on fire. As the fire department responded, 300 protesters, on foot and in automobiles, blocked them. Even though they were close by, the fire department was not allowed to put out the fire. When the State Police returned, they intervened in the situation, however Josie's was

---

at Akwesasne and Kahnawake." Alfred and Lowe, "Warrior Societies," 8,15, 21.

[143] Hogansburg, NY (44.973N, -74.663W), is a hamlet at Akwesasne on the US side of the border on route 37 at the cross streets of Church St., St. Regis St. W. Main St., and Hogansburg Rd.

totally destroyed.[144] Without a written complaint, New York State Police could not respond and close bars on the reservation. Troopers said that Mohawks were uncertain about filing a complaint with the state police against other Indians and preferred to handle it within the community.[145]

The Canadian side of the reservation had its own set of circumstances and problems. Police had closed down two bars since December 1985.[146] Chief Mike Mitchell and the Mohawk Council of Akwesasne (Canadian Mohawk government) wanted to change the status of their ten-member Mohawk Police Force to a more autonomous, private reserve force, similar to the Peace Keepers at Kahnawaka that had been in service since 1979. Mitchell said that this was the direction the reservation had been moving in, but because of Ontario Provincial Police (OPP) harassment the council had been trying to expedite the change. The first incident considered harassment by the Mohawks, was over the Stetson-style police hats the Mohawk force had decided to wear. The OPP of the Long Sault detachment said that the US-style hats did not meet uniform standards. When asked about the hats Sergeant Wes Prosser of the OPP said, "personally, I'm a Canadian."[147] OPP Commissioner

---

[144] Robert O. Boorstin," A Tavern Is Burned to the Ground on SL Indian Reservation Upstate," *New York Times*, May 11, 1986; Esther B. Fein, "Indians' Rage at Illegal Bar Fuels Upstate Fire," *New York Times*, May 12, 1986.

[145] Ibid.

[146] Ibid.

[147] CP, "Mohawk Band Council Wants OPP Kept Off the Reserve," *The Toronto Star*, October 6, 1986.

Archie Ferguson, however agreed with the Mohawks' rationale, stating that the Stetsons reflected the geographical setting of the reservation.[148]

This next confrontation between the Mohawks and the OPP concerned the right of reservation conservation officers to carry guns. Chief Mitchell said that as officers had to charge people with crimes such as speeding, unsafe boating, polluting, using the wrong firearms, and fishing and hunting without permits, they should be able to carry weapons. The Mohawk Police Force, since they were affiliated with the auxiliary police, had to bring their prisoners before a justice of the peace. The Mohawk Council originally wanted the officers trained by the OPP but when they did not cooperate the council had the officers trained at the New York State Police Academy. In discussing the Mohawk Police Force, Sergeant Prosser said, "[Mohawk Officers] do not fall into the group of people generally empowered by federal legislation to carry arms." Additionally, Prosser wrote a memo instructing OPP officers to arrest any conservation officers (Mohawk Police) who were carrying weapons. The police officers were told not to let the media sway them in carrying out their duty. Fred Longechamps, OPP Superintendent, supported Prosser's memo and said that the Cornwall Island portion of the reserve was within OPP jurisdiction for routine patrols. Chief Mitchell said the routine patrols had become a problem since the OPP was waging a "campaign of intimidation" by issuing a

---

[148] Ibid.

glut of tickets against Mohawks on the island. [149] The OPP denied targeting Mohawks, saying the tickets were issued on routine patrols.

During October 1986, the Mohawk Council passed a resolution and informed the OPP not to enter the reserve unless they were specifically requested by the council to act as backup for the Mohawk police. Copies of this resolution, approved by the council, were sent to the federal and provincial officials.[150] This was not the end of conflict; there continued to be friction on the border over the paying of duty and free passage.

During the 1980s, Port Cornwall was the only Canadian customs post where the employees were prohibited from talking about the risk they faced every day. The custom workers described themselves as "hostages under siege."[151] Mansel Legacy, National President of the Customs Excise Union, stated that the situation was more than just a scandal. Legacy said that the situation was at a point that, "if something isn't done, people are going to get very seriously hurt, or killed." [152] He said that the Customs Union was being hamstrung by the federal government and by the department (of revenue), and said, "let me say, very adamantly, that we are under siege at the Port of Cornwall. We are being held hostage. If our officers do not enforce the Customs Act, as they were hired to do, then they are culpable - they could even be charged with

---

[149] Ibid.
[150] Ibid.
[151] CP, "Customs Wants Probe of Alleged Smugglers," *The Toronto Star*, January 22, 1988.
[152] Ibid.

violation of the federal statute." [153] Legacy continued that, according to their instructions, "unless we're 100 per cent sure there is smuggling going on, we're not to send those cars in for any kind of secondary examination, which is ludicrous."[154]

Custom officers had problems on the border because of the Mohawks' belief that they could cross the border at will and with any goods in their possession. Until September 1987, the customs department had not been diligent in charging duties on items bought in or brought from the US. After September, the Canadian Customs began enforcing the law.[155] On July 23, 1987, two hundred Mohawks threatened to force a mobile home through Canadian Customs. Initially, the customs officials were going to resist but eventually decided on a compromise so there would not be a "confrontation over the historically volatile customs issue."[156] Jim Brenner, Chief of Customs Operation of the Canadian Port of Cornwall, stated, "We did not want a confrontation with the native people either in the past . . . or now, and in the future," Chief Mike Mitchell argued that the 14 feet by 66 feet mobile home was a personal possession and not

---

[153] Ibid.

[154] Ibid.

[155] CP, "Mohawk Chief Fights for Right to Shop on U.S. Side of Reserve," *The Toronto Star*, November 12, 1987.

[156] AP, "St. Regis Mohawks, Canadian Guards Clash at Border," *The Post-Standard*, July 24, 1987.

subject to the thirty-two hundred dollar duty.[157] More confrontations over duty were to come.

On November 22, 1987, Chief Mitchell was arrested bringing groceries across the border without paying duty. In a speech to one hundred and fifty Mohawk supporters Mitchell said, "This is a symbolic gesture to underline our rights. I won't tolerate outside people arresting our people for living here."[158] Mitchell was involved again on March 22, 1988, pushing the point of sovereignty and free access across the border. Mitchell, with 300 supporters following silently behind, crossed the border, bringing Mohawk clothes and furniture through customs without paying duty. Mitchell was arrested but released on his own recognizance to appear in court at a later date. Speaking to the crowd, Mitchell said, "as far as we're concerned, we're citizens of the Mohawk Nation and our rights of survival are at stake. We're caught between the United States and Canada as a community. . . We need to show our unity and fight for border rights."[159]

Other chiefs of the Mohawk Council spoke concerning customs, "We're willing to stop at customs and declare what we bring across. But, . . . the people in the community are having their clothes and groceries and personal items confiscated and taken away from them."[160] Mitchell said,

---

[157] Ibid.

[158] CP, "Mohawk Chief Fights for Right to Shop."

[159] Janis Barth, "Mohawk Chief Arrested During Protest at Canadian Border," *The Post Standard*, March 23, 1988.

[160] Rosalie MacEachern, "Mohawk Chief Faces Charge in Border Protest," *The Toronto Star*, March 23, 1988.

"Smuggling has blackened the name of every Mohawk and it is giving the federal (Canadian) government an excuse not to listen to us."[161]

Warriors

During the 1980s, as much as five million dollars-worth of Canadian cigarettes passed through the Akwesasne reservation in the smuggling network.[162] The Warrior Societies of Akwesasne and Kahnawake were intertwined in this trade. Another problem connected to the Warriors in a peripheral way and certainly ideologically, was the bingo, gaming, and gambling enterprises. Over the years there had been bingo, and gambling halls operating on the reservation. The Warriors, although not directly connected to them, supported the idea of sovereignty and, therefore, the rights of the Mohawks to own and operate their gambling establishments. The Warriors and the elected US Tribal Chiefs of Akwesasne supported bingo. Although there had been overtures for high stakes bingo on the Canadian side of Akwesasne, Canada's Indian policies were significantly different than the US's and would not allow it. When speaking of the sovereignty differences between the US and Canadian portions of the reservation, Chief Mike Mitchell said that he did not want to, "argue

---

[161] Ibid.
[162] CP, "Border Reserve Called Smugglers' Den up to $250 Million of Cigarettes Handled a Year, Newspaper Says," *The Toronto Star*, January 19 1988.

sovereignty for the basis for bingo."[163] The Mohawk government on the US side, however since 1985, was a fifty percent partner in the Mohawk Bingo Palace. There were protests by some Mohawks on the first day of business, but the elected tribal council sanctioned it.[164] "In 1987, the US Supreme Court rendered a six to three decision upholding the rights of Indians to use their land for bingo and gambling enterprises provided they were approved by the elected chiefs and authorities."[165] On August 15, 1987, there was a referendum on the US side of the border that passed by 600 votes prohibiting gambling, but allowing bingo and similar games. The owners were given until September 19, 1987, to remove their slot machines.[166]

Early on the morning of December 16, 1987, the New York State Police, acting on the request of the US elected tribal officials, raided the reservation. The police used seven trucks to confiscate and remove 203 slot machines from the reservation. Those who opposed state intervention in tribal affairs did not cause any confrontations as had been expected. Head Chief (on the US side) Rosemary Bonaparte stated that the casino owners had been given adequate time to voluntarily remove their slot machines. She said, "everybody knew it

---

[163] Rudy Platiel, "Reserve Reaps High Stakes Indians Hit Jackpot on Bingo," *Globe and Mail*, July 25 1985.
[164] Ibid.
[165] Hornung, One Nation under the Gun, 33.
[166] Janis Barth, "Mohawk Land Raided Slot Machines Seized," *The Post Standard*, December 17, 1987.

was just a matter of time before they were removed. It's been almost three months . . . We told them we had turned the matter over to the state. I hope they [slot machines] are gone for good now."[167]

Smuggling

Another point of conflict involved the smuggling of contraband.[168] It has occurred across the border, along the St. Lawrence River at Akwesasne, since the War of 1812, but has changed over time in its complexity. It was connected to the idea of unencumbered travel with personal items. In this case, it included the transporting of commercial stock from one side of the border to the other without duty. Gasoline and cigarettes were the two commodities that were transported the most. Canadian and US taxes were the issue. The reservation is exempt from NYS tax on the US, and in Canada the property of an individual Indian or of the tribe is tax-exempt on the reservation. At this time, Mohawks could buy a car in New York and only have to pay federal tax on the sale as long as they could provide proof of their Indian status. In the 1980s, a Mohawk also could buy gas and

---

[167] Ibid.

[168] "Contraband is any substance, object, or product that has been deemed illegal, by law or treaty, to transport across the international border. Typically, at the Akwesasne border area, this would include drugs (prescription or illegal), cigarettes and other tobacco products without proper duty and taxes paid, or alcohol products without proper duty and taxes paid and transported across the border." The Free Dictionary, s.v. "Contraband," http://legal-dictionary. thefreedictionary.com/contraband (accessed October 15, 2007).

cigarettes on the reservation without paying NYS sales tax. The reservation stores were open not only to residents of the reservation, but to outsiders too. People from outside the reservation could buy gas and cigarettes, state tax-free, on the reservation and then leave. State and provincial authorities frowned on this. The main problem that concerned the state and provincial authorities was smuggling. A perfect example of the smuggling problem is the movement of cigarettes. (See Figure 5. Akwesasne Cigarette Smuggling Routes. Page 126)

Cigarettes transported from their US manufacturer to a Canadian location on the reservation were shipped wholesale and tax-free. This was legal on the Canadian side of the reservation; however, these same US cigarettes were then smuggled across the border at Akwesasne back into the US, and sold tax-free on the US side. Even worse, retailers from off the reservation, such as in Syracuse or Rochester, New York, would drive to Akwesasne with tractor trailers and buy untaxed cigarettes to sell at a profit at their establishment at home. The same was done with Canadian cigarettes. They were shipped to the US and then smuggled back into Canada. The Canadian government lost a great deal more revenue than the US government. Canadian Mohawks processed about $250 million in cigarettes a year. Canadian loses in federal taxes in 1988 were $38.80 per one thousand cigarettes, and the province of Ontario lost an additional $28.30 per one thousand cigarettes lost.[169]

---

[169] CP, "Border Reserve Called Smugglers' Den up to $250

The money that could be amassed through cigarette smuggling was enormous and made a small number of people millionaires. In between May 1987 and October 1988, more than $3 million was seized in contraband, with 110 arrests by five different police agencies.[170] The Mohawks government tried to control the cigarette trade too. During November 1986, Joseph Swamp and Chief Mike Mitchell confiscated $88,000 worth of cigarettes in an attempt to disrupt distribution.[171] The Mohawk leaders attempted to establish their own justice system to eradicate bootlegging, cigarette smuggling, drug trafficking, and illegal gambling on the reservation. It would require, along with a judiciary, a law enforcement agency to enforce the court's decisions.[172]

A number of the Mohawks did not see this as smuggling. They felt that the US-Canadian border was a 'white-man's' border and did not pertain to them. The Mohawks perceived themselves as part of one nation, and that the St. Lawrence River was merely a waterway in the reservation, not a border dividing it.[173] Bringing the cigarettes across made economic sense to the Mohawks, yet the US government and especially the Canadian government, tried to interdict this trade. The

---

Million of Cigarettes Handled a Year, Newspaper Says," *The Toronto Star*, January 19 1988.

[170] CP-Staff, "Police Arrest 7, Seize $200,000 in Illegal Goods in Reserve Raid," *The Toronto Star*, October 14, 1988.

[171] Hornung, *One Nation under the Gun*, 68.

[172] Darcy Henton, "Mohawk Reserve Setting up Plans for Court System," *The Toronto Star*, June 29, 1988.

[173] Henton, "Smugglers' Haven a Zone of Fear."

Traditionalists' view was voiced by former chief Julius (Speed) Herne. He said that what they were doing was not smuggling because the Mohawks own the land on both sides of the border. Herne said that this land is not just "land covered by reservations, but lands of untold acres that were stolen from us. For an Indian to smuggle from his land on one side of the border to his land on the other side is just as impossible as someone smuggling goods from his kitchen to his living room. It's all his house; it's all our land."[174]

Cigarettes and gasoline were not the only articles being smuggled. There is a history of contraband being smuggled across the border at Akwesasne, as well as up and down the St. Lawrence River. During the days of prohibition, liquor and other spirits were smuggled across the border out of Canada. During the 1980s-smuggling centered on marijuana, hard drugs, liquor; even people were bought back and forth.[175]

---

[174] Ibid.

[175] "Mohawk leaders, meanwhile, watched in dismay as the Canadian government began to focus their attention on Akwesasne and publicly identified the territory as "smuggler's alley." Although Akwesasne was now only one of many access points used by smugglers, the mass media picked up on the romantic and racist image of the "renegade Indian smuggler" and helped to convey the misconception that Mohawks were solely to blame for the loss of Canadian tax revenue. They ignored the fact that for many, many years, the Mohawk leaders had warned the Canadian government that their tobacco taxation policies would lead to the creation of a black market that would exploit Akwesasne's geographical situation. They proposed the creation of a Mohawk border patrol which would protect the community from being used as a corridor for this kind of activity. These proposals were rejected by the Canadian government

Smuggling became a point of contention and culturally factional between the Traditionalists, Tribalists, and Warriors, who each had their own, take on the situation. However, all three agreed the situation centered on the concept of sovereignty and that it was influenced by the economic rewards connected to smuggling. As an illegal activity, smuggling brought outside forces, such as the NYSP or RCMP, onto the reservation. This contributed to contentions between the Native and non-Native cultures when they interacted.[176]

A massive police raid was conducted on the reservation on October 13, 1988. Because of smuggling and illegal activity occurring on the reservation five agencies were involved: the RCMP, OPP, Cornwall City Police, NYSP, and Border Patrol. The force was augmented with 250 heavily armed Canadian Police, 75 police cruisers, 15 vans, unmarked cars, helicopters, boats, bulldozers, and dogs trained to sniff out illegal drugs.[177] The police went from person to person arresting people as if following a list. James Benedict, who owned a

---

on the grounds that the Mohawks did not have the legal power to enact such laws. " Darren Bonaparte, "Border Crossing Rights," Wampum Chronicles, http://wampumchronicles.com/history.html (accessed August 17, 2005).

[176] Rudy Platiel, "Treaty at Root of Mohawk Woe Akwesasne / Cigarette Trade Alone Does Not Explain the Reserve's Recent Bloody History, Mourners Say," *Globe and Mail*, February 16, 1994.

[177] CP-Staff, "Indians Vow Revenge after Massive Raid on Mohawk Reserve," *The Toronto Star*, October 14, 1988; AP, "Indians Block Bridge to U.S. In Dispute over Reservation Raid," *The Associated Press*, October 15, 1988.

smoke shop, arcade, and junkyard, was surprised by fifteen officers who handcuffed him, threatened to shoot his dog, and searched his house looking for cigarettes. The process was repeated all over the reservation, eventually resulting in seven arrests and the seizure of $160,000 worth of cigarettes.[178] Chief Mike Mitchell said, "They [the police] scared a lot of people. I'm having a lot of trouble restoring calm in the community."[179]

The day after the raid, a group of Indians who called themselves the Militant Mohawk Warriors took control of the Seaway International Bridge for a half hour to protest the police raid. After a group of Akwesasne residents convinced the Warriors that they were not speaking for everyone the Warriors backed the cars away and opened the bridge back up. Custom and immigration officials felt threatened during the entire operation. Six immigration officers left the station saying they feared for their lives, and five more left two hours later. Serge Charette, First Vice President of the Customs and Excise Union, said, "The Island either belongs to the Indians or belongs to Canada. Right now, we're not really sure."[180] After a two-hour meeting on October 17, 1988, between the Mohawks and acting Federal Deputy Solicitor General Ian Glen, Chief

---

[178] Dale Brazao, "Outraged Mohawks Block Bridge," *The Toronto Star*, October 15, 1988; Warren Perley, "Mohawks Threaten War over Cigarette Seizures," *United Press International*, October 14, 1988.

[179] CP-Staff, "Indians Vow Revenge."

[180] Dale Brazao, "Outraged Mohawks Block Bridge," *The Toronto Star*, October 15, 1988.

Mitchell said, "We told them that if there is another raid the consequences would be very serious. You will be putting the people in the position of having to defend their territory and their community right or wrong."[181]

During the 1960s, 70s, and 80s, there had been a great deal of reservation unrest. It centered around three issues: free unencumbered crossing of the US-Canadian border, smuggling of contraband, and the gambling casinos. These issues pointed to one major subject for the Mohawks, sovereignty. The idea of sovereignty was an important concept to Indians in general, and Mohawks specifically.

Not only was reservation unrest an important factor during the 1960s, 70s, and 80s, but so were ecological concerns. When the Love Canal tragedy was exposed 1978, communities began to investigate their own problems. This was true of the community at Akwesasne. Up river, from the western boundary of the reservation, there were industrial complexes from Massena, New York to the area around the international bridge across the St. Lawrence River and access to Cornwall Island, Ontario, Canada. With the building of the St. Lawrence Seaway in 1959 and the construction of the power dams and locks at Massena, an abundance of cheap hydroelectric power was available. Access to international waterways of the St. Lawrence made the area near Akwesasne ideal for foundries, factories, and paper mills.[182]

---

[181] Southam News, "Further Raid on Reserve Could Lead to Violence, Ottawa Told," *The Toronto Star*, October 18, 1988.

[182] Mary Esch, "The Mohawks Call Their Homeland Akwesasne, 'Land Where the Partridge Drums.' It's a 25-Square-Mile

After the industrial development of the area, the Mohawks noticed that their crops and livestock seemed diseased. They found cattle and crops dead and the health of the residents of the island impaired. Upon investigation, it was found that the crops and animals were poisoned by fluoride. The Reynolds Metals Company (Reynolds), Aluminum Company of America (Alcoa), and General Motors Corporation, Powertrain Division Massena (GMPT), industrial plants seemed to be polluting the Canadian islands downwind and downstream. In 1978, two US doctors conducted a study investigating the emissions from the Reynolds plant and the downwind consequences of the two smelters. They found that in nineteen years after the smelters opened in1959, twenty-five million pounds of fluoride had drifted over and settled on Cornwall Island and other areas of the reservation.[183] They found the children "were showing the brittle and stained teeth characteristic of excessive fluoride exposure."[184] By April 1981, "Judge Howard G. Munson of the Northern New York District Court ruled that the band has a case against Reynolds, and Alcoa and ordered that the matter go to trial."[185] Although the aluminum companies used legal

---

Reservation Spanning the St. Lawrence River, a Place Where They Once Could Hunt and Fish for Food. Today the White Man's Chemicals Have Poisoned Akwesasne and the Mohawk Way of Life Is in Peril," *The Associated Press News features*, January 24, 1988.

[183] Yves Lavigne, "US Court Upholds Indian Band's Right to Sue Metals Firms," *The Globe and Mail*, April 17, 1981.

[184] Janis Barth, "A Land Lost, a People in Agony," *The Post-Standard*, April 15, 1990.

[185] Lavigne, "US Court Upholds Indian Band's."

tactics to delay the action, the Mohawks were given the 'go-ahead' by the court to sue for $50 million.[186]

On October 30, 1980, Health Minister Monique Begin announced a $1,600,000 study on the effects of the pollution on the health of the Mohawks at Akwesasne. The study investigated the "presence of such contaminants as mercury mirex, PCBs, and fluoride, on the health of the reserve residents."[187] In 1985, a wildlife pathologist with the New York State Department of Environmental Conservation, Dr. Ward Stone, tested the animal life. Capturing animals within three hundred yards of the GM dump, he dissected them and found that there was 875 parts per million[188] of PCBs and insecticides such as Dieldrin in the turtles.[189] Jay Palter, spokesman for Greenpeace Toronto, stated that a chlorine plant upstream, on the Canadian side of the border, was allegedly discharging mercury into the St. Lawrence River. "'Fish taken from those waters,' Palter said, 'have been found with one part per million of mercury in their flesh, twice the limit for human consumption set by the province of Ontario.'"[190]

---

[186] Ibid.

[187] CP, "Ottawa Backs Study of St. Regis Band," *The Globe and Mail*, October 31, 1980.

[188] ". . . 3 parts per million of PCBs in poultry is considered unfit for human consumption; 50 parts per million in soil is hazardous waste. . ." Barth. "A Land Lost, a People in Agony."

[189] Ibid.

[190] Janis Barth, "Greenpeace Plan St. Lawrence Pollution Protest," *The Post-Standard*, May 13, 1988, B3.

Since 1983, both the US and Canadian governments have tried unsuccessfully to respond to the pollution found at Akwesasne. Their attempts have been more bluster than actual solution. By 1985, the tribe was $2.5 million in debt from fighting Reynolds over fluoride contamination.[191] Reynolds paid $650,000 in damages to the tribe and cut emissions by seventy-five percent.[192] The Environmental Protection Agency (EPA) did attempted to help and raised the tribe's funding 250 percent a year for air and water quality improvement programs. However, that meant they still only received $120,000.[193] In June 1989, the Mohawk tribe filed intent to sue the Alcoa, Reynolds, and GMPT for damaging the Raquette, St. Lawrence, and Grasse river systems.[194] By the end of 1989, nothing had changed for the Mohawks. They were confronted with the pollution and found no real answers or solutions. The Mohawks were losing out on their sovereignty with their land taken once more, this time ecologically.

Looking at the background of Akwesasne, we discover a contentious past with a number of points of cultural conflict that increased over time between Native and white communities. One was the lack of free unencumbered crossing of the US-Canadian border. The Mohawks wanted the ability to bring

---

[191] Barth, "A Land Lost, a People in Agony."
[192] Ibid.
[193] Barbara Stith, "St. Regis Mohawks Find Environment a Unifying Issue," *The Post-Standard*, February 25, 1990.
[194] CP, "Mohawk Tribe, NY State Suing Three Us Firms over Pollution," *The Toronto Star*, June 1, 1989.

their used or new personal property across the border and not be detained or have to pay duty. Test crossings with personal property were attempted from both the US and Canadian sides of the border. Their methods were effective at times, but did not reap lasting success. The episodes usually involved the RCMP or the NYSP and, at times, both of them. Usually, the respective government's fines or charges were not administered to abate the situation and avoid violence. Although different factions of Mohawks confronted each other during this time, serious violence never erupted. There were times when arms were taken up and factions splintered, but this only occurred when outside influences such as the RCMP, the AIM, or the NYSP were involved.

Smuggling was a second point of contention and culturally factional. Traditionalists, Tribalists, and Warriors each had their own take on the situation. But all three agreed it centered on the concept of sovereignty and that it was influenced by the economic rewards connected to it. Smuggling, by its very activity, brought outside forces such as the NYSP or RCMP onto the reservation. This too contributed to contentions between the Native and non-Native cultures.[195]

Gambling casinos was a third point that contributed to the cultural conflict and created

---

[195] Rudy Platiel, "Treaty at Root of Mohawk Woe Akwesasne / Cigarette Trade Alone Does Not Explain the Reserve's Recent Bloody History, Mourners Say," *The Globe and Mail*, February 16, 1994.

tension on the reservation.[196] There had been low-stakes bingo on the reservation for years, some games operating in local churches. The community radio station used radio bingo to raise revenues. The majority of the reservation accepted low-stake games, and in May 1985 the Tribal Council became a fifty percent partner in the Mohawk Bingo Palace, a high stakes bingo establishment. This caused some dissension initially, but was accepted. Over time, a number of other private high stakes gambling establishments opened, and some of these added casino style gambling.[197] Eventually, slot machines were added, and changed the factions on the reservation once again. Casino gambling shifted traditional alliances and caused increased tensions.[198] The Tribal Council called in the state police to have the slots removed. This created conflicts for those who did not want to see outside forces come onto the reservation. As outside forces interfered on the reservation, the cultural conflict, and the threat of violence increased. It all condensed down to the concept of sovereignty and the definitions held by the numerous factions involved.

---

[196] Timothy Appleby, "Tensions Simmer on Reserve as Gambling Supporter Convicted," *The Globe and Mail*, April 14, 1990.

[197] Casino's: Tony's Vegas International, Burn's Casino, Lucky Night, Silver Dollar, Club 21, Golden Nugget, Hart's Palace. Other establishments with slot machines: Bear's Den, Onkwe Bingo Jack, Billy's Bingo Palace, Mohawk Bingo Palace.

[198] Appleby, "Tensions Simmer."

CHAPTER 4

The Gnashing of Nations

At the beginning of 1989, business on both sides of the Akwesasne reservation were operating as usual. In January 1989, the Canadian side of the reservation signed a trade agreement with the Cree Indians of James Bay, Québec. This agreement removed non-Native entrepreneurs who transported food, clothing, and other household necessities to James Bay, Québec from the southern portion of Ontario. At the time, the Cree spent eighty-seven million dollars on food and supplies annually.[199] The agreement allowed them to buy food from Akwesasne stores that would deliver the cargo to the Cornwall Airport, where Cree planes would fly it north. In return, the Cree would invest in Akwesasne development projects.[200]

In February, after months of the elected Chiefs condemning gambling, the Warrior society countered that the American and Canadian elected councils were pawns enforcing non-Indian law.[201]

---

[199] OANDA, "Fxhistory®: Historical Currency Exchange Rates," OANDA Corporation, http://www.oanda.com/convert/fxhistory (accessed March 18, 2008). The exchange rate in 1989 was: Canadian Currency, $0.85 CD to $1USD; CP, "Mohawks, Québec Crees to Sign 'Free-Trade Deal,'" *The Toronto Star*, January 5, 1989.

[200] CP, "Mohawks, Québec Crees to Sign 'Free-Trade Deal.'"

[201] Hornung, *One Nation under the Gun*, 29.

The Warriors felt that when the councils tried to close the gambling casinos, the Chiefs were turning their backs on their own people. They labeled Chief Harold Tarbell, a traitor to the Mohawk Nation.[202]

In March, on the American side of the border, the St. Regis Band of the Mohawks signed an agreement with the EPA that they believed would acknowledge their status as a sovereign nation. The agreement would fund a number of government programs, such as the *Clean Waters Act* and the *Superfund Act*, for Akwesasne. Additionally, the US government helped the tribe set up environmental ordinances offices. [203]

Problems appeared again in April, when the anti-gambling faction of the reservation held a protest rally on Route 37 outside Massena. Later, two elected Chiefs, Harold Tarbell and Brenda LaFrance, led a group protesting the casinos on the reservation to the county seat in Canton, New York where a Republican fundraiser was being held.[204] Problems over sovereignty continued on May 9, when a group of Mohawks took a construction trailer from the Canadian Customs house. Chief Mike Mitchell had said if the smuggling situation at Akwesasne was not solved, renovations would not be allowed to move forward at the Customs House. This was a continuation of customs problems that

---

[202] Ibid.

[203] Staff, "Signing of E.P.A.-Indian Agreement Slated," *United Press International*, March 27, 1989.

[204] Hornung, *One Nation under the Gun*, 29.

began in the 1950s with the construction of the original building on Cornwall Island.[205]

The situation began to change on May 16, when nine traditional chiefs, not recognized by the US government, sent a letter to President Bush asking him to end and remove casino gambling from the reservation. New York State law enforcement had long contended that slot machines were illegal on the reservation. On May 25, Eli Tarbell owner The Bear's Den contacted the NYSP on behalf of the casino operators and asked for a meeting. "Later that day at Troop B headquarters at Ray Brook, [NY], Maj. Ronald R. Brooks and three of his top officers met with four Mohawk casino operators: Eli Tarbell of The Bear's Den; Anthony Laughing of Tony's Vegas International; Rudy Hart, proprietor of Hart's Palace; and Paul Tatlock Jr., proprietor of the Golden Nugget."[206] The four stated that rumors were 'flying around' the reservation that the police were going to raid them soon. The owners said they would voluntarily surrender their slot machines to avoid violence. A memo written by Captain Robert B. Leu stated, "they went as far as to say unanimously that if we were planning on seizing the slot machines they would make the removal of the machines as advantageously as possible to the state police and would offer no resistance whatsoever."[207]

---

[205] CP, "Indians Take Trailer from Customs Site," *The Toronto Star*, May 10, 1989.

[206] Matthew Cox and Tom Foster, "State, Mohawks Try to Set House Rules for Gambling," *The Post-Standard*, October 25, 1989.

[207] Ibid.

The same day on the Canadian side of the reservation the RCMP was trying to stop a car that allegedly was being used for smuggling. The RCMP followed the car onto the reservation when twenty-five Mohawk Warriors surrounded them. The Warriors saw themselves as the Mohawks' traditional police force and demanded the RCMP let the Mohawk police assigned to the area handle with the incident. When the Mohawk Police, an arm of the Mohawk Council of Akwesasne and the OPP, came to take over the situation, they were also surrounded by the Warriors and not permitted to interfere, allowing the alleged smugglers to drive away.[208]

During the 1989 campaign for the elections, Harold Tarbell turned off the water to three of the casinos and kept it turned off for six days. When he turned the water back on, he wrote a letter to the New York State and the US governments complaining about the continuation of gambling continuing and asked that they step in and take care of the situation.[209] On June 2, Chief Mike Mitchell of the Mohawk Council of Akwesasne on Canadian side of the reservation thought that the New York State Police were backing down and not enforcing the law. Mitchell said the NYSP were being intimidated and were ordered off the reservation by the Warrior society.[210]

---

[208] CP, "RCMP Forced from Reserve," *The Toronto Star*, May 25, 1989.

[209] Hornung, *One Nation under the Gun*, 30.

[210] AP, "Troopers Back Off, Mohawk Chief Says," *The Post-Standard*, June 4, 1989.

The June 1989, elections saw two factions vying for power: the anti-gambling ticket that included Harold Tarbell, Brenda LaFrance, and Rosemary Bonaparte; and the pro-gambling faction that included L. David Jacobs and Lincoln White. On June 3, the electorate returned Harold Tarbell to office, but also elected Jacobs and White, giving the pro-gambling side a majority on the tribal council.[211] Even with a majority the contentions over gambling were not eased.

Clashing at the Casino

On June 6, a fight started after last call at a local bar called Shaft's on the US side of Akwesasne. Apparently, the fight was between two suitors over a woman. The fight expanded to more people and was coincidently split between the pro- and anti-gambling factions. As the fight got worsened, it moved into the parking lot of Tony Laughing's casino. Eventually, the elected Chiefs summoned the New York State Police to defuse the situation.[212] According to New York State Trooper Sgt. Michael Downs, who was on the scene, by 11AM it was apparent that the anti-gambling faction had the support of both the traditionalists and elected Chiefs. With this encouragement, the anti-gambling faction was getting bolder and louder. It was also clear that Tony Laughing and the people in the casino wanted the fight to end so the gambling could continue. The Warriors who were involved

---

[211] Hornung, *One Nation under the Gun*, 30.
[212] Ibid., 9-12.

just wanted the state police to leave and let the different factions work through the problems.[213]

With the situation growing worse the police knew something had to be done. After an hour of negotiations between Laughing and the New York State Police, they decided that the police would arrest Laughing on a minor charge of promoting gambling so that it would not look as if the police were protecting him. The plan was that once Laughing was gone the police could clear the area. At 12:30 PM unmarked NYSP cars arrived, put Laughing and some slot machines in the car and drove away. The Warriors, who had not taken sides between the pro- and anti-gambling factions, simply wanted the police to leave. Once they did the Warriors also left. Art Montour, a Warrior, said, "We figured our job was done and the police had kept their word, we left."[214] However, the police never cleared the crowd away, and as soon as they left about one hundred people stormed the casino. They destroyed slot machines and broke gambling tables with sticks and chairs. The crowd pulled the slot machines out into the parking lot and made a big pile. No one employed by the casino or who was pro-gambling got involved to try to stop the vandalism.[215] Cindy Terrance, editor and publisher of *The People's Voice*, a pro-gambling paper, said, ". . . that was a real riot, Tribal Officials were

---

[213] Ibid., 13.

[214] Hornung, *One Nation under the Gun*, 14. Art Montour is known as Kakwirakeron.

[215] CP-Staff, "Mohawk Indians Trash Casino in Bid to Eliminate Gambling," *The Toronto Star*, June 7, 1989.

photographed walking in and out of the casino while it was being ransacked."[216] Police Chief Ernie King of the Mohawk Police from the Canadian side of the reservation and nine of his officers stood by and watched the destruction. King felt that the raid went smoothly, and no one was injured. Chief Mike Mitchell from the Canadian side of the reservation stood outside the casino with other anti-gambling supporters and said that they would stay until the casino was closed down.[217] By 1:30 PM the riot had created around four hundred thousand US dollars in damages.[218] The NYSP returned at 2 PM.

When the NYSP returned to the reservation, they brought one hundred troopers and trailers to remove the slot machines. The police took one hundred and fifty slot machines from Tony's Vegas International and fifty from the Bear's Den Trading Post. The Warriors tried to interfere, but they had no effect on the operation. A NYSP spokesman said they carried out the operation to promote public safety; the Warriors retorted that this was a typical excuse.

The next morning, June 7, Tony Laughing, returned from the police station, and said, "it was planned, the crowd didn't come until after the police left and I think there was a connection. The cops said they would stay and protect the building. They didn't. They got me off the reservation and the crowd burst in. ."[219]

---

[216] Hornung, *One Nation under the Gun*, 14.
[217] CP-Staff, "Mohawk Indians Trash Casino."
[218] Hornung, *One Nation under the Gun*, 14.
[219] Ibid.

It is illegal in New York for private citizens or corporations to have gambling casinos. Small stakes bingo has been allowed for decades in New York, and it is familiar to see Catholic churches, towns, and communities having bingo night. Raffles, fifty-fifty draw, pull-tabs, and other forms of gambling are used for income for many different organizations. Organization can obtain permits for roulette nights, or casino nights to raise money for charities and other special, time-limited events.[220] In New York, the Mohawks' gambling establishments were viewed as illegal; however, there was concern over how valid New York's jurisdiction was over Indian gaming. The US federal government believed it had jurisdiction by treaties and through the Bureau of Indian Affairs. The Mohawks viewed themselves as a sovereign nation that was not obligated to outsiders. *The Indian Gaming Regulatory Act* (1988) gave the Mohawks the right to have gambling on the reservation because the state already permitted gambling.[221] The "law called for a commission

---

[220] New York State Statutes "Article 9-A. Local Option for Conduct of Games of Chance by Certain Organizations: §185... This article shall be known and may be cited as the games of chance licensing law. The legislature hereby declares that the raising of funds for the promotion of bona fide charitable, educational, scientific, health, religious and patriotic causes and undertakings, where the beneficiaries are undetermined, is in the public interest. . ." Chuck Humphrey, "Charitable Gaming Laws of New York. gambling-law-us.com," http://www.gambling-law-us.com/Charitable-Gaming/New-York/ (accessed October 15, 2007).

[221] "Findings, 25 USC 2701 The Congress finds that - (1) Numerous Indian tribes have become engaged in or have licensed gaming activities on Indian lands as a means of generating tribal

within the Federal Bureau of Indian Affairs that would oversee arrangements between reservations and the states in which they are located."[222] This complicated the issues even further.

A solution to gambling, or any other problem, had to include all of the factions. Federal, state, and provincial authorities had to interact the elected

---

governmental revenue; (2) Federal courts have held that section 81 of this title requires Secretarial review of management contracts dealing with Indian gaming, but does not provide standards for approval of such contracts; (3) Existing Federal law does not provide clear standards or regulations for the conduct of gaming on Indian lands; (4) A principal goal of Federal Indian policy is to promote tribal economic development, tribal self-sufficiency, and strong tribal government; (5) Indian tribes have the exclusive right to regulate gaming activity on Indian lands if the gaming activity is not specifically prohibited by Federal law and is conducted within a State which does not, as a matter of criminal law and public policy, prohibit such gaming activity." U.S. Congress, *Indian Gaming Regulatory Act Public Law 100-497*, 100th Congress, http://www.nigc.gov/
LawsRegulations/IndianGamingRegulatoryAct/tabid/ 605/Default .aspx (accessed September 25, 2007).

"The act establishes three categories of gaming: Class I, which encompasses religious and ceremonial games, and which is not subject to government scrutiny; Class II, which includes bingo and its many variations, and which is supposed to be regulated by a yet-to-be-formed National Indian Gaming Commission; and Class III, which includes high-stakes casino gambling, horse racing and jai alai. Class III gaming is permitted in states that already allow some form of those games. But before they may be sanctioned, the state and the tribe must come to an agreement on how they will be conducted." Matthew Cox and Tom Foster, "State, Mohawks Try to Set House Rules for Gambling," *The Post-Standard*, October 25, 1989.

[222] Dan Kane and Elizabeth C. Petros, "Both Sides Say the Law Backs Them in Dispute," *The Post-Standard*, July 27. 1989.

tribal officials and the traditionalist chiefs. Dr. Henrik Dullea, Director of State Operations in New York, said that traditionalists were an important faction to include for any program or process to be successful. They must be included, "especially on the levels of the local councils because the New York Council does not have any power in Québec or Ontario and vice versa. In many ways, it's easier to get something done for millions in New York City."[223]

On the morning of June 7, one hundred and fifty New York State Police officers in police cruisers raided the casinos on the reservation. The police drove down Route 37 and divided into teams, sealing off Burn's Casino, the Golden Nugget, Club 21, and Hart's Place. The police saw the raid as a success that was accomplished without many problems or interference. When the police had answered the call about the fight at Tony's Vegas International the day before, they sensed they were swept into tribal politics. The sole objective of the June 7 raid was to remove slot machines.[224] The Warriors were upset about the raid and thought that the NYSP was an alien force on the reservation. Francis Boots, a spokesman for the Warriors Society, explained in a news conference that the Warriors were peacekeepers and had no intention of starting violence or trying to hurt anyone.[225] On June 9, Harold Tarbell and others encouraged anti-gambling proponents to identify themselves as

---

[223] Hornung, *One Nation under the Gun*, 21.
[224] Ibid, 14-15.
[225] Ibid., 30.

Determined Residents United for Mohawk Sovereignty (DRUMS). The next day DRUMS distributed one hundred black armbands to symbolize lost rights due to gambling.[226]

As gambling continued on the reservation the NYSP and FBI agents raided it on July 20, at 5 AM and seized slot machines, cash, and gambling records.[227] The "authorities confiscated business records and a large quantity of cash from Hart's Palace, Burns' Casino, Club 21, and the Golden Nugget."[228] (See Figure 6. Map of Akwesasne Roads. Page 127) They arrested ten people and closed down seven casinos.[229] Sergeant Michael

---

[226] Ibid., 31-32.

[227] Janis Barth and Mike Fish, "Indians, Police in Standoff Gambling Raid Met with Force," *The Post-Standard*, July 21, 1989.

[228] Ibid.

[229] "Charged with operating an illegal gambling business and possession of slot machines within Indian country were: Anthony Laughing, 45, proprietor of Tony's Vegas International, a casino where 173 slot machines were seized during a June 6 raid by state police; Hattie R. Hart, 24, an operator of Hart's Palace, a casino where an FBI agent observed 17 slot machines in business July 9; Paul A. Tatlock, 50, and Terak Tatlock, 23, identified as operators of the Golden Nugget casino, where 70 slot machines were seized in a Dec. 16, 1987, raid by state police; Audrey Burns, 32, an operator of Burns Casino; and David Mainville, 21, identified as operator of Club 21 casino. They face maximum penalties of five years in prison and $20,000 fines. Peter Burns Sr., 57, identified as an operator of Burns Casino, was charged with the same offenses and also using a deadly weapon to impede execution of a federal search warrant. Police said he pointed a shotgun at state police and FBI agents. Charged with one or more counts of possession of a slot machine within Indian country were: Roderick Cook, 35, operator of the Night Hawk Arcade, where 62 slot machines were seized by state police Dec. 16, 1987; William Sears, 40, an operator of Wild Bills Grocery and Deli, where 30 slot machines were seized the same day; and James Burns, 31, who has identified himself as the owner of the Silver Dollar Casino, where 49 slot machines were seized the same day. All of those charged live on

Downs of the NYSP said sixty to seventy Mohawks resisted the raids. "It was pretty evident to us they maybe had some advanced warning."[230] When the police attempted to serve federal search warrants to Tony's Vegas International and the Bear's Den the police encountered two roadblocks with fifteen Mohawks armed with AK-47 assault rifles. No shots were fired and the police decided not to challenge the situation.[231]

Around 9AM, after the police left the reservation, gambling proponents built a barricade across Route 37 using logs and a tanker truck. The NYSP also built a barricade across Route 37 and diverted traffic onto secondary roads around and away from the reservation. A group of Mohawks, the Mohawk Sovereign Security Force, manned the barricades.[232] Their leader and spokesman, Art Montour, warned the police, stating, "we will meet their level of aggression with like force."[233] By the next day an "uneasy calm" had settled over the area. Armed Mohawks stayed behind the logs and vehicles, and the police kept traffic away from the reservation.[234]

This was more than just a raid to the Mohawks; some saw it as an incursion into sovereign territory.

---

the reservation or nearby. They face a maximum penalty of two years in prison and $5,000 in fines." Ibid.

[230] William Kates, "F.B.I. And State Police Raid Indian Gambling Casinos," *The Associated Press*, July 21, 1989.

[231] Barth and Fish, "Indians, Police in Standoff."

[232] This group morphs into the Warriors Society.

[233] CP, "Armed Indians Blockade New York Highway," *The Toronto Star*, July 21, 1989.

[234] Ibid.

In a letter to Governor Mario Cuomo, Tribal Chiefs David Jacobs and Lincoln White wrote that the "invasion was an act of war."[235] Opinions on the reservation were split. Some felt that gambling was harmful to Indian culture, while others were upset over the police intruding on reservation sovereignty.[236] The government said that they had been invited in. U.S. Attorney Frederick J. Scullin said the raid was orchestrated to respond to complaints that a small group of people within Indian country were profiting from illegal activities not approved by the tribal government. "Most of our complaints came from the Indian nation itself. A lot of people are morally against gambling. It brings an undesirable element in."[237]

Jacobs and White, in their letter, said they would "hold Cuomo and an unnamed Mohawk informant responsible for 'any abuses or acts of racism that may occur.'"[238] Sergeant Downs (NYSP) commented, "The potential for violence is definitely there. I would say at this point, personally, they're quite volatile. Every hour we're kind of reassessing things to see what should be done, what needs to be done."[239]

On Friday, July 21, the original Mohawks manning the barricades were joined by one hundred

---

[235] Ibid.

[236] AP, "Gambling Raids on Indian Land Divide a Tribe," *The New York Times*, July 21, 1989.

[237] Barth and Fish, "Indians, Police in Standoff."

[238] Liz Petros and Janis Barth, "St. Regis Reservation Sealed Off Following Gambling Raid Armed Indians Fend Off Troopers near Massena," *The Post-Standard*, July 21, 1989.

[239] Barth and Fish, "Indians, Police in Standoff."

and fifty members of the Warriors Society from Kahnawake reservation near Montreal, Québec. There were two hundred or so Mohawks armed with shotguns and AK-47s; the police chose not to response. In an interview, Sergeant Downs stated that the state police were not negotiating with the Warriors. Their understanding was that the different factions on the reservation were trying to work through the situation.[240] In fact there was a meeting between the tribal chiefs and the casino owners. The meeting included Tony Laughing of Tony's Vegas International and Eli Tarbell of the Bear's Den and centered on barricades and the casino employees.[241]

The Mohawks took down their barricades on Sunday, July 23, and announced that they would be holding a news conference the next day at 12:30 PM. The NYSP kept the reservation off limits by diverting traffic. The police stated that until they could guarantee it was safe for traffic the barricade on the west end of the Racquette River Bridge on Route 37, seven miles west from Hogansburg, New York, would remain up.[242] The next day, July 24, approximately seventy-five Mohawks, including men, women, and children, went to meet with news reporters to complain about the police barricade.[243]

---

[240] AP-CP, "Mohawks Maintain Blockade at Reserve," *The Toronto Star*, July 22, 1989.

[241] Petros, and Barth, "St. Regis Reservation Sealed Off."

[242] Hornung, *One Nation under the Gun*, 45; CP, "Mohawks Take Down Roadblocks," *The Toronto Star*, July 24, 1989. Hogansburg, NY on the Akwesasne/St, Regis Reservation.

[243] Dan Kane and Elizabeth C. Petros, "Mohawks Claiming Brutality 11 Hurt in St. Regis Clash," *The Post-Standard*, July 25, 1989.

As they approached the area they found the reporters were being held a quarter mile farther west on Route 37 beyond the barricade.[244] As the Mohawks went to meet the reporters, over one hundred New York State Police in riot gear attacked them. Art Montour was the target of the police.[245] He was accused of interfering with "Thursday's raid."[246] Not only were the police wielding clubs, but the various factions within the Mohawks also began to fight. Verna Montour and Minnie Garrow reported seeing a three-year-old girl who had been clubbed in the face, and whose lip was so swollen that it could not be stitched.[247] Sgt. Michael Downs (NYSP) denied any police brutality. "We did take Art Montour out of there, we did what we had to do with minimum force necessary. They naturally will have their side of the story."[248] Vera Montour showed the deep purple bruises on her arms to reporters. She said the police caused them when her husband was arrested.[249] At least eleven people were injured during the incident.[250] (See Figure 7. Conflict between NYSP and Mohawks,1989. Page 128)

---

[244] CP, "Mohawk Indians Battle State Police," *The Toronto Star*, July 25, 1989.

[245] Kane and Petros, "Mohawks Claiming Brutality."

[246] Ibid.

[247] Ibid.

[248] Mike McAndrew and Lori Duffy, "Group Promises Bail, Testimony for Leader of Indian Force," *The Post-Standard*, July 26, 1989.

[249] Ibid.

[250] William Kates, "Violence Grows on Indian Nation Divided by Gambling," *The Associated Press*, September 2, 1989.

The incident prompted Warrior Society members to set up manned checkpoints to prevent further raids by the New York State Police. The group professed that they were protecting the sovereignty of Akwesasne.[251] Mark Maracle, spokesman for the Warrior Society, said, the "[state police] has no authority in here. These people [residents] have been intimidated by an outside force coming in here."[252] Edmund Culhane, First Deputy Superintendent of the New York State Police, said that the police would keep the roadblock on Route 37 as long as public safety was concerned.[253] Reverend Jon Regier, retired Director of the NYS Council of Churches, said in an interview, "this issue is a lot bigger than gambling. It is whether the Indian people will be allowed to live as Indian people."[254]

On July 25, Art Montour was arraigned on charges of forcibly impeding the execution of a federal search warrant through the use of a deadly weapon. He hired Seth Shapiro, an attorney in William Kunstler's office at the Center of Constitutional Rights in New York City.[255] In a pre-trial detention hearing FBI agent John McEligot testified that the Mohawk chiefs did not want

---

[251] Elizabeth C. Petros, "Facing Camps Stick to Vigils Reservation Remains Quiet, Tense as Police, Mohawks Keep Distance," *The Post-Standard*, July 26, 1989.

[252] Michael Killian, "State Police Presence Debated," *The Post-Standard*, July 28, 1989.

[253] Petros, "Facing Camps Stick to Vigils Reservation Remains Quiet."

[254] McAndrew and Duffy, "Group Promises Bail."

[255] Ibid.

Montour back in the community. They were afraid that he would make a volatile situation worse.[256] After eleven days, Montour was freed on $200,000 bail. He owed another $500 to the Town of Salina's town court, where he was originally arraigned. Montour went home to his farm in Bombay, New York, about four miles southwest from the reservation.[257] One condition of his federal bail arrangements was that he could not be on the St. Regis Mohawk Reservation (US side of Akwesasne) except from 6 AM to 8 PM during his work hours at a construction company. When asked about the situation, Montour said he thought the problems would end peacefully when the US sat down at the negotiating table with the Mohawks to talk about sovereignty. He said his feelings about gambling were mixed, however, he felt the government's raids violated Mohawk rights of self-determination.[258]

Within the reservation, away from the New York State Police barricades and the casinos, life went on as usual. Families had picnics and children rode their bikes, but conversations still centered on the police raids and gambling.[259] Some thought that

---

[256] William Kates, "Government Says Warrior Leader Would Renew Reservation Tension If Released," *The Associated Press*, July 27, 1989.

[257] Measured from Hogansburg, NY (44.973N, -74.663W), which is on the Akwesasne/St, Regis Reservation.

[258] Gary Gerew, "Mohawk Freed after 11 Days without Bail Judge Finds No Evidence of Danger," *The Post-Standard*, August 1, 1989.

[259] Elizabeth C. Petros, "Facing Camps Stick to Vigils Reservation Remains Quiet, Tense as Police, Mohawks Keep Distance," *The Post-Standard*, July 26, 1989.

the police should take down the barricades and leave. Others said that Mohawks needed to resist incursions when they were made. Others were on another side of the gambling situation. The situation drew external comments, too, such as from the Onondaga Council of Chiefs.[260] They issued a seven-page statement asking questions of the supporters and owners of casino gambling.[261] These

---

[260] "The entire Haudenosaunee has 50 chiefs. The chiefs are all considered equal. To show that they are leaders, the Peacemaker places the antlers of the deer on the Gustoweh (headdress) of every Hoyane. When in council, every chief has an equal responsibility and equal say in the matters of the Haudenosaunee. The Peacemaker envisioned the chiefs holding hands in a large circle. Inside the circle are the laws and customs of our people. It is the responsibility of the chiefs to protect the people within the circle and to look forward seven generations to the future in making decisions. If individuals do not follow the laws and customs of the Haudenosaunee, they have "left the circle" and are no longer under the protection of the chiefs.

Each nation was allocated a certain number of leaders by the Peacemaker. At Onondaga, there are 14 Hoyane or Chiefs. The chief titles originate from the original 50 leaders' names from long ago. Tadadaho is a chief still sitting at Onondaga. Hiawatha, is still a chief among the Mohawk nation (he was adopted by the Mohawks to help form the first councils there). Each chief works with his Clan Mother and their clan. In council, they are the voice of the people. When a decision by council has been passed, it comes with the backing of all chiefs in agreement and is said to be "Of One Mind."
Onondaga Nation, "*Onondaga Nation: People of the Hill*," Onondaga Nation, http://www.onondaganation.org/gov/chiefs.html (accessed November 27, 2007).

[261] "1st: Do they have outside non-Indian business partnerships? If they do, and they did not get the consent of the Council of Chiefs, they themselves have violated the sovereignty of the Mohawk people by bringing into sovereign Mohawk territory

questions included: Who is involved with the finances? Are any finances going to the tribe? Does the Mohawk Council approve of casino gambling? The Onondaga Council of Chiefs said these questions needed to be answered before a gaming establishment began operation. Their statement intertwined the issue of sovereignty and the effect of gambling's impact on the community then and in the future. The statement, although eloquent, had one major theme: gambling should not have occurred if it was not sanctioned by the Traditionalists and by the chiefs of the Mohawk tribal government that is recognized the US federal government.[262] Gambling cut across pro- and anti-gambling factions. The Traditionalists, Tribal Council, and the Warrior Society all "seem to be in favor of sovereignty, but each has a different idea of what that means and how it should be accomplished."[263]

---

non-Indian people as business partners. 2nd: Are there revenues taken off the Mohawk Nation territories without the consent of the Mohawk Nation? Then, Mohawk sovereignty is being violated again by non-Indians and their Indian partners. There should be an accounting of these revenues to the people. 3rd: the sovereignty of the Mohawk people is being violated everyday by the invasion of non-Indian people crossing Mohawk boundary lines to take part in illegal gambling activities on Mohawk Nation territories, also violating the laws of the Mohawk Nation and the Haudenosaunee." Staff, "We Have Witnessed the Corruption of Young People by These Businesses," *The Post-Standard*, July 28, 1989.

[262] Staff, "We Have Witnessed the Corruption of Young People by These Businesses," *The Post-Standard*, July 28, 1989.

[263] Connie Bramstedt, "Chief Says State Exploits St. Regis Gambling Issue," *The Post-Standard*, July 30, 1989.

Originally on July 29, there had been a referendum scheduled concerning the continuation of gambling on the reservation. However, because of the heightened tensions about gambling mixed with the police roadblocks, the vote was postponed until August 7 and 8.[264] David Jacobs, a tribal chief on the US side of Akwesasne, accused the NYSP of "exploiting the tribes feud over gambling to help undermine the tribe's governing body. I think they used the gambling issue to come onto the reservation to determine who is in power."[265] It seemed that the issue was more about which government is supreme rather than just the issue of gambling.[266]

On that same day, Jacobs and Chief Lincoln White met at the Mohawk Bingo Palace with about 100 residents of the reservation. They discussed the situation and possible solutions; the idea of a separate Mohawk Police force was suggested.[267] Later, 100 Mohawks protested peaceably at the roadblocks that the NYSP were still manning outside the reservation. The marchers said that sealing the reservation off was hurting the local economy.[268] Others had the same idea but expressed it differently. Doug George, editor of the Indian

---

[264] Nancy Bonvillain, *Ethnographic Exploratory Research: The Census Process at St. Regis Reservation* (Albany, NY: State University of New York at Stony Brook, 1989), Report # 3.

[265] Bramstedt, "Chief Says State Exploits St. Regis Gambling Issue."

[266] Ibid.

[267] Ibid.

[268] AP, "Mohawks Protest Reservation Roadblocks," *New York Times*, July 30, 1989.

Time and Akwesasne Notes newspapers, said, "gamblers, they don't want any order. We [anti-gamblers] want to unify Akwesasne. We want to make it one nation, no Canada, no US. We want justice, peace, and economic development."[269]

The New York State Police, five Mohawk leaders, representatives of the BIA, and Governor Mario Cuomo's staff met on July 31, 1989. They agreed that the ten-day closure of the reservation would end with the removal of the barricades and the excess police presence.[270] The NYSP's costs for 200 troopers' overtime, food, motel rooms, and other expenses was around $500,000. The state police defended the expenditures by asking, "What is the price of public safety?" State Police officer, Richard Garcia said there were armed Mohawks "from as young as fourteen on up. Young men without military training handling weapons and pointing them at people at checkpoints . . . we are charged with a position of protecting public safety."[271]

The three chiefs from the US side of Akwesasne, who were recognized by the BIA as the legitimate government, proposed that the NYSP patrol the reservation's state roads until the US Mohawks had their own police.[272] On August 2,

---

[269] Bramstedt, "Chief Says State Exploits St. Regis Gambling Issue."

[270] AP, "Police Removing Roadblocks at Reservation," *The New York Times*, August 1, 1989.

[271] Erik Kriss, "The Blockade's Other Cost," *The Post-Standard*, August 1, 1989.

[272] Jonathon D. Salant, "St. Regis to Have Its Own Police, Courts If Senate, House Ok Funds," *The Post-Standard*, August 1, 1989.

Tony Laughing and the Warriors came to an agreement that they would close the casinos at 9 PM on August 3 until after the referendum on August 7 and 8.[273] On August 5, the elected Mohawk council and the NYSP signed an agreement to allow the police to resume patrols on Route 37 through the reservation and remove the barricades across the main routes. The start date was uncertain because the council had a planned meeting with the Warriors first. Under the agreement, by August 8, the NYSP could patrol Route 37 until September 15 to enforce traffic laws and respond to needs of motorist. The police would not leave the main highway unless they had permission from the tribal council.[274] The Warrior Society also set guidelines. The NYSP had to notify them in advance before coming onto the reservation, arrive in an unmarked car, and be escorted to the scene of the incident.[275] The NYSP did leave manned police cruisers near the reservation entrance on the side of the road and in the center median.

Referendum and the Results

The gambling referendum was held on August 7 and 8; however, the controversy did not end. On August 7, pro- and anti-gambling forces confronted

---

[273] Hornung, *One Nation under the Gun*, 60.

[274] Janis Barth and Elizabeth C. Petros, "Pact Would Let Police Resume St. Regis Patrol," *The Post-Standard*, August 8, 1989.

[275] Kates, "Violence Grows on Indian Nation Divided by Gambling."

each other in a field where ten slot machines were found. A tug of war erupted, that the pro-gambling force won. The conflict occurred about one quarter of a mile from the Bear's Den and across the road from the tribal building.[276] Even the three head chiefs on the Tribal council did not agree among themselves. Chief Harold Tarbell thought the referendum was "totally discredited" and called for a "fair referendum."[277] Chiefs Lincoln White and David Jacobs planned the referendum and considered the opposition's complaints as political squabbling.[278] White's comments included his belief that legalized gambling would be important in future economic development. He added that tribal government "is endeavoring to set up tribal police, rules, and regulations that will be in full compliance with federal law."[279] Chief David Jacobs agreed that the poverty on the reservation was the biggest problem. He said they had to find a way for the tribe to prosper within the confines of the law and their rights as American citizens. "On this side of the border," he said. "the law gives us a chance to start our bingo and gambling businesses and we should." With increased numbers of gamblers, there was a corresponding increase in jobs on the reservation. "In Canada, the government won't

---

[276] Janis Barth and Elizabeth C. Petros, "Gambling Foes Boycott St. Regis Election 'We're Considering This an Illegal Vote,'" *The Post-Standard*, August 8, 1989.

[277] Ibid.

[278] Ibid.

[279] Janis Barth, "BIA Claims Referendum Has No Clout Lt," *The Post-Standard*, August 9, 1989.

allow gambling. That's their problem. Let Ottawa or Québec keep dishing out grants and subsidies. Washington and Albany want us to go on our own. And it's hard, but it can work if we do it right." The Americans and Canadians have two culturally different approaches to the problems. Jacobs said, "I'm choosing to stay with the Americans."[280]

Dean White (no relation to Lincoln White), a field representative for the US Bureau of Indian Affairs, said that no matter what the referendum determined, casino gambling at this time was illegal according to federal and state law.[281] On August 8, 1989, after the ballots were counted, 480 voted to approve all forms of gambling, 57 voted against gambling, and there were nine abstentions.[282] Chief Harold Tarbell said that even though only 57 voted against gambling there were many more who did not vote because they questioned the legitimacy of the referendum.[283] Tarbell said the referendum was "a charade and that it was not a mandate for casinos to open, [further the low turnout] made a mockery of the idea the casinos enjoyed wide spread support in the community."[284] The anti-gambling faction called for a boycott because only US Akwesasne residents could vote. Those living in Ontario and Québec were ineligible because they were not US

---

[280] Hornung, *One Nation under the Gun*, 21.

[281] Barth, "BIA Claims Referendum Has No Clout Lt."

[282] Hornung, One *Nation under the Gun*, 62.

[283] AP, "Mohawks Vote for Resuming of Gambling at Reservation," *The New York Times*, August 10, 1989.

[284] CP, "Residents Vote in Support of Gambling on Reserve," *The Globe and Mail*, August 10, 1989.

residents.[285] However, within an hour of the vote tally, "the reservation's largest casino reopened for business."[286] Tony Laughing said the referendum gave him a license to reopen. "People voted the slot machines back in. I can't let those people down."[287]

---

[285] Ibid.
[286] AP, "Mohawks Vote for Resuming of Gambling at Reservation," *The New York Times*, August 10, 1989.
[287] CP, "Residents Vote in Support of Gambling on Reserve."

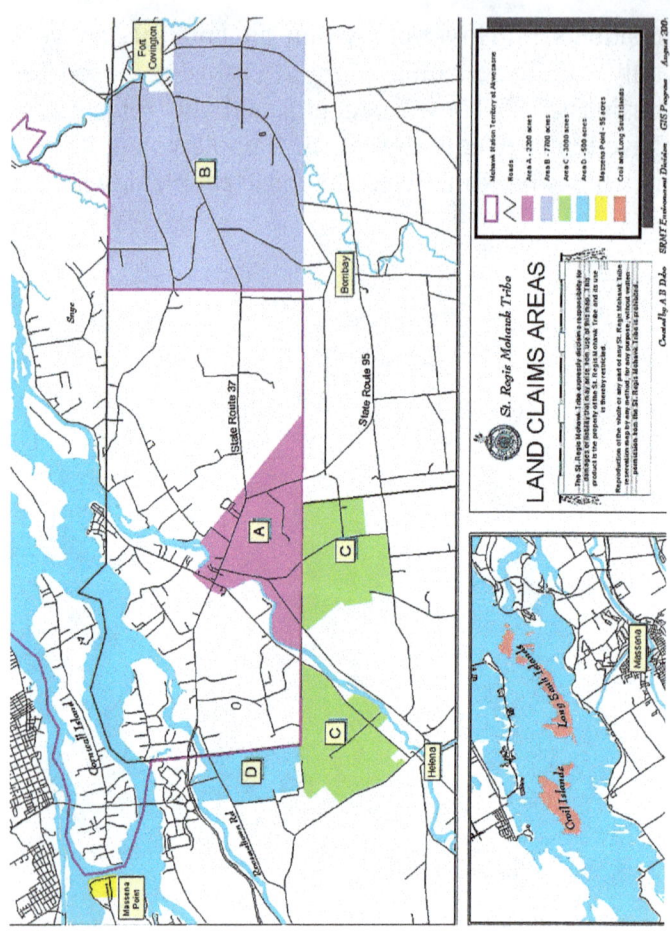

Figure 1. Map of Akwesasne and the Surrounding Area. Source: St. Regis Mohawk Tribe Land Claims Areas., Created by AB Debo, SRMT Environment Division GIS Program, August 2004.

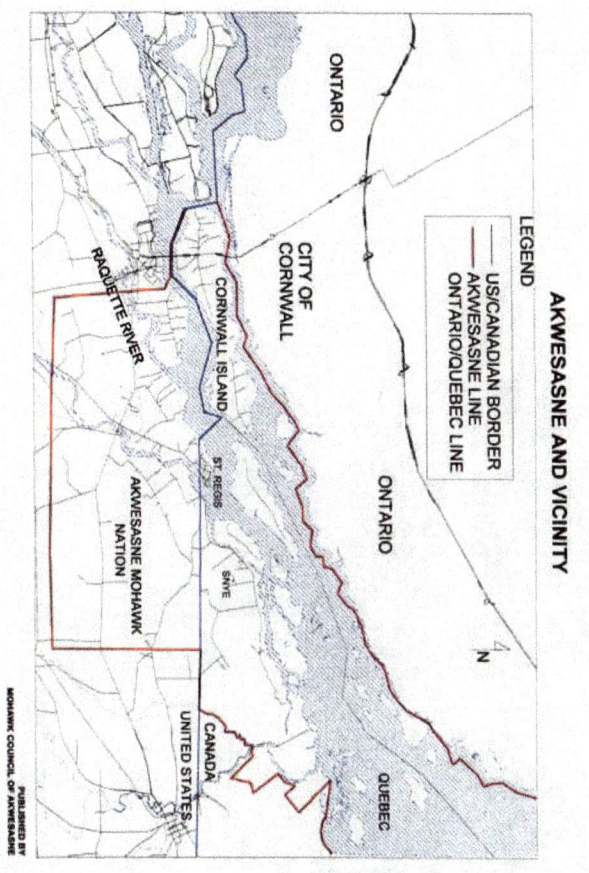

Figure 2. Jurisdictional Map of Akwesasne.
Source: Mohawk Council of Akwesasne

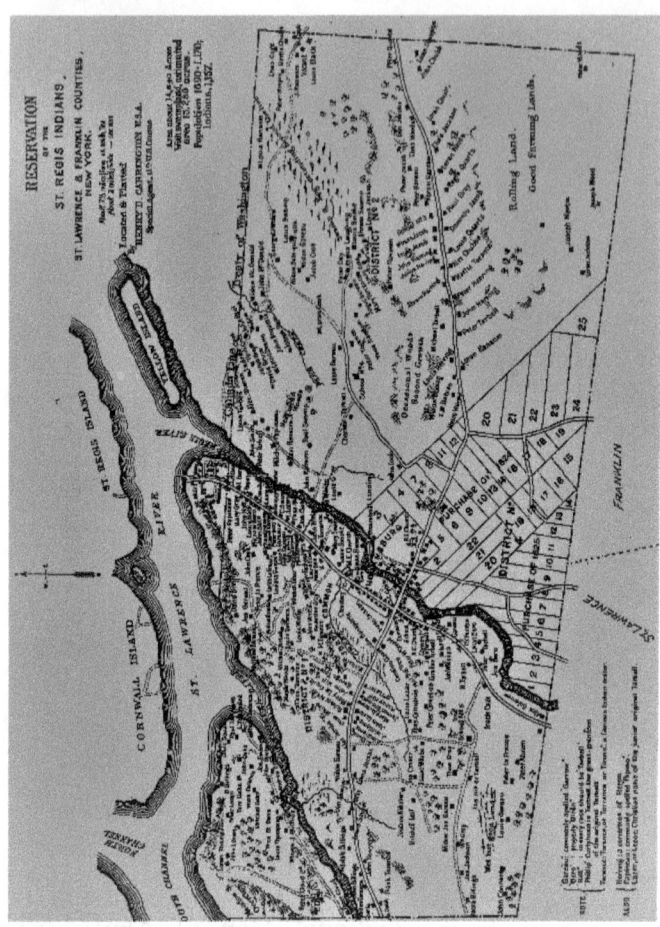

Figure 3. *Reservation of the St. Regis Indians. St. Lawrence & Franklin Counties, NY 1890.*
Source: *Located and Platted by Henry B. Carrington, USA*

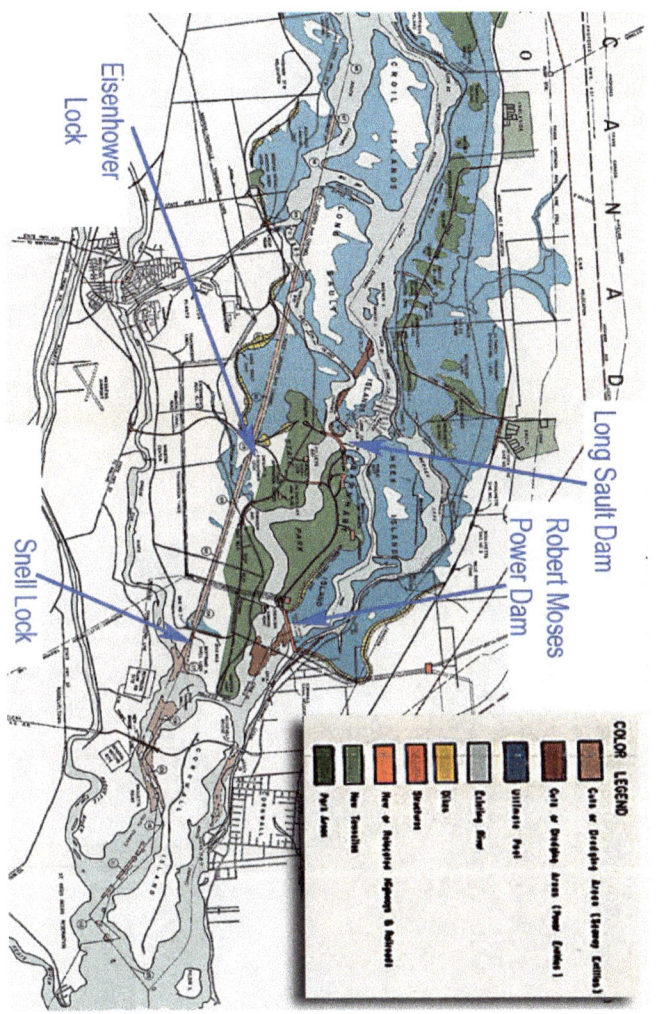

Figure 4. Ontario Hydro Blueprint for Cornwall-Massena Section of the Seaway July 1958

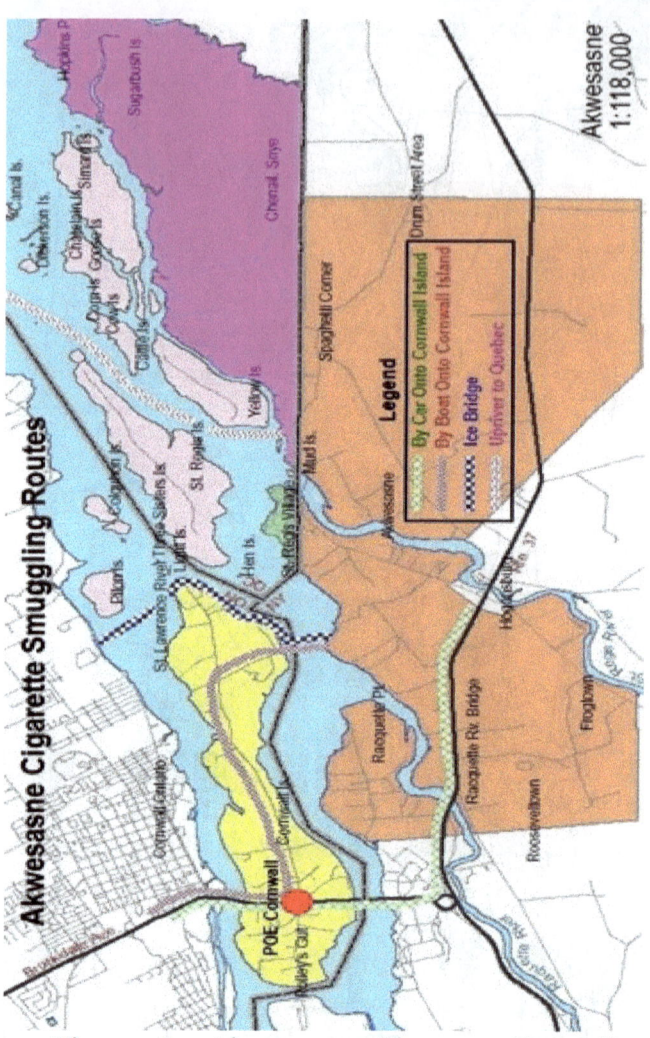

Figure 5. Akwesasne Cigarette Smuggling Routes. Source: Marsden, William, *Canada's Boom in Smuggled Cigarettes.* The International Consortium of Investigative Journalist. March 27, 2009

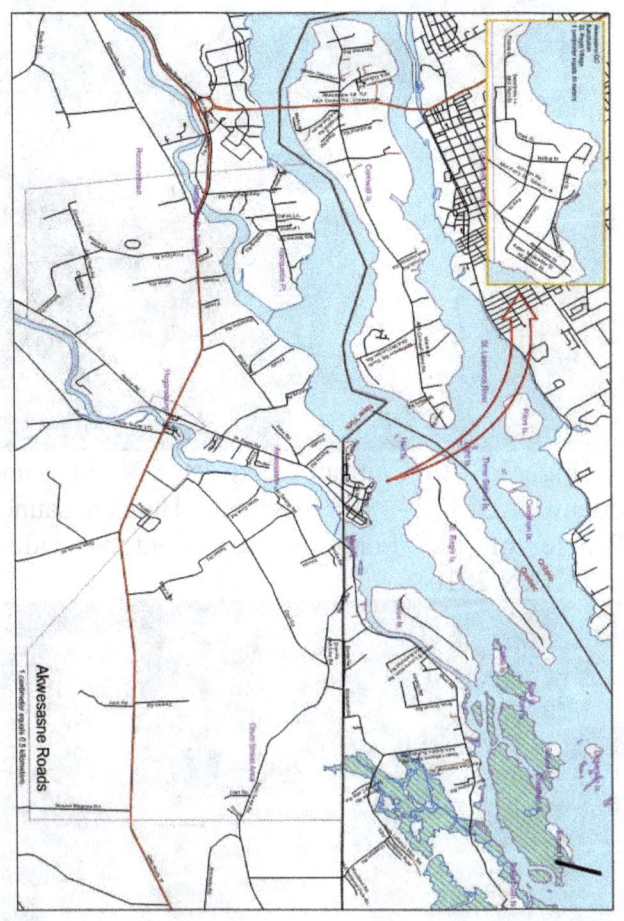

Figure 6. Map of Akwesasne Roads. Source: Mohawk Council of Akwesasne, GIS/OVS "Akwesasne and Surrounding Area," 2005.

Figure 7. Conflict between NYSP and Mohawks July 24, 1989. Source: Haudenosaunee (People of the Long House) Youtube video, AZTKIAN 2010

Figure 8: Anti-Gambling Roadblock, Akwesasne. Source: Video News Report, NBC Universal Media, LLC. 1989

Figure 9. State Police examine one of several bullet marks on a National Guard medivac helicopter, fired upon when flying low over Ganienkeh in Altona. A physician onboard was wounded in the March 30, 1990 incident. (AP)

Figure 10. Map of Ganienkeh. Source: Image © 2017, TerraMetrics Tele Atlas, "Ganienkeh," Mountain View, CA: Google, 2008.

Figure 11. St. Regis Catholic Church, St. Regis, Quebec, Canada Source: Narratively: *Where Sunday Mass is in Mohawk*, Photo by Adrienne Surprenant

Figure 12. Famous stand-off during the Oka Crisis between Pte. Patrick Cloutier, a perimeter sentry, and Anishinaabe warrior Brad "Freddy Krueger" Larocque. Shaney Komulainen of Canadian Press 1990

THE OKA STANDOFF

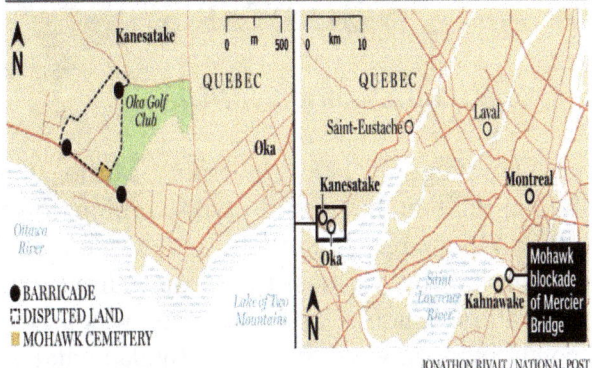

Figure 13. Map of Kanesatake, Oka, Québec

Figure 14. Mohawk Bingo Palace Akwesasne (St. Regis Mohawk Reservation, Rt. 37 & Frogtown Rd,)

CHAPTER 5

Cops, Culture, and Conflicts

On August 14, Governor Mario Cuomo announced that he would start working toward a solution to the recent conflicts and devise guidelines and limits for various types of gaming on the reservation. Cuomo said the state was now in a "position to address the more fundamental issues pertaining to law enforcement and gambling, outside of a crisis environment." He further said that there was a need to address "the legitimate" interests of the Native Americans in reasonable ways. "After more than 200 years we have yet to resolve a number of fundamental issues that stand in the way of a continuing harmonious relationship between" the original inhabitants of this continent and those who came here to build a better life.[288]

Chief Mike Mitchell (from the Canadian side of Akwesasne) and 150 of his followers crossed the US-Canadian border on August 27, 1989. They marched to the Mohawk Tribal headquarters (US) and demanded that the "pro-gambling" Warriors leave Akwesasne. The Canadian Mohawks saw the Warriors as lawless, pro-gambling militants who were tied to the monetary fruits of gambling and who were leading the community astray. During the episode, 500 Mohawks confronted each other; this

---

[288] Elizabeth C. Petros, "Cuomo Vows to Help End St. Regis Reservation Conflict," *The Post-Standard*, August 15, 1989.

appeared to be a decoy operation. While this was going on, some anti-gambling Mohawks snuck away from the crowd, and destroyed the Lucky Night Casino using Molotov cocktails.[289] Along with the arson at the casino, two power transformers were shot out near Tony's Vegas International Casino. Laughing put snipers on roofs to protect the village from violence.[290] During the conflict, Mark Maracle, a Warrior spokesman, was caught by the crowd, beaten, and humiliated.[291] Maracle said, "We'll stand our ground against people or state troopers . . . whatever it takes. If it takes a baseball game, we'll do that."[292] Summing up the police's position since being allowed back on the reservation Lieutenant Peter Burns, of Troop D of the New York State Police said, "at this point we go on the reservation only when requested, but we would like this to change. I think we'd like to go in and do what we do in any other part of the state."[293]

The Canadian Mohawks at Akwesasne declared a state of emergency. After anti-gambling supporters allegedly shot out the power transformers Chief Mike Mitchell declared, "We've

---

[289] CP, "Mohawks Threaten Fight in Dispute over Gambling," *The Toronto Star*, August 29, 1989.

[290] Gary Rosenberger, "Armed Patrols Guard against Violence by Security Force," *United Press International*, August 30, 1989.

[291] Ibid.

[292] CP, "Mohawks Threaten Fight in Dispute over Gambling;" The reference to a baseball games concerns the carrying and using of baseball bats in fights.

[293] Scott Scanlon, "Troopers. Mohawks to Discuss Renewed Patrol Service," *The Post-Standard*, August 27, 1989.

taken this action because lawlessness on Akwesasne is out of control."[294] On August 30, armed Warriors were reported to have made telephone threats; they said they would burn down the CKOW radio station and the *Akwesasne Notes* newspaper office because of their anti-gambling stance. Armed guards protected the offices after the threats.[295]

At the end of August 1989, three days of meetings were planned between all the factions in Cornwall, Ontario to discuss gambling. Three Cornwall Police detectives escorted Chief Mike Mitchell, who had been in hiding, to the meetings each day.[296] Other chiefs from the Canadian side participated, as did Tarbell, one of the three head chiefs, and some sub-chiefs from the American side of the reservation. Traditionalist chiefs from both sides of the border attended the meeting, as did business leaders. Because the meetings were held in Canada at Cornwall, many of the casino owners could not attend because of pending warrants and outstanding charges in the US. The Warriors' leaders protested the meeting by not attending; however, they did send observers. The Warriors thought that the imposed, non-traditional institution of elected tribal chiefs made the respective tribal governments the puppets of the US and Canadian governments. Fearing more violence the leaders and

---

[294] CP-AP, "Power Cut, Mohawks Say Reserve 'Lawless,'" *The Toronto Star*, August 29, 1989.

[295] Rosenberger, "Armed Patrols Guard against Violence by Security Force."

[296] Darcy Henton, "'All-out War' Looms over Reserve Gambling," *The Toronto Star*, September 3, 1989.

attendees of the conference asked the NYSP to immediately begin patrols on roads on the US side of the reservation.[297]

The three days of meetings were unproductive. On September 3, 1989, the NYSP sealed off the reservation for eight hours because anti-gambling forces were attacking the Warriors Society's acting headquarters.[298] While Canadian Grand Chief Mike Mitchell, American Head Chief Harold Tarbell, and casino owner Tony Laughing were giving a news conference about getting the Warriors to the table, anti-gambling forces were battering down the front door where the Warriors were headquartered with a four-wheel drive truck.[299] About 40 anti-gambling Mohawks, many who were ironworkers back from working off the reserve, fought with about 25 Warriors (of which ten were women).[300] The Warriors barricaded themselves in a bingo hall, blocked the doors with tables, and fought the attackers with fire extinguishers.[301] Windows were

---

[297] Elizabeth C. Petros, "St. Regis Leaders Urge Restraint During Conflict," *The Post-Standard*, August 31, 1989; CP, "Gamblers Boycott Mohawk Meeting," *The Toronto Star*, August 31, 1989; Darcy Henton, "Little Progress in Mohawk Conflict," *The Toronto Star*, September 1, 1989; Darcy Henton, "Mohawks Fear Bloodshed over Gambling," *The Toronto Star*, September 2, 1989; William Kates, "Violence Grows on Indian Nation Divided by Gambling," *The Associated Press*, September 2, 1989.

[298] Darcy Henton, "'All-out War' Looms over Reserve Gambling," *The Toronto Star*, September 3, 1989.

[299] Staff, "Police Close Road as Mohawks Clash," *The Toronto Star*, September 3, 1989.

[300] Ibid.

[301] AP, "Fight on Indian Reservation as Casinos Divide Mohawks," *New York Times*, September 3, 1989.

broken and cars were smashed. Even some photographers who were at the skirmish were attacked with clubs and lacrosse sticks. Loran Thompson, a Warrior leader, said, "these guys [anti-gamblers] didn't want to talk, they wanted blood."[302] Leaders of the Warriors Society sent a request to the Peace Chiefs of the Six Nations Iroquois Confederacy to oversee discussions to end the conflict. Warrior leader Loran Thompson "had contacted Six Nations leader, Leon Shenandoah, to request the chiefs help restore harmony to the Mohawks."[303]

Even with all the commotion on the reservation, gamblers kept coming, oblivious and unconcerned about the situation. Buses came carrying gamblers from Québec, Toronto, and parts of New York State.[304] During the 1980s, it was common to find two or three busloads of gamblers from Rochester, New York headed to Akwesasne each weekend. The gamblers would leave on a charter bus (for example, Peter Pan Bus Lines) from Rochester and arrive at the Flanders Inn at Massena, New York by 9 or 10 PM. [305] Over the weekend, the charter buses ferried the gamblers back and

---

[302] Staff, "Police Close Road as Mohawks Clash."
[303] Darcy Henton, "Mohawks Can't Rule out More Clashes," *The Toronto Star*, September 4, 1989.
[304] Darcy Henton, "Casino Stays Open Despite Violence," *The Toronto Star*, September 5, 1989.
[305] Massena, NY is approximately 12.4 miles west of Hogansburg, NY (44.973N, -74.663W), which is on the Akwesasne/St, Regis Reservation.

forth from the reservation.[306] At times anti-gambling forces threw rocks and stones at the buses, and cars parked at the casinos were damaged.[307] Doug George, a local Native newspaper editor said, that residents on the reservation were weary of looking for peaceful solutions.[308]

Before sunrise on September 4, a group of allegedly hooded Warriors attempted to raid the Akwesasne Police Headquarters on the Canadian side of the border. They were stopped by residents who surprised them in front of the police station.[309] John Boots, a Warrior spokesman, said that the Warriors were not involved and tried to keep away from these situations. "We never advocate events of that nature, it would seem counterproductive, I know we had people driving around and observing, but it would be very unlikely they would be involved in something like this."[310]

On September 6, after speaking with Governor Cuomo by phone, Chief Lincoln White and Chief David Jacobs issued new operating permits to casino owners. Chief Harold Tarbell would not support the issuance and said that Jacobs and White

---

[306] Ernest R. Rugenstein, *Remembering the Busloads from Rochester to Akwesasne*, to Ernest K. and Donald K. Rugenstein, April 20, 2006.

[307] Darcy Henton, "Casino Stays Open Despite Violence," *The Toronto Star*, September 5, 1989.

[308] Staff, "Police Close Road as Mohawks Clash," *The Toronto Star*, September 3, 1989.

[309] Darcy Henton, "Mohawks Block Raid on Police Building," *The Toronto Star*, September 5, 1989.

[310] Ibid.

had misinterpreted Cuomo's remarks.[311] "Cuomo in a taped conversation, agreed to negotiate some gaming operations such as high stakes bingo . . . 'but we have to live by federal laws.'"[312] Because of the provisions of *The Indian Gaming Regulatory Act* (1988), if the state did not permit that type of gambling, the reservation could not have it, this meant no slot machines.

The anti-gamblers predictably were unhappy with the issuing of permits. They immediately wanted to circulate a petition to have the two chiefs impeached. Doug George, editor of *Akwesasne Notes*, said, "what they did was illegal and they must be removed from office."[313] Although the anti-gambling faction would have preferred to have gambling disappear quietly, they would not limit the possibilities for action. George added that with "what has happened on Akwesasne recently, it looks like we're in for another hot weekend."[314] Warrior spokesman Francis Boots said the Warriors' only goal was to protect the "territorial integrity of the reservation."[315] Their goal was to keep outside forces from violating Mohawk land. New York State Police Troop B Commander, Major Ronald Brooks asked the factions to not increase tensions on the reservation or raise the likelihood of

---

[311] CP, "Anti-Casino Natives Want to Impeachment of Two Chiefs," *The Toronto Star*, September 8, 1989.

[312] Ibid.

[313] Ibid.

[314] Ibid.

[315] Elizabeth C. Petros, "State Police Say Warriors Ok Not Needed Troopers Will Enter Reservation If Called," *The Post-Standard*, September 8, 1989.

violence. "State Police would like to see residents of Akwesasne develop peaceful solutions to their internal problems without intervention, but if further violence occurs troops will respond immediately to provide protection to uninvolved public."[316] While Brooks said that the NYSP would notify the Warriors before entering the reservation to answer a complaint, in a written statement he wrote that the "provision of this service is not dependent on any such system, and the state police will continue to provide response to call for service regardless if the Warriors give their consent."[317]

DRUMS held a protest in downtown Massena, New York, on September 9. Thirty anti-gambling members held a peaceful demonstration, marching down the main streets with signs condemning non-Native businesses and residents that they believed supported gambling.[318] David Cole, DRUMS spokesman, explained that, "basically we're just asking them to stay out of the internal affairs of the reservation."[319] Later that night a transformer was shot out on the reservation that knocked out power to the casinos, and cut power to five hundred homes for over eight hours. The Warriors Society investigated the shooting, and said that the anti-gambling faction did not care if the whole

---

[316] Elizabeth C. Petros, "Cops Would Enter Reservation, Ok or Not," *The Post-Standard*, September 8, 1989.

[317] Petros, "State Police Say Warriors Ok."

[318] CP, "Gambling Foes Stage Peaceful Protest," *The Toronto Star*, September 10, 1989.

[319] AP, "Reservation Gambling Protest," *New York Times*, September 11, 1989.

community suffered. Loran Thompson, a Warrior spokesman, felt "whoever's doing this terrorism can't have much of a mind." Tony Andre of the Niagara Mohawk Power Company said that a number of smaller transformers had also been shot. "It's very frustrating, it's [transformer] an expensive item."[320]

The situation was wearing down the people on the reservation, and was costing the State of New York financially. The cost to the NYSP through September 13, was $1,534,901, and of that amount, overtime was $1,386,470. Other costs were $20,000 for 27,400 road-flares and $10,800 for auto fuel. Each New York State Police officer's expenses were about $26 per day for food and between $32 and $42 per night for rooms.[321] The proprietors of Massena, New York were doing well financially. They provided lodging and meals for the patrons gambling at Akwesasne, and for the police officers parked on Route 37 at the edge of the reservation.

Tony Laughing, casino owner and one of thirteen facing gambling charges, was arrested on September 21, outside Fort Covington, New York, small town ten miles east of the reservation, with $11,000 on him and another $76,000 in the car he was driving.[322] That evening a large group of women went to the New York State Police Barracks

---

[320] CP, "Gunshots Cut Power to Mohawk Casinos," *The Toronto Star*, September 11, 1989.

[321] Michaell Kilian, "Cost of Indian Unrest Flares to $1.5 Million," *The Post-Standard*, September 21, 1989.

[322] Measured from Hogansburg, NY (44.973N, -74.663W), which is on the Akwesasne/St. Regis Reservation.

in Massena, NY. The group was assured by Major Ronald Brooks that Laughing was fine and would stay that way. That night he was taken to Syracuse, New York to be arraigned. A two-car escort followed him as he was transported to Syracuse.[323] Art Montour, still free on bail, said, "our concern is that the Indian people wanted to make sure his life was not in danger. We wanted to make sure he was not beaten on the way to Syracuse like I was on July 21 [1989]."[324]

There were strange twists in the gambling situation. In September, New York State was sued by Atlantic and Pacific Amusement Corporation, headquartered in New Jersey. The corporation sued to recover $77,500 for the thirty-one slot machines taken from the casinos during the NYSP raid. Atlantic and Pacific Amusement Corporation claimed that the state did not have the jurisdiction over Indian gaming to take the machines. The machines had been sold and shipped to the tribal government not to the casinos directly. When confronted, the chiefs said someone must have stolen the tribal council stationery.[325] Simultaneously, New York State opened talks with the Mohawk Tribal Council about legalizing certain types of gambling on the reservation under *The Indian Gaming Regulatory Act* (1988). The first

---

[323] Sue Weibzahl Naylor, "Casino Owner Arrested Laughing Caught Off Reservation," *The Pot-Standard*, September 22, 1989.

[324] Ibid.

[325] Tom Foster, "Firm Sues State for Seizing Slots," *The Post-Standard*, September 27, 1989.

meeting was held in Albany, New York and was attended by all Chiefs Jacob, Tarbell, and White. Chief Tarbell initially was unaware of the meeting and upset that the other two chiefs had set it up without his knowledge. The three chiefs, NYS officials, and attorney John Peebles of Omaha, Nebraska, attended the meeting. Peebles was an Indian gaming specialist and did not represent the tribe. Although Tarbell disapproved of his presence because he was Tony Laughing's attorney, Jacobs had invited him.[326]

The Ferociousness of Borderlands

In the fall of 1989, gambling on the reservation continued. The buses full of gamblers kept rolling in, the NYSP kept shadowing the border and handling calls along Route 37, and the factions became more violent. On October 8, 1989 while *en route* to the various bingo halls and casinos four buses were attacked at the intersection of Racquette Club Road and Route 37 with stones, rocks, and other debris. Bus windows were smashed and paint was thrown at them. Flying glass from broken windows hurt two women. One of the women, Janet Langly from Ottawa, was treated for cuts at the hospital. Another bus was hit in the side with a single shotgun blast at the Canadian Customs Office on Cornwall Island.[327] In response to the growing

---

[326] Matthew Cox and Tom Foster, "State, Mohawks Try to Set House Rules for Gambling," *The Post-Standard*, October 25, 1989.

[327] AP, "Bingo Buses Attacked at Indian Reservation," *New York Times*, October 10, 1989; Elizabeth C. Petros, "Police Lift St.

violence, the federal government recruited the OPP for round-the-clock patrols of the customs compound.³²⁸

Later that day, a transformer providing power to a casino was shot out for the fourth time in two months. The NYSP accused it to the anti-gambling faction. Around 8:30 PM that night, shots fired near a patrol car forced officers to seal off the reservation for 24 hours to investigate.³²⁹ In a written statement, the Warriors stated that those who have been terrorizing them had "previously confined their physical attacks to the Mohawk people and private property in Akwesasne." The statement continues that the attackers had recently begun "attacking, harassing, and threatening non-native people." The Warriors further declared their intent to "protect, preserve, and defend the sovereignty and jurisdiction of the Mohawk Nation at Akwesasne according to the *Great Law of Peace*." The statement ended with the Warrior Society's commitment to seek a peaceful coexistence of all people of the Mohawk nation.³³⁰

The weekend of Sunday, October 15, was a repeat of the previous one. A scuffle between anti- and pro-gambling supporters caused eight buses filled with gamblers for the bingo halls and casinos

---

Regis Blockade," *The Post-Standard*, October 10, 1989.

[328] CP, "Customs Officers Threaten Walkout," *The Toronto Star*, October 20, 1989.

[329] Elizabeth C. Petros, "Police Lift St. Regis Blockade," *The Post-Standard*, October 10, 1989.

[330] Elizabeth C. Petros, "Warriors Denounce Weekend Violence at Reservation," *The Post-Standard*, October 12, 1989.

to turn back. Five of the buses were from Montreal and two were from Ottawa. The buses had crossed the border, but were confronted by 100 Mohawks blocking Route 37.[331] In one incident cars were beaten by baseball bats to get them to turn around.[332] The anti-gamblers also distributed leaflets that warned motorists to stay away, stating that the residents of the reservation wanted to resolve the gambling situation internally. The leaflets asked anyone planning on visiting the casinos not to. The anti-gamblers stated that "continued participation in the illegal establishments have added to the unrest that our community is experiencing."[333] The State Police set up roadblocks on Route 37 to divert non-residents from crossing the reservation. Sergeant Michael Downs said, "We know of a couple of cars that were damaged when they were hit with bats."[334] Public safety was the reason why the NYSP sealed off the reservation again.

About ten days later, October 25, New York State officials met with the chiefs from the American side of the reservation in Lake Placid, New York. This meeting was a continuation of the initial meeting in Albany, New York in September. There was a hope that an agreement would be

---

[331] CP, "Mohawks Repel 8 Bingo Buses," *The Toronto Star*, October 16, 1989.

[332] Staff, "Anti-Casino Violence Breaks Out," *United Press International*, October 15, 1989.

[333] Ibid.

[334] Ibid.

reached.[335] Chief White said, "The fact that we are able to sit down around the table and discuss these matters brings about a feeling of optimism." White continued, "If we weren't able to sit around the table, then I would be very disappointed."[336] Robert Batson, counsel to the State Office of Rural Affairs, attended the meeting and said, "We have to negotiate with the tribe some sort of regulatory scheme that will guarantee the integrity of the games."[337]

Gambling on the US side of the reservation continually involved the Canadian side through the Mohawk Council of Akwesasne that had no legal jurisdiction over the US side's gambling. Canada did not allow gambling and the Canadian Mohawks did not want to challenge the government. However, because of the uniqueness of the reservation Mohawks freely voiced their opinion on the cultural aspects of issues. The anti-gambling faction on the Canadian side did not appreciate buses from Québec and parts of Ontario driving across their part of Akwesasne. Buses had been fired upon at the border, and the protests were sometimes large. The OPP officers stationed at the Cornwall Island border crossing provided a sense of relief to the customs officials who worked there. Mansel Legacy, President of the Customs Excise Union, said, "custom officials will walk out if

---

[335] Matthew Cox and Tom Foster, "State, Mohawks Try to Set House Rules for Gambling," *The Post-Standard*, October 25, 1989.
[336] Ibid.
[337] Ibid.

Ontario Provincial Police officers guarding the Cornwall Island Border Crossing are withdrawn."[338] On October 27, the two OPP officers stationed at the customs compound were withdrawn and replaced by two armed RCMP officers. Chief Mitchell had wanted the OPP off Cornwall Island and wanted the Canadian Mohawk Police force to police their part of the reserve. Mitchell wanted the RCMP gone in a week. Of them, Mitchell said, "This is the last compromise we're going to make."[339]

On October 30, a car jumped the border at Canadian Customs and headed toward the east end of Cornwall Island. A high-speed chase ensued by the RCMP. According to Ernie King, Police Chief of the Mohawk Police Force, the car, which was allegedly driven by Arthur Montour Jr., went to Duane Jock's house. It was reported that the car was full of contraband cigarettes. The Warriors Society intervened and prevented the RCMP from arresting the Warriors leader's son, Montour Jr. The six RCMP and six Mohawk Police Officers were pelted with rocks and had to stand up to between 40 to 200 people for four hours.[340] A potentially related incident on November 3, when at 4:45 AM, a Mohawk Police car was shot at six times. The two on-duty officers could not identify the car because it

---

[338] CP, "Customs Officers Threaten Walkout."
[339] CP, "Mounties Man Border near Reserve," *The Toronto Star*, October 30, 1989.
[340] Tom Foster, "Police Car Hit by Shots at Regis," *The Post-Standard*, November 3, 1989.

had its lights off.[341] A local newspaper noted that with all the incidents of violence, arson, and other illegal activity between July 20 and November 2, the police had not made any arrest other than casino owners.[342]

At 8:30 PM on November 12, and again at 9:30 AM on November 13 the building that housed the weekly newspaper *The Voice*, located at the four-corners in Hogansburg, New York, was shot at nine times with a .22 caliber rifle. The paper's editor Cindy A. Terrance, reported that five windows were broken, but no one was hurt. The paper, was started in 1986, and owned by Eli Tarbell the owner of the Bear's Den.[343]

Four officers of the Sûreté du Québec, who had been working by request of Mohawk Police Chief Ernie King, were withdrawn by their superiors on November 16, 1989. The Warriors had expressed their disapproval and said the officers should leave, the Sûreté du Québec complied. Denis Pelletier of the St. Jean Division said, "we feel this is a First Nations problem and should be resolved by them. . . [however if the band council] makes a formal request, we would have no alternative but to return."[344] The Sûreté du Québec had two-dozen officers on stand-by in Huntington, Québec in case

---

[341] Ibid.
[342] Elizabeth C. Petros, "Shots Fired at St. Regis Newspaper," *The Post-Standard*, November 14, 1989.
[343] Ibid.
[344] CP, "Police Leave Mohawk Reserve," *The Toronto Star*, November 17, 1989.

trouble arose.[345] When the officers were removed, Chief Mike Mitchell and the council declared a state of emergency and asked the residents for 40 volunteers to serve as deputies to help the Mohawk Police force. Mitchell said, "obviously, they [deputies] are going to have to carry firearms if they are to be of any help to the [reserve] police.[346] By November 22, 70 people had volunteered to support the Mohawk Police Force. Security checks were conducted on the applicants, who were scheduled to start a 24-week training program in January 1990. Thirty volunteers who had already been deputized were held in reserve in case of an emergency.[347]

At 3:10AM on November 27, a Mohawk police cruiser was rammed into at a parking lot next to the station by a vehicle with no plates or insurance. As police officers arrived to investigate, they identified James Oaks of St. Regis, Québec fleeing the scene in another car. As police tried to follow Oaks, the Warriors blocked them. The standoff allowed Oaks and his accomplice to get away. After two hours, the Warriors dispersed peacefully. Around 7AM, while on a routine patrol a Mohawk Police car was shot at from a four-wheel drive brown and white vehicle. No one was hurt, and the car was not hit.[348]

---

[345] Ibid.

[346] CP, "Emergency Declared as Police Leave Reserve," *The Toronto Star*, November 18, 1989.

[347] Elizabeth C. Petros, "Mohawks Forming Auxiliary Police Force," *The Post-Standard*, November 22, 1989.

[348] Janis Barth, "Reservation Violence Targets Police Patrols," *The Post-Standard*, November 28, 1989.

The next day, the Mohawk Council of Akwesasne declared that the Warriors Society were terrorists and had no legal or moral authority over the Mohawk nation. Because of the violence, the Council suggested that the residents of the community to remain at home and limit use of public roads after 10 PM to help prevent violence. The suggested cur 10 PM suggestion includes making sure all minors are home or supervised by an adult. Further the Council prohibited the use of "all-terrain vehicles by minors on public roads and limit the use of firearms to authorized personnel."[349]

A number of situations that occurred ended 1989 and bookmarked the decade. Eli Tarbell, charged with three accounts of possession of slot machines, accepted a plea deal.[350] Tony Laughing pleaded guilty to one count of operating an illegal gambling business, resisting arrest, and possessing slot machines. Laughing had six other counts dismissed through a plea deal with federal prosecutors.[351] In an interview, Laughing said, "my business employs 240 people and none of those jobs are minimum wage."[352] However, Doug George, editor of the Indian Times had an opposing view, ".

---

[349] Janis Barth, "Mohawk Council Urges Reservation Curfew," *The Post-Standard*, November 29, 1989.

[350] Charles Miller, "Mohawk Pleads Guilty Tarbell Admits Having Lots," *The Post-Standard*, November 28, 1989.

[351] AP, "Mohawk Pleads Guilty in Illegal Casino Case," *New York Times*, December 19, 1989.

[352] John Larrabee, "Mohawks Divided over Casinos; Debate Rages as Trial Starts; Details About Reservation," *USA Today*, December 15, 1989.

. . [gambling] is destroying the fabric of Mohawk society. Ten years from now we won't recognize ourselves as Mohawk people."[353]

Another situation that had a major impact, not just in the 1986 but also in 1989, was the ruling of Judge Condon A. Lyons, New York State Court of Claims, in White et el v. New York. In May 1986, there were nine fatalities involving drunk driving and people drinking at unlicensed bars. When the police arrived at the bar they arrested Josephine White for running an unlicensed bar and serving alcohol to intoxicated people. After the police left a crowd broke down the door, smashed the interior, and burned down the building.[354] Lyons ruled that the New York State Police did not have a special duty to protect the bar owner's property from the crowd.[355] This implied that the New York State Police did not have special directives or responsibilities to protect the casinos that had been burned down or trashed in the current situation. This was especially true with Tony Laughing's casino, where the police took him into custody and told him they would disperse the crowd. While they were gone, the casino was trashed and tables and chairs destroyed.

Governor Cuomo, in an end-of-the-year press conference on December 20, 1989, announced that if the Chiefs wanted him to come and if he could be

---

[353] Ibid.
[354] Josephine White was the owner of Josie's Bar. See Chapter 3, page 84.
[355] Gary Spencer, "State Police Cleared by Judge of Not Protecting Bar Owners," *New York Law Journal*, December 12, 1989.

helpful to the situation, the Governor would travel to Akwesasne. Cuomo said, "if they really need me, I'll be around, I like to move around. I'm easy."[356] Harold Tarbell said, "If the governor is going to come, he's going to have to be willing to talk about a lot more than gaming. He's going to have to be willing to talk about law enforcement and the environment, and the intervention of non-Indians in the affairs of our community."[357]

Conflicts and Convictions

At 12:30 PM on January 13, 1990, Gerald McDonald, 26, from Bombay, New York, shot-up Tony's Vegas International using a pump-action shotgun. In just over an hour he had fired thirty times. Bill Patterson a gambler from Watertown, New York, said, "He shot the place up real good . . .He [McDonald] said, 'Why don't you people learn? We don't want you here.'"[358] Another gambler from Montreal, Québec said, "he was mad, real mad, but he didn't want to hurt anyone because he shot the floor or the wall or the ceiling."[359] McDonald was charged with first-degree reckless endangerment, third degree assault, and second-degree criminal mischief.[360] On January 15, he was arraigned before the court in Fort Covington, New York and released

---

[356] Matthew Cox, "Cuomo Willing to Meet with St. Regis Factions," *The Post Standard*, December 21, 1989.
[357] Ibid.
[358] CP, "Gunman Opens Fire in Casino on Reserve," *The Toronto Star*, January 14, 1990.
[359] Ibid.
[360] Ibid.

on $500 bail.[361] It was reported that McDonald caused $5,000 worth of damage at the casino.[362]

About 12 hours after McDonald shot-up Tony's Vegas International, two or three truckloads of armed Warriors parked next to the Akwesasne Police Headquarters in St. Regis, Québec. Each side said the other fired first, however, there ensued a 2 1/2-hour gun battle between the Warriors and Police.[363] Police Chief Ernie King said the Warriors used semi-automatic shotguns, AK-47 assault rifles, and Uzi machine guns in the attack. The police had only started to purchase assault rifles. King said, "No other police force in Canada has had to face what we've been through."[364] Lloyd Benedict, one of the twelve chiefs on the Canadian side of the border, said it was time to bring in the National Guard.[365] He felt it was a "miracle no one has been killed in the many exchanges of gunfire that occurred over the past year."[366] During the 2 1/2 hour gun battle neither the New York State Police nor Sûreté du Québec responded to calls for help

---

[361] Timothy Appleby, "Mohawks Want Cuomo to Act in Dispute," *The Globe and Mail*, January 16, 1990. Ft. Covington is thirteen miles east of Hogansburg, NY, (Akwesasne/St, Regis Reservation) on Route 37.

[362] Thomas Fine, "Chief: Troopers Ignoring St. Regis Gunplay," *The Post-Standard*, January 30, 1990.

[363] Timothy Appleby, "Mohawks Want Cuomo to Act in Dispute."

[364] Darcy Henton, "Mohawk Leaders Fear Deaths in Gambling Feud," *The Toronto Star*, January 17, 1990.

[365] Ibid.

[366] Darcy Henton, "Border Reserve's Gambling Crisis Turning into War," *The Toronto Star*, January 16, 1990.

from the Mohawk Police.[367] Bill Hutton, OPP Inspector, said that even though the province established, trained and equipped the Native force it had no jurisdiction to go to its aid. The Native police headquarters were located in "Québec and the only land access is through New York State." Because of the international border, OPP officers could not carry weapons into that portion of Akwesasne or the United States without special permission. Even if they could cross the border with their weapons, they could "not use them because they have no jurisdiction in the United States or Québec."[368]

Over 100 Mohawks, along with representatives of other Indian Nations traveled to Albany, New York on January 15. They made the trip to request in person that Governor Cuomo intervene in the uprising at Akwesasne. Four days later, on January 19, the Canadian Customs House was fired on. When local police responded, they said they were outgunned. When the police went to replenish their ammunition in Cornwall, Ontario, after the last firefight, they found their attackers had already been and had bought out the entire supply of ammunition.[369]

On Friday, January 29, the Warriors society building, containing about 40 people was hit with five gunshots. No one was injured, but the attack kept anxieties high. Many feared retaliations similar

---

[367] Ibid.
[368] Darcy Henton, "Gambling Feud Puts Indians on Brink of War," *The Toronto Star*, January 20, 1990.
[369] Ibid.

to the one on January 14. Art Montour, speaking for the Warriors Society, said that the Warriors would not retaliate because they were more interested in "defending Akwesasne sovereignty against any outside forces of the U.S. or Canada."[370]

The Traditionalist chiefs could not understand why the NYSP had not intervened the violent attack on the US portion of the reservation. Edie Gray, a member of the Mohawk Council of Chiefs, said, "I don't know what sort of games they're [New York State Police] playing. They showed no interest. . ."[371] Traditionalist Chief Gray said, "every time something happens, I call the state police, nothing's done at all."[372] Chief Mike Mitchell said the reservation had become "victims of gambling. The reserve is in a state of lawlessness and it has been that way for the better part of a year. There's no law on the American side. It's a free for all."[373]

Events occurred that caused all sides of the gambling issue to come together. The Internal Revenue Service (IRS) said that Tony Laughing owed $2,385,564.99. "The lien covers income and Social Security taxes for 1988 and the first three quarters of 1989, as well as the unemployment taxes that should have been submitted in 1988."[374] The

---

[370] Thomas Parry, "Shooting Worries Police on Reserve," *The Globe and Mail*, January 29, 1990.

[371] Thomas Fine, "Chief: Troopers Ignoring St. Regis Gunplay," *The Post-Standard*, January 30, 1990.

[372] Ibid.

[373] Darcy Henton, "Gambling Feud Puts Indians on Brink of War," *The Toronto Star*, January 20, 1990.

[374] Tom Foster, "I.R.S. Slaps $2.4m Tax Lien on Casino Owner," *The Post-Standard*, February 6, 1990.

IRS filed in the Franklin and St. Lawrence county clerks' offices. When the FBI and the state police had tried to force Tony's Vegas International to close, they were met with armed resistance. Mohawks both for and against gambling did not believe the federal government had the right to tax Natives or Native businesses. The Indians did not think the IRS had jurisdiction on the reservation and their claims were null and void.[375]

Laughing was not the only person affected by the government. Art Montour went to trial on February 15, 1990 for forcibly interfering with the execution of a federal search warrant and rallying armed Mohawks to prevent State Police and the FBI from raiding gambling casinos. Montour faced a possible $5,000 fine and up to three years in prison His lawyer Seth Shapiro, an associate of William Kunstler, said that the raid was in violation of the Helsinki Accords that state all nations of the world are to respect the sovereignty of the other nations of the world.[376]

On February 27, U.S. District Judge Neal P. McCurn sentenced Laughing to 2 1/4 years in prison. He was found guilty of operating an illegal gambling business and possessing slot machines on Indian land. Although sentenced, Laughing was released until the New York State Court of Appeals determined jurisdictional issues with the raid. Laughing contended that Mohawk land was sovereign, and that New York State could not stop

---

[375] Ibid.
[376] Dan Kane, "Mohawk Activist Goes to Trial," *The Post-Standard*, February 15, 1990.

him from having a casino. In an interview, Laughing said, "sovereignty means I can do what I damn well please on my land."[377] When he left the courtroom Laughing said, "we're going to beat them. I don't believe this court has jurisdiction over any reservation in the country."[378] The next day the owner of Burns' Casino, Peter Burns, was sentenced to twenty-one months in prison and a $5,000 fine. "He was charged with possession and use of slot machines, operating an illegal gambling business and forcible interference with the execution of a search warrant."[379] The judge also ordered him to subsidize his prison stay by paying $1,000 per month. After prison, he would then have three years' probation when he would have to pay $96 per month.

Henry Lickers, a Seneca who had lived at Akwesasne since 1975 and who worked on environmental issues, captured the essence of the situation. He said, "The non-natives point their fingers and say, 'How can they do such things?'" concerning Mohawk gambling, casinos, and smuggling. Lickers knew that the environmental destruction of the water and land is what motivated many of the Mohawks' socially and economically. Lickers continued, saying, "all of this, we've tried to maintain our traditional ways and found we couldn't. When you destroy a man's environment,

---

[377] Mike McAndrew, "Mohawk Casino Owner to Appeal Sentence," *The Post-Standard*, February 27, 1990.
[378] Ibid.
[379] Dan Kane, "Casino Owner Gets 21 Months in Prison," *The Post-Standard*, February 28, 1990.

you destroy the man. Akwesasne can very much be the example."[380]

May Day

The different jurisdictional areas splitting Akwesasne created problems for the Mohawks. The mandates imposed upon these different jurisdictional areas further complicated the picture. Although Mohawk sovereignty was the end goal there was the reality of borders. The elected tribal councils were the only authorities that their respective federal governments recognized. Legally, the elected tribal governments had to use the sanctioned authorities to resolve problems in their jurisdictional area. The problem was that the governmental agencies did not respond to pleas for help by the recognized governments of the reservation. Combined with different factions each having its own ideas on how to achieve these goals, and the situation was ripe for violence to occur.

On Saturday night, March 3, the Mohawk police force truck on the Canadian side of the reservation was struck by gunfire three times. The police retaliated by ramming a truck and exchanging gunfire for hours with the unknown assailants in the truck. Later that night, the police station at St. Regis, Québec was fired upon with automatic weapons. Twenty-five people were inside, but no one was injured. The police alleged

---

[380] Barbara Stith, "St. Regis Mohawks Find Environment a Unifying Issue," *The Post-Standard*, February 25, 1990.

that members of the Warriors Society were responsible. They denied it. The Warriors blamed the incident on the police. They declared the police were Chief Michael Mitchell's "personal goon squad."[381] With the escalating violence, Mitchell, on March 6, called for the community to resist violence. He said if that did not work, the reservation would need to be shut off from the outside. Chief Mitchell opened the decision-making process to the community at large. Beginning on March 6 meetings were held, starting with women, and then met subsequent nights with the elders, men, and youth. Mitchell said that after this, a decision would be made about closing the reservation to outside traffic.[382] Steven Lazore, a senior constable with the Mohawk Police force, felt shutting down the reservation would have effects internally and externally to the community. With the reservation shut down the businesses inside the reservation would suffer. The casinos would suffer as well as legitimate businesses such as the office supply store, gas stations, tourist shops, and other small businesses. Externally closing the reservation would force non-Indians to drive further to travel across northern New York. It would mean driving an extra thirty miles to cross over into Canada. Non-Indians would have to cross over at the Ogdensburg–Prescott Bridge instead of the Cornwall Island Bridge. The hope was that both

---

[381] Barbara Stith, "Leaders Consider Closing Canadian Reservation," *The Post Standard*, March 7 1990.
[382] Ibid.

effects would force public opinion against the Warriors.[383]

Chief Mitchell, the police, and the residents on the Canadian side of the reservation were planned to join the anti-gambling forces on the US side of the reservation to block off Route 37 and the Cornwall Bridge.[384] On March 10, 400 Mohawks met to consider closing the reservation to cut off the flow to the casinos and to stop the illegal cigarette trade. As they were discussing closing the reservation, businesses continued to do well, especially the Golden Arrow, the French Riviera, Tony's Vegas International, Bear's Den Truck Stop, and the Mohawk Bingo Palace.[385]

On the US side of the reservation some people were working toward a similar solution. Chief Harold Tarbell had written a letter to President Bush, in January, asking him to intervene in the situation at Akwesasne. In the letter, he wrote, "I fear that if an aggressive initiative is not undertaken at the highest levels of our government now, we will soon be living under 'the rule of outlaws.'"[386] There was no response to the letter. When asked about the letter in March, Tarbell said he was trying to get someone to pay attention to the serious of the situation at Akwesasne. Tarbell said they could not get help from the various bureaucracies. "The

---

[383] Ibid.

[384] Ibid.

[385] Thomas Fine, "Reservation Quiet, Open to Traffic During Weekend," *The Post Standard*, March 12 1990.

[386] Thomas Fine, "St. Regis Head Chief Asks Bush for Help," *The Post Standard*, March 13, 1990.

reservation," he said, "needs assistance from the Bureau of Indian Affairs, the Commerce Department, the Justice Department, Congress and the State Department." Tarbell's message was "we're not going ... to let them sit back and hem and haw."[387] The state police did not see the arguments between the factions at Akwesasne as a sign of trouble. Major Robert Leu, Commander of New York State Police, Troop B, said, "right now the situation at the reserve is like a family where two sides are yelling and shouting at each other, getting out the aggressions, but no one is getting hurt."[388]

In the middle of March, a report from the US Senate Select Committee on Indian Affairs stated that the Akwesasne reservation was in the "worst situation in Indian country."[389] U.S. Sen. Daniel K. Inouye, Committee Chairperson, Democrat from Hawaii, said, "you have a community in effect under the control of a band of outlaws, armed with automatic weapons and clearly acting in collusion with casino owners."[390]

On March 15, the Mohawk Business Committee issued a press release that said in part that they were against the proposed blockade of the borders. They said they would hold "Mike Mitchell and Harold Tarbell and their few supporters on this political issue responsible for all the violence,

---

[387] Ibid.

[388] Hornung, *One Nation under the Gun,* 118.

[389] Barbara Stith, "Mohawks Situation Called Worst in Decades," *The Post Standard*, March 14, 1990.

[390] Ibid.

damage, vandalism, loss of income and loss of jobs as a result of their closing or attempting to close the various borders of this reservation."[391]

On the same day, the Mohawk Tribal Council (US), the Mohawk Council of Akwesasne (Canada), and the Traditionalists (Mohawk Nation Council of Chiefs) met at Flanders Inn, in Massena, New York. It was the culmination of meetings that began on March 6, 1990, with the community residents. Returning from the meeting in Massena, the leaders asked the reservation residents to consider having a forum and referendum on law enforcement, gambling issues, and on the cross-border smuggling.[392] Additionally, the leaders agreed that the residents of the reservation had to eliminate violence completely and that the idea of a blockade was "ridiculous."[393] In a news conference held on Friday, March 16, Mitchell, speaking about the agreement said, "If we didn't commit ourselves to this last night, we would be looking at sealing off the community."[394]

After the news conference, the Warriors Society met at 2 PM. The meeting lasted late into the night, while they discussed the recent developments. Warriors' spokesman John Boots told with reporters that the Warriors did not see the need for a judicial system or a police force on the US side of the reservation. Relying on the 200-year-

---

[391] Barbara Stith, "Possible St. Regis Closure Angers Merchants," *The Post Standard*, March 16, 1990.

[392] Barbara Stith, "Mohawks Want Vote to Resolve Conflicts," *The Post Standard*, March 17, 1990.

[393] Ibid.

[394] Ibid.

old Iroquois Constitution they were already patrolling the American side and providing peacekeeper services. Boots said the Warriors would participate with a referendum if the community called it. The Warriors viewed the elected tribal governments as dupes of their respective federal governments.[395]

Agreements began to break down between the three councils. The Canadian council was still at odds with the Warriors, blaming them for past attacks and anticipating possible future ones. Because of this the Mohawk Council of Akwesasne decided to close their tribal offices. The council office and the police station are located in St. Regis, Québec, but to reach the other parts of the reservation such as Cornwall Island or Snye, Québec, the police had to cross the American side of the reserve. This is when trouble could occur because the Warriors patrolled the US portion of the reservation. Although the council offices were closed, the police office remained open.[396]

On Friday, March 23, anti-gambling protestors closed two highways with a school bus, a dump truck, and a number of other vehicles. Three of the protesters were hurt.[397] Virgil and Allen White, brothers who lived on the US side of the reservation, were walking home and hit with objects at a roadblock on Frogtown Road. Both were taken

---

[395] Ibid.

[396] Barbara Stith, "Canadian Mohawks Close Council Office," *The Post Standard*, March 21, 1990.

[397] CP, "Mohawks Blockade Casino Roads," *The Toronto Star*, March 25, 1990.

to Massena Memorial Hospital. At another roadblock, a woman was hurt, treated at Cornwall Hospital, and then released.[398] (See Figure 8: Anti-Gambling Roadblock, Akwesasne Page 128)

Early the next morning, at 2 AM, New York State Police went on the reservation to investigate an accident at the corner of Route 37 and 37C. On the way, back to the station, a group of Warriors stopped the squad car. They started a verbal confrontation about the legitimacy of the state police being on the reservation. As the police drove away someone threw a beer bottle that hit the back window and shattering it. The police continued back to the barracks and investigated the incident later.[399]

Around 10 AM, 30 people began stopping traffic on Route 37 on the western edge of the reservation. By 4 PM people started to stop traffic on the eastern end of the reservation. Gil White, a member of the Mohawk Business Committee and partial owner of the Mohawk Bingo Palace, said that if the blockade was longer than a couple of days 700 people could be out of work, "It's hurting everybody. It's a little radical group that has no support whatsoever."[400]

Although the three governing councils had just a few days earlier met and they agreed that the reservation should not be closed off, they issued a press release that called the barricaded roads an, "an act of sovereignty. . . That restricting traffic are

---

[398] Barbara Stith, "Indians Block Roads 3 Hurt," *The Post Standard*, March 24 1990.
[399] Ibid.
[400] Ibid.

calling attention to the current violence associated with the gambling and the Warrior force, which protects the gambling industry."[401] Harold Tarbell, the only American Chief who agreed with the press release, said, "I think it is effective . . . it's not something we asked them to do, but they're sick of talking to themselves."[402]

The response from the NYSP ranged from indifference to guarded concern. From their barracks near Massena, New York the police coordinated four checkpoints surrounding the reservation. They warned motorists of the situation and detoured them around the problem areas. A state police officer from the Massena headquarters said, "it appears their only intention is to keep the gambling traffic out."[403] In fact their attention was diverted to Ganienkeh Mohawk Territory, near Altona, New York in Clinton County, approximately 50 miles east from the Akwesasne reservation.[404] This situation involved Mohawks, the Warrior's Society, the NYSP, and the concept of sovereignty.

---

[401] Ibid.
[402] Ibid.
[403] Ibid.
[404] Measured from Hogansburg, NY (44.973N, -74.663W), which is on the Akwesasne/St, Regis Reservation. See Figure 6 page 127.

CHAPTER 6

Ganienkeh, Oka, Warriors, and the Governor

On March 30, a Vermont National Guard helicopter was shot at during an emergency medical fight. Its flight plan took it across Ganienkeh when it was hit three times, forcing it to land. One of the passengers, Dr. James Van Kirk (27), was shot in the right arm. The Mohawks would not allow state and federal authorities to investigate the shooting. They said that the police and FBI did not have jurisdiction on their territory.[405] The next day the police sealed off the community.[406] NYSP and New York Corrections Officers manned the barricades. NYSP Officer, Fred Curns said, "We've turned back everybody . . . We'll turn back everybody until the powers that be decide it's safe to let them through."[407] Talks broke down on April 3. The arrival of Fletcher H. Graves, a conciliation specialist with the US Justice Department of Manhattan on April 4. Dale Dione, a Ganienkeh resident, said she was "hopeful Graves will get the

---

[405] AP, "Indians Stand Off Troopers after Copter Hit by Shot," *New York Times*, April 1, 1990.

[406] Matthew Cox, "Federal Mediator Agrees to Help Resolve Tensions at Ganienkeh," *The Post-Standard*, April 4, 1990.

[407] Staff, "Police Blockade Mohawk Territory after Helicopter Shooting," *The Associated Press*, March 31, 1990.

deadlocked talks moving again."[408] When the Mohawks proposed that the investigation be turned over to a third party, the NYSP rejected the idea.[409] (See Figure 9. State Police examine one of several bullet marks on a National Guard medivac helicopter, fired upon when flying low over Ganienkeh in Altona. Page 129)

These problems at Ganienkeh were not the only events on March 30; it was also the beginning of Art Montour's trial. He was in US District Court in Syracuse, New York, accused of the three felonies. Montour's defense lawyer Seth Shapiro intended to prove at trial that Montour had not planned to keep the police from serving their warrants-the barricades had been set up to protect the Mohawks from a feared massacre.[410] (See Figure 10. Map of Ganienkeh. Page 129)

As events were occurring at Ganienkeh, problems arose again at Akwesasne. NYSP officer Mark Klosowski stopped a car driven by John T. Lazure at a barricade, for drunk driving. As Klosowski was walking back to his patrol car he was struck by Lazore's car as he was driving away. Lazore made it into Canada and outside the jurisdiction of the NYSP.[411] Later the same, day Lazore turned himself into the police. He faced

---

[408] Cox, "Federal Mediator Agrees to Help Resolve Tensions at Ganienkeh."

[409] Ibid.

[410] Mike McAndrew, "Police: Mohawk Manned Barrier," *The Post-Standard*, March 30, 1990.

[411] Thomas Fine, "Driver Runs into Trooper. Flees to Reservation," *The Post-Standard*, April 3, 1990.

charges of "attempting to murder a trooper by running him over, assaulting a trooper with a vehicle, driving while intoxicated and leaving the scene of a personal-injury accident."[412]

On April 5, 1990, Douglas George, editor of the Akwesasne Notes, spoke at *The Iroquois/Jesuit Study Symposium*. He expressed his views on the uprising at Akwesasne. George thought it was entirely connected to the Mohawks' lawsuits against the state of New York. They were suing for $1 billion because the Mohawks believed that 1500 acres had been illegally taken from Akwesasne and nine million acres from the border to the Mohawk Valley. Ultimately George blamed New York State for the reservation's problems. He was upset with how Governor Cuomo had handled the situation and had not heeded the elected Chiefs request to close the casinos. George said, "They were hoping that the gambling and smuggling would cause a breakdown in unity . . . If the Indians are not united, some of them may be willing to accept a lesser settlement from the state."[413]

Meanwhile on April 10 at 6:20 PM a federal jury convicted Art Montour "of forcibly impeding the execution of a federal search warrant and conspiracy. . . the jury spared Arthur Montour a stiffer charge of using a weapon to forcibly impede the execution of a search warrant."[414] His lawyer,

---

[412] Staff, "Police Say Man Rammed Officer," *The Post Standard*, April 5, 1990.

[413] Karen Nelis, "Iroquois, Jesuits Try to Heal Old Wounds," *The Post-Standard*, April 6, 1990.

[414] Dan Kane, "Defender of Sovereignty Convicted Mohawk Activist Gracefully Accepts Federal Court Verdict," *The

Seth Shapiro, said the jurors were "obviously confused... [and that this was] another indication of the malignant paternalism of the United States government."[415]

The situation at Ganienkeh began to change on April 12, when the eleven-day standoff ended. The Mohawks allowed investigators to spend two hours on the reservation to investigate the shooting. The situation was complicated when the FBI arrived with arrest warrants for 14 Mohawks for obstruction. The residents of Ganienkeh did not recognize the FBI jurisdiction and said they would fight back if the FBI entered without permission.[416]

At Akwesasne the situation started to change quickly. On April 19, two of the three elected Chiefs from the American council asked the state police to enter the reservation and remove the roadblocks that had been in place since March 23. The Warriors Society, who had been opposed to any interference by the NYSP, backed the request. However, a spokesman for the Division of State Police in Albany said that the police would not remove the barricades unless all three chiefs requested it. The police's non-responsiveness turned out to be a disservice to the elected representatives of Akwesasne and to the surrounding communities.[417] Communities from around

---

Post Standard, April 11, 1990.

[415] Ibid.

[416] Sam Howe Verhovek, "Standoff Ends, but Not Mohawk Defiance," *The New York Times*, April 14, 1990.

[417] Barbara Stith, "Troopers Busy with Roadblocks," *The Post Standard*, April 19, 1990.

Akwesasne became upset and decided that they were going to place their own barricade across Route 37.[418] One of the organizers, Dick Lavigne, the owner of WICY Radio in Malone and a motel in Moira, said, "our problem is not with the Indians, it's with the governor. We don't feel he's upholding the laws of New York."[419]

Later at noon on April 19 around 500 people, along with elected officials, barricaded Route 37 in Westville, New York, about 15 miles from Akwesasne, for 90 minutes. Their goal was to accentuate two different standards being used. While it was against the law to block a road in Westville on Route 37, it was not illegal on the same route through the reservation. Norman Treptow from Fort Covington, New York, said, "just because they (the Mohawks) can't solve their internal problems, they don't have to affect all of Northern New York adversely . . . The governor has the means at his disposal to take care of this problem. . . We want to see law and order restored."[420] When asked Malone Mayor, Richard Gokey said, "I'd like to tell the governor that he wanted the job, he got the job, and damn it, I wish he'd do his job."[421]

Cuomo's office responded that they were assisting the tribal council on the US side of the border work through its difficulties. Jeff Cohen, an

---

[418] Ibid.

[419] Ibid.

[420] Barbara Stith, "Non-Indians Erect Barrier to Protest Unrest at St. Regis," *The Post Standard*, April 20, 1990.

[421] Ibid.

aide to Governor Cuomo, said, "We understand their concern and frustration, but we are doing what we can to resolve the situation peacefully, in a way that doesn't beget violence."[422] Ernie King, the police chief from the Mohawk Police on the Canadian side, said that he came to the barricade, "to show them what we're up against. It's really upsetting to a lot of people, with all these violent tactics and no response from the [New York] state."[423] In an editorial to *The Post Standard* in Syracuse, Doug George wrote that the Mohawk people "do not suffer lightly the political manipulations of an administration whose attitude seems to indicate to us that as long as no non-native is hurt or killed, the problem can be ignored." George continued that during Cuomo's time in office the Mohawk people had been exposed to the worst violence "to our existence since the American Revolution." He added that this "'friend of the Indian' has alleged the people of Altona might have shot at a medical helicopter in order to discredit the people of Ganienkeh, sabotaged our land claims by refusing to take our proposals seriously, challenged the credibility of our traditional leadership by refusing to meet with the Mohawk Nation, fostered the rise of the casinos here by ordering the state police not to work with us on closing these dens of corruption and given benign support for the outlaw "Warrior society" by allowing the troopers [NYSP] to work with them despite repeated requests by our

---

[422] Ibid.
[423] Ibid.

leaders not to do so."[424]

Violence returned four days later, when, on April 23, three reserve buildings were firebombed and the police station was attacked three times with Molotov cocktails.[425] In one attack a hand grenade was thrown into the crowd.[426] The next night, at 7:30 PM, the Warriors attacked the west barricade, first using AK-47s. The unarmed anti-gambling residents who were manning the roadblock were pinned down by the gunfire for almost two hours. By 11:30 PM over 2000 rounds, including tracers, were shot at them. The barricade along with two-dozen cars were burned and the Mohawk police were pushed back across the river. The eastern roadblock was abandoned and destroyed after midnight.[427]

While no one was injured during the attack Horace Cook, 50, a diabetic ran away from the gunfight and disappeared. Gary McDonald and others searched for him, worried that he was injured in the attack. As they were searching, two pro-gambling women attacked them; one began throwing rocks, while the other brandished a shotgun. McDonald said, "We had no chance against them. We were unarmed. First they started throwing rocks and then they came on us with

---

[424] Douglas M. George-Kanentiio, "Struggle at Akwesasne Mohawks Need Time to Heal Wounds," *The Post-Standard*, April 23, 1990.

[425] Bill Taylor, "Heavily Armed Mohawks Overrun Cornwall Reserve," *The Toronto Star*, April 26, 1990.

[426] CP, "Grenade Wounds Three," *The Toronto Star*, April 24 1990.

[427] Taylor, "Heavily Armed Mohawks Overrun Cornwall Reserve."

baseball bats."[428]

US Chief Harold Tarbell was furious with the Governor Cuomo's lack of leadership. He claimed that the governor was courting the criminals and making the legally recognized government negotiate with them.[429] Tarbell told a reporter that those who opposed gambling had been fleeing to Cornwall Island on the Canadian side of the reservation for safety. He said that he had contacted the US federal government and had asked the NYSP to end the two–year situation at Akwesasne.[430] John Boots, a Warrior leader, was upset that Tarbell had contacted Cuomo to ask him to send in the state police. Boots said it was unnecessary because peace was returning and traffic was beginning to move again.

By April 26, most families had been affected by the violence in one-way or another. Many houses on the US side had either been smashed, shot at, or burned.[431] Canadians suffered also. The Snye, Québec house of Ken Lazore, brother of Chief John Lazore of the Canadian Mohawk Council of Akwesasne, was burned down in retaliation for his anti-gambling stance.[432] Officials in the Ontario Solicitor-General's office acknowledged the jurisdictional problems and asked NYSP to become involved. The NYSP refused intervene. NYSP

---

[428] Darcy Henton, "4 Mohawks Hurt in Clash as Anger Boils Over," *The Toronto Star*, April 27, 1990.

[429] Ibid.

[430] Darcy Henton, "War over Gambling Heats Up Elderly Mohawks Rescued by Boat," *The Toronto Star*, April 27, 1990.

[431] Ibid.

[432] Thomas Fine, "Canada Pressures Cuomo on St. Regis," *The Post-Standard*, April 27, 1990.

Major Robert Lea, said, "we're viewing this as an internal matter. Our orders are to stay out."[433] The Canadian Embassy in Washington, DC, contacted the State Department and asked for an end to the New York State policies.[434] The Canadian government wanted the US State Department to persuade Governor Mario Cuomo to stop the violence on the US side of the reservation. Anti-gambling proponents hoped that the Canadian government could do even more by bringing in the RCMP or Canadian Forces troops.[435]

Darren Dopp, Governor Cuomo's spokesman, in response to the Canadian requests that the governor was not changing his policies and that he was determined not to use state police or National Guard in the situation. Dopp said, in "our judgment the best way to settle this is through mediation. What we're not going to do is confrontation . . . [reservation violence is] part of an internal conflict within the Mohawk community."[436] Dopp stated that state mediators and the three elected chiefs from the American side were meeting in Syracuse on April 26 to work out a solution.[437]

While meetings were going on in Syracuse, preparations were made to move Mohawks from the south side of the St. Lawrence River in Québec to

---

[433] Bill Taylor, "Heavily Armed Mohawks Overrun Cornwall Reserve," *The Toronto Star*, April 26, 1990.

[434] Henton, "War over Gambling Heats Up Elderly Mohawks Rescued by Boat."

[435] Thomas Fine, "Canada Pressures Cuomo on St. Regis," *The Post-Standard*, April 27, 1990.

[436] Ibid.

[437] Ibid.

near Cornwall, Ontario. Because they could not leave where they were by land without going through the US and crossing Warrior barricades boats would be used to ferry them. The next day, over 200 residents left St. Regis, Québec by barge across the St. Lawrence River. First onto the barge were 21 people from the Senior Citizen Lodge in Québec. The Cornwall City Police, the Sûreté du Québec, and emergency service personnel helped the Mohawks to the Cornwall Hockey Arena.[438] During the evacuation there was one bright light: Horace Cook, who disappeared and was presumed dead by many during the violence on April 24, was found. Fearing that everyone at the barricade had been killed, he hid in the woods for three days, controlling his diabetes by eating tree bark and cedar wood.

People blamed Canadian Grand Chief Mike Mitchell for all of the problems. One evacuee blamed Mitchell saying, "[He] wants everyone to be poor and he'll be the only one making money. The casinos should be kept open. They bring employment and get people off welfare."[439] Mohawks who were against gambling said that the Warriors had a hit list of 250 names. The anti-gamblers said the Warriors seemed peaceful during the day but at night they broke out automatic weapons and Molotov cocktails. The uprising had split families and friends apart. One man pointed and said, "See that guy? I fished with that guy all

---

[438] Darcy Henton, "Mohawks Flee Border Reserve to Escape Gambling Showdown," *The Toronto Star*, April 28, 1990.
[439] Ibid.

winter. I might have to shoot him tonight."[440] Louis Terrence, a Program Director of a drug and alcohol treatment programs on the reservation, said, "The fact that no one has been shot to death is a miracle beyond belief."[441] The Canadian Mohawk Police had asked repeatedly for help from three Canadian police forces, but none had committed officers, stating they would not intervene if New York State did not intervene.[442]

As of April 28, New York State had refused to take action at Akwesasne. The government in Ottawa continued to talk to American officials to try to get them to address the violence. Cuomo faced increasing pressure from Indian leaders too. Chief Harold Tarbell asked the governor to bring in the National Guard and separate the heavily armed factions.[443] US Senator Daniel K. Inouye wrote Cuomo, stating that a majority of Mohawk leaders felt the community was living with "clear threats of deadly violence . . . [and that this situation] …would not be tolerated by state or federal government in any other community or under any other circumstances."[444]

Despite the repeated requests of the Canadian government, the US Senate, and the leaders of the Mohawk community to send NYSP onto the

---

[440] Ibid.

[441] Sam Howe Verhovek, "Mohawks Ask Cuomo to Join a Peace Effort," *New York Times*, April 28, 1990.

[442] John Lichfield, "Mohawks Go to War over Bingo," *The Independent*, April 29, 1990.

[443] Verhovek, "Mohawks Ask Cuomo to Join a Peace Effort."

[444] Ibid.

reservation to stop the violence, Governor Mario Cuomo refused.[445] Cuomo had no intentions of sending the NYSP or the National Guard onto the reservation. In a news conference, Cuomo said, "This will be resolved by negotiation, not with a cannon. You have to be careful because most incendiary statements are coming from individuals who are seeking to advance their own political causes."[446] Cuomo rejected the idea that he or she should take a harder stance against the uprising at Akwesasne. Major Robert B. Leu confirmed Cuomo's response. Leu said, "It's simply because of the amount of fire power they have. We're not a military operation."[447] Traditional Mohawk Chief Tom Porter, speaking about the various provincial, state, and federal authorities' refusal to help, said, "We're resting now and we are rethinking everything, but we cannot run away because we're afraid. That is our home . . .it looks like we will have to clean our own house . . . What does that mean? That remains to be seen. What lies ahead, we will place in the Creator's hands. But people want to go home."[448]

Significant events occurred on April 29 on both sides of the border. Georges Erasmus, the leader of the Canadian Assembly of First Nations, asked the

---

[445] Ibid.

[446] Donatella Lorch, "Behind Violence, Tensions Roil Mohawks," *New York Times*, April 30, 1990.

[447] Verhovek, "Mohawks Ask Cuomo to Join a Peace Effort."

[448] Darcy Henton, "Anti-Casino Mohawks Vow to Resolve Reserve War Alone Reserve Becomes War Zone over Gambling," *The Toronto Star*, April 29, 1990.

Canadian police associated to take the initiative and intervene. "If they [police] don't respond on the weekend, there could be a serious loss of life. Is that what they're [New York State Police] going to do - just come in and pick up the bodies?"[449] Erasmus was right about the need for police. That day armed Mohawks dug bunkers on Cornwall Island and watched the US mainland. The Mohawks who were evacuated to the Cornwall Hockey Arena said on April 30 they had decided to return home and take back over the reservation and put an end to gambling.[450]

On April 30, Governor Cuomo announced a peace plan that would "negotiate legalized gambling on the reserve, provided the casinos close, the US road through the reserve remains open, and the violence stops."[451] The governor appointed Henrik Dullea, to start the negotiations.[452] Harold Tarbell replied, "As far as I'm concerned the prerequisites have not been met yet. We've been shot by people who want gambling and he's prepared to negotiate what they want."[453] John Boots, Warriors spokesman, accused Mike Mitchell of being a Canadian government agent. Boots said that

---

[449] John Lichfield, "Mohawks Go to War over Bingo," *The Independent*, April 29, 1990.

[450] Darcy Henton, "Uneasy Calm Falls on Reserve," *The Toronto Star*, April 30, 1990.

[451] Darcy Henton, "500 Mohawks Waiting Off Reserve Amid Peace Talks in Casino War," *The Toronto Star*, May 1, 1990.

[452] Staff, "Mohawk Violence Escalates; Two Killed in Gun Battles," *United Press International*, May 1, 1990.

[453] Henton, "500 Mohawks Waiting Off Reserve Amid Peace Talks in Casino War."

Mitchell was "hungry for power because he sees so many millions of dollars here. He doesn't want to close down the casinos – he wants to control them and we're the only ones who are standing in his way."[454]

In response Chief Mitchell said, "the American side is an outlaw town. The Warriors society doesn't have any rules, they just make them up."[455] Canadian Indian Affairs Minister Tom Siddon criticized Cuomo's actions saying that Canada wanted to see New York State "cooperate and assist in dealing with" the pro-gambling faction "on the New York side that appears to be provoking the incident." Siddon said that his government was dissatisfied with New York State's response to the crisis.[456]

On the evening of April 30, around 9:30 PM, a Canadian Press (CP) reporter, and a photographer arrived for interviews at David George's house near Snye, Québec.[457] A group of Mohawks were guarding George's two-story log cabin armed with shotguns and hunting rifles all day. From the cabin, one could see the surrounding area and the river even by the light of a half moon. The first gunfire between pro- and anti-gambling factions began around 10:30 PM. Mohawks at the log cabin fired at

---

[454] Donatella Lorch, "Behind Violence, Tensions Roil Mohawks," *New York Times*, April 30, 1990.

[455] Ibid.

[456] Mike Hill, "Reservation Feud over Gambling Turns Deadly," *The Associated Press*, May 1, 1990.

[457] Darcy Henton, "Two Mohawks Shot Dead in Casino War on Reserve Police Asked to Stop Gun Battles," *The Toronto Star*, May 2, 1990.

a speedboat crossing the border on the St. Lawrence River. This was a typical route for smugglers coming across the river. From a wooded area on the New York State side of the river anti-gambling gunfire was returned. During the exchange, a tanker, going up the Seaway toward Kingston, Ontario, found itself in the middle. From the first shot of the firefight thousands of rounds were fired from shotguns, hunting rifles, and automatic weapons between the two positions. The CP reporter and the photographer hid in the basement of George's cabin all night.[458] Gunfire erupted sporadically throughout the night, escalating between 4 AM and 7 AM.

Around 5:30 AM on May 1, May Day, Matthew Pyke and some anti-gambling traditionalists were protecting themselves inside David George's Snye, Québec house.[459] Pike was "a twenty-two year old gas station attendant who was a brother of a Mohawk leader in the Akwesasne territory and a strong supporter of traditional ways."[460] After the exchange of gunfire Pyke ended was helping people leave Snye and trying to keep vehicles out of the area.[461] Joe Lazore was walking with Pyke when Pyke was shot in the back. The

---

[458] Ibid.

[459] Darcy Henton, "Two Mohawks Shot Dead in Casino War on Reserve Police Asked to Stop Gun Battles," *The Toronto Star*, May 2, 1990. David George was the brother of Doug George, anti-gambler and editor of the Indian Time and Akwesasne Notes newspapers.

[460] Thomas Fine and Sean Kirst, "2 Victims Differed in Views of Dispute." *The Post-Standard*, May 2, 1990.

[461] Ibid.

gunfire came from a wooded area on the American portion of the reserve.[462] His sister Beverly Pyke said that Warriors were shooting over the heads of people trying to get her brother. "They wanted him dead and that's what they got."[463] Pyke was taken to Alice Hyde Hospital in Malone and died at 10:30 AM.[464]

Around 7:30 AM, the CP reporter and photographer emerged from the house while still under fire. Sometime between 8 and 9 AM, Harold "Junior" Edwards Jr. was shot dead during sporadic gunfire.[465] He was near the house of his uncle, Raymond Lazore, on River Road. A Warrior, Thomas Square, and a Daily-Courier-Observer reporter, from Massena, New York, found Edwards body about six hours later around 3 PM. He was said he have been acquainted with most of the Warriors but was also seen as a friend to many of the anti-gambling people.[466] The nine-hour battle ended around 12:00 noon, leaving most of the houses in the area, shut up, and in some, cases guarded. Beverly Pyke's anti-gambling neighbors

---

[462] Hill, "Reservation Feud over Gambling Turns Deadly."

[463] Fine and Kirst, "2 Victims Differed in Views of Dispute."

[464] *Ibid.*; Staff, "Escalating U.S.-Canadian Indian Conflict Claims First Life," *The Xinhua General Overseas News Service*, May 1, 1990.

[465] Edwards was thirty-two-year-old Mohawk "born on the US side of the reservation." Lazore said his nephew "wasn't on either side... You could see him laughing or joking around at the anti's blockade or up around here." Fine and Kirst, "2 Victims Differed in Views of Dispute."

[466] Ibid.

guarded her parents' house.[467] Before Edwards' body had been found, Chief Harold Tarbell said, "I'm going to tell Cuomo, he got his body. . ., two attempted murders I guess is not good enough."[468] Barbara Barnes, a spokeswoman for the anti-gambling faction, said, "people are in shock and angry but not just at the Warriors. They are angry with Governor Cuomo. This could have been avoided."[469]

As May Day progressed it became politically dynamic. Cuomo ordered the New York State Police to investigate and assist the Sûreté du Québec. The shootings had occurred on the Canadian side of the reserve in Québec, and the NYSP escorted the Sûreté du Québec through New York State and back to the Canadian border.[470] Canadian External Affairs Minister Joe Clark contacted US Secretary of State James Baker and asked for the US's cooperation and to use law enforcement to stop the violence.[471] Around 8:30 PM, the New York State Police and the Sûreté du Québec sealed off the reservation. The police set up roadblocks on all roads onto the reservation and did not allow anyone, even residents, to pass. Families were waiting off the reservation for the police to allow them by. Tisha Jacobs waiting at a service

---

[467] Ibid.

[468] Henton, "Mohawks in 9-Hour Gunfight on Reserve."

[469] Joanne Zipperer, "Mohawk Feud Escalates; 2 Slain," *USA Today*, May 2, 1990.

[470] Sam Howe Verhovek, "2 Mohawks Killed in Feud over Reservation Gambling," *The New York Times*, May 2, 1990.

[471] Darcy Henton, "500 Mohawks Waiting Off Reserve Amid Peace Talks in Casino War," *The Toronto Star*, May 1, 1990.

station, with her family, remarked, "The troopers told us we couldn't get in."[472] The Mohawks who had been evacuated from the south shore of the St. Lawrence River decided to stay a few more days at the Cornwall Hockey Arena. They felt peace needed to return to the reserve first. Chief Mike Mitchell said, "The people who evacuated think it's worthwhile. Somebody said: 'What's two days out of our lives?' We're still seeking a peaceful solution."[473] When the Warriors were asked about the situation, their spokesman John Boots said, "As far as can be determined, a fire fight happened between two groups of antis [anti-gamblers] and, unfortunately and sadly, Matthew Pyke took a round."[474] Editor Doug George blamed Cuomo for the deaths, saying that if there was another fight, "we'll fight back [holding an AR15 semi-automatic rifle].. This is the first time in my life I have picked up a gun to shoot a human being, but they would have killed us one by one if we had stayed in our homes." George continued, saying that he had not had a choice and that the fighting was thrust upon him and the others.[475] The Canadian Defense Department stationed about 100 troops from both the 1st Battalion Royal Canadian Regiment, in London, and the Canadian Forces Base (CFB)

---

[472] Hill, "Reservation Feud over Gambling Turns Deadly."

[473] Darcy Henton, "500 Mohawks Waiting Off Reserve Amid Peace Talks in Casino War."

[474] Darcy Henton, "Two Mohawks Shot Dead in Casino War on Reserve Police Asked to Stop Gun Battles," *The Toronto Star*, May 2, 1990.

[475] Ibid.

Petawa near the reservation to support the RCMP.[476]

Gunfire continued overnight. Early on May 2, over 400 police officers entered the reservation in a multinational operation. New York State Police, along with the OPP, RCMP, the Sûreté du Québec and 100 Canadian Armed Forces personnel took control of the area and ended the nightly gunfire. Cuomo stated that the American elected Chiefs and the Warriors Society had approved the operation. The police checked the names and identifications of everyone attempting to enter or leave the reserve. Some Mohawks feared that the violence had gone beyond the issue of gambling and had become a blood feud between families. People were dead and injured, and houses and businesses had been burned down. Vehicles had been destroyed. Most people on the reservation just wanted the nightmare to end. Canadian Federal Solicitor General Pierre Cadieux, announced, in Ottawa that on May 3 the five governments would meet in Montreal to hold talks on the Akwesasne violence. The assumption was that the state and provinces would handle the policing aspects and the two federal governments would handle jurisdictional concerns. Although Ontario Attorney General Ian Scott had hoped that the Canadian and American Chiefs would attend, they were not invited.[477] Cadieux said that it was impractical to search house to house for weapons, but if police found any illegal weapons they would

---

[476] Ibid.
[477] Jonathan Ferguson and David Vienneau, "Leaders to Discuss Joint Police Force," *The Toronto Star*, May 3, 1990.

confiscate them. At this point the New York State Police were allowing only residents onto the reservation and, even then, their cars were searched. There had been two arrests, one for carrying tear gas and the other for possession of brass knuckles.[478] Federal Indian Affairs Minister in Ottawa Tom Siddon said although the chiefs had not been invited to Montreal there would be immediate discussions with them after the five jurisdictions had met.[479]

On the morning of May 3, during a news conference in Albany, New York Governor Mario Cuomo said that units of the National Guard, although on alert, would not be sent to the reservation. Cuomo said he had sent his representative Henrik N. Dullea to the scene to negotiate a peaceful solution. Cuomo said. "Before you use a military force, you should use the force of reason."[480] Further, Cuomo denied any responsibility for the death of Pyke or Edwards. Cuomo said, "The violence was on the Canadian side. Our state police don't go on the Canadian side. Our politicians don't go on the Canadian side."[481]

As Cuomo denied responsibility at the news conference, about thirty Canadian and US government officials were meeting at a hotel near

---

[478] Darcy Henton and Dale Brazao, "Show of Force Halts Gambling War," *The Toronto Star*, May 3, 1990.

[479] Ferguson and Vienneau, "Leaders to Discuss Joint Police Force."

[480] Sam Howe Verhovek, "Indian Reservation Sealed Off after 2 Killings," *The New York Times*, May 3, 1990.

[481] Matt Maychak, "Cuomo Denies Blame in Native Deaths," *The Toronto Star*, May 3. 1990.

Dorval Airport in Montreal. These leaders and their police forces from throughout Canada and the US were trying to devise a plan to coordinate a response to the uprising. After three and one-half hours, they told reporters that the multi-national forces would remain in the reservation. They, like Cuomo, had rejected the idea of a military response. However, they failed to establish a long-range plan.[482] Although they met to come up a solution for the Mohawks, they had not invited the Mohawk leaders. Because of the desire for peace the meeting had their blessings. The government leaders proposed the idea of a single Native-run government regardless of jurisdiction.[483] The proposal was passed to the Mohawk Council of Akwesasne (Canada), St. Regis Indian Tribal Council (US), and the traditional Mohawk Longhouse Chiefs for their approval. The originators proposed that the three sets of Indian councils be formed into one powerful council that could achieve a unified peaceful solution.[484] Eddie Brown, Assistant Secretary for the BIA, said, "before any solutions can be implemented it will have to be accepted by the legitimate tribal government. The future must be

---

[482] Staff, "Mohawk Gambling Dispute Erupts," *Facts on File World News Digest*, May 4, 1990; Peter Kopvillem and Greg W. Taylor, "Tribal Warfare," *Mclean's*, May 14. 1990.

[483] Sandro Contenta, "Single Native Governing Body May Be Solution Officials Say," *The Toronto Star*, May 4, 1990; Kopvillem and Taylor, "Tribal Warfare."

[484] Darcy Henton, "Guns Silent but the Fury Remains Mohawks' Gambling War About Power and Money," *The Toronto Star*, May 5, 1990.

decided by the Mohawks themselves."[485]

Members of the Warrior society did not want anything to do with the meeting or any outside forces. Although seen as illegal by both federal governments, the Warriors refused to give up their arms. They saw themselves as protectors of Mohawk sovereignty and described the police forces as foreign invaders and occupiers. They refused to negotiate "until the occupation and state of siege ends, the foreign armies are removed, martial law lifted, and our fundamental human rights restored."[486] A Warriors' spokesperson, Diane Lazores, said, "The state police have blown it. And now, if they want an international incident, they'll get one."[487] Two elected Canadian Council members rumored that the Warriors had a hit list for anti-gambling leaders. Minnie Garrow, a Warrior representative said the whole idea was "total fabrication."[488] However, they produced a list that contained about 200 names, with one of the names being the deceased Matthew Pyke. The Warriors said that the list was for use in a possible court case and that in was not a death list.[489]

Later the same day, Chief Harold Tarbell, speaking on the US side, said that problems began

---

[485] Kopvillem and Taylor, "Tribal Warfare."

[486] Sam Howe Verhovek, "Mohawk Reserve Quiet as Officials Meet," *The New York Times*, May 4, 1990.

[487] Sam Howe Verhovek, "Indian Reservation Sealed Off after 2 Killings," *The New York Times*, May 3, 1990.

[488] Sam Howe Verhovek, "Mohawk Reserve Quiet as Officials Meet."

[489] Dale Brazao, "Dead Man Was on 'Hit List,' Chiefs Claim," *The Toronto Star*, May 4, 1990.

over gambling but had moved into a battle for the continued existence of the Akwesasne community. "We're asking that all Mohawks must lay down their weapons so peace can return to Akwesasne. In our view blaming each other and promoting further hatred and encouraging further violence will not bring these two young men back."[490] Mary David, one of the twelve elected chiefs in Canada said, "The urgency remains to find a solution to disarm and to guarantee safety in our community. External governments cannot let themselves believe that the solution has been found."[491] Hundreds of Mohawks were refugees from the violence. Many were housed in dormitories for air-traffic controllers and other government workers. Others were staying at the Bob Turner Memorial (Hockey) Center in Cornwall, Ontario. Hundreds more went to Ogdensburg, Saranac Lake, and Malone, New York.[492] James Ransom, a sub-Chief on the American side, when asked, said that most of refugees left with just a small suitcase, however, some came with only the clothes on their backs. "There is a sense of frustration building up again as far as how long people are going to be here, how long this is going to go on, when everyone will be able to go home."[493] Ontario Premier David Paterson, suggested that an international police force might be

---

[490] Darcy Henton and Dale Brazao, "Show of Force Halts Gambling War," *The Toronto Star*, May 3, 1990.

[491] Ibid.

[492] Jim Reilly, "Residents Flee Powder Keg St. Regis Still Calm, for Now," *The Post-Standard*, May 3, 1990.

[493] Ibid.

a way to keep peace. He said setting up a police force "would not be easy when two sovereign national governments are involved like the US and Canada."[494]

On May 4 and 5, with over 400 police officers still controlling and patrolling the reservation, hundreds of Mohawks returned home. The police presence had brought a modicum of calm to the area.[495] In Albany, Cuomo reiterated his stance on the National Guard where he said, "it would only provoke violence."[496] He stated that he had "no constitutional right" to take weapons that are legal under New York State law.[497] Captain Chris Hand, of the Canadian Armed Forces, said their job was, "to aid the Royal Canadian Mounted Police and the civilian police authorities in whatever task they ask of us. So far these tasks are mainly transport and communication support."[498]

Matthew Pyke funeral was held on May 4. Prior to the funeral, the RCMP searched every car going onto the Canadian side of the reservation. Overhead helicopters ensured that no incidents would take place. Mohawk leaders hoped that the police would allow a time of healing. Over 500 people were in

---

[494] Jonathan Ferguson and David Vienneau, "Leaders to Discuss Joint Police Force," *The Toronto Star*, May 3, 1990.

[495] Staff, "Evacuees Back to Canada-U.S. Indian Reserve as Violence Ends," *The Xinhua General Overseas News Service*, May 4. 1990; Sam Howe Verhovek, "Mohawk Reserve Quiet as Officials Meet," *The New York Times*, May 4, 1990.

[496] Ibid.

[497] Ibid.

[498] Darcy Henton and Dale Brazao, "Show of Force Halts Gambling War," *The Toronto Star*, May 3, 1990.

attendance chanting, "Give peace a chance."[499] Rev. Thomas Egan, the Pastor of the St. Regis Catholic Church, officiated at the funeral. During the homily, he said that it was going to take a very long time for the community to heal and for things to return to normal. Gambling had split the community and turned people against one another, even within families. "It's like the spirit of the border-states during the Civil War. There have been other battles in the past between Christian Indians and the traditional Indians but this has split everybody. In my congregation, there are people who think both ways."[500]

The next day, state police thought things on the reservation were fairly calm. New York State Police officer Ronald Clark said, "Things are still touchy. We want to try to keep things stable here to allow the negotiations to begin."[501] Another officer said, "We're taking care of the situation. Our position is that we take what comes as it comes."[502] Cuomo had stated that he would "negotiate legalized gambling on the reserve, provided the casinos close, the US road through the reserve remains open and the violence stops."[503] Cuomo viewed the situation as one that the Mohawks had to try to solve first, and then the state would become

---

[499] Dale Brazao, "Give Peace a Chance, Mourners Chant," *The Toronto Star*, May 5, 1990.

[500] Ibid.

[501] Doug Schneider, "Police Report Quiet Night," *The Post-Standard*, May 5, 1990.

[502] Ibid.

[503] Darcy Henton, "500 Mohawks Waiting Off Reserve Amid Peace Talks in Casino War."

involved. He had consistently framed the problem as a delicate balance of state and federal jurisdiction and Mohawk sovereignty. However, Cuomo expressed other thoughts about Akwesasne saying there were a number of associated problems. One was the Indian concept of sovereignty. He said many of the Mohawks "regard themselves as a part of a nation. They are a nation. They're a conquered nation. And they, some of them, will not accept that you obliterate their existence as a nation just because you're more powerful than them."[504] He continued that under an Act of Congress of 1948, the New York State Police had full jurisdictional authority to enforce the NYS codes on the US portion of the reservation even though they did not always have to do so.[505] Tom Siddon, Canadian Indian Affairs Minister, said, "We have to keep in mind that governments must not impose solutions that are not welcome. So, there's no magic formula for governments to pull out of a bag somewhere and say here's the answer to your problem."[506] Chief Harold Tarbell was upset that Cuomo wanted the elected chiefs negotiate with the casino owners and the Warriors to legalize gambling. "He's dancing with the criminal element and he's making us negotiate with them and we don't understand that."[507] The anti-gambling faction drafted a peace proposal to ease the tension. Their proposal

---

[504] Sam Howe Verhovek, "Whose Law Applies When Lawlessness Rules on Indian Land?" *New York Times*, May 6, 1990.

[505] Ibid.

[506] Doug Schneider, "Police Report Quiet Night."

[507] Henton, "Guns Silent but the Fury Remains Mohawks' Gambling War About Power and Money."

included:

> 1) Mutual disarmament and regular police patrol until a single Mohawk Police force could be established.
>
> 2) Immediate closure of Casinos.
>
> 3) An end to barricades that were erected to keep non-Indians away.
>
> 4) An independent referendum on gaming.
>
> 5) Counseling to speed community healing.[508]

Harold Edwards Jr. funeral took place on May 7. Hundreds of Mohawks showed up at St. Regis Catholic Church again to pay their respects. Both sides of the gambling issue agreed that Edwards had not taken sides.[509] Barbra Barnes, a spokesperson from an 'anti' group, said that both pro- and anti-gambling supporters attended the funeral. Warrior spokesperson Francis Boots, "He was a friend of everyone. He always had a smile. He was a total victim."[510] During the funeral Rev. Thomas Egan said, "he was just in the wrong place at the wrong time."[511] (See Figure 11. St. Regis Catholic Church, St. Regis, Quebec, Canada. Page 130)

A Change or A Coup?

---

[508] Ibid.

[509] John Tierney, "Mohawks Mourn Victim of Reservation Violence," *New York Times*, May 7, 1990.

[510] Leslie Zganjar, "Indians Agree to Set Aside Differences to Bury One of Their Own," *The Associated Press*, May 7, 1990.

[511] CP, "Mohawk Victim Was Innocent Bystander," *The Toronto Star*, May 7, 1990.

On May 8, hundreds of military personnel from the Canadian side of the reservation tactically supported the OPP, the Sûreté du Québec and the RCMP to maintain the peace. At the same time, five hundred state police officers were present on or around the reserve on the American side barricading the roads.[512] With this clampdown Cuomo decided the reservation finally met the conditions for direct negotiations between New York State representatives and Mohawk leaders on gambling.[513] He also called for the formation of a Native police force, with the NYSP remaining on patrol until this force was established. While the Canadian side had a police force, the American side had not had one since 1980.[514] Tom Siddon, from Ottawa, said that Cuomo's support for an independent police force was welcomed.[515]

Cuomo's representative, Henrik Dullea met for the first time with the three US chiefs on May 9. It was the beginning of negotiations for gambling and to redress sovereignty issues. Both sides agreed that the state police would remain in place until a Native police force was created. The chiefs wrote in a letter to Cuomo that law and order was important to them and without it they would not be able to address the

---

[512] Zganjar, "Indians Agree to Set Aside Differences to Bury One of Their Own."

[513] AP-CP, "New Mohawk Police Force Proposed for Reserve," *The Toronto Star*, May 8, 1990.

[514] Kevin Sack, "Cuomo Urges Internal Police for Mohawks," *New York Times*, May 8, 1990.

[515] Zganjar, "Indians Agree to Set Aside Differences to Bury One of Their Own."

other needs and matters that concerned them such as, "the uninterrupted education of our children, the reopening of tribal community services and business that are vital to our community and full employment of our Mohawk people."[516] That day, there was also a meeting at the reservation at the Mohawk Bingo Palace. It was an open forum so that everyone had a chance to talk.

Some problems that existed prior to the uprising continued. The police on both sides of the border still arrested smugglers and they continued to crack down on any contraband they found, including illegal drugs, cigarettes, and weapons. Naturally, the Warriors were unhappy with the role of the police in dealing with these matters. The Warriors believed that they should handle these situations internally. In a telephone interview, Minnie Garrow, a spokeswoman for the Warriors, said that "while the Warriors disapprove of the police action on what they consider sovereign territory they don't condone the use of drugs on the reserve." [517]

On May 12, with an election upcoming in the near future, hundreds of Mohawks attended a picnic supporting Russell Lazore for chief. Lazore was running against Harold Tarbell. Elections on the American side of the reservation were held annually of the positions of chief and were scheduled for June 2. Many families that went to Bill's Bingo Hall

---

[516] Barbara Stith, "3 St. Regis Chiefs Agree to Trooper Presence," *The Post-Standard*, May 10, 1990.

[517] Lisa Priest and Darcy Henton, "14 Mohawks Arrested in $1 Million Drug Raid," *The Toronto Star*, May 10, 1990.

wanted to see Lazore run and bring stability back to the community.[518] Tony Laughing, owner of Tony's Vegas International, said that a new election for the tribal council would return stability. "With new leadership on the council, the turmoil will come to an end."[519]

Four of the five Mohawks with outstanding arrest warrants from the Canadian side of the reservation were arrested on May 13. They were charged with conspiracy or complicity in the death of Harold Edwards. Two of the four arrested were members of the St. Regis (Mohawk) Police force from the Canadian side of the reservation. Those arrested included: David George, an anti-gambling activist; Ken Lazore, the owner of a small business on the reservation; Steve Lazore, a constable with the St. Regis police department; and Roger Mitchell, a sergeant with the St. Regis police department.[520]

On the same day, Doug George, who was wanted by the police, turned himself in. George was the editor of two newspapers on the reservation and an anti-gambling activist. He was charged with second-degree[521] murder in the death of Harold

---

[518] Barbara Stith, "4 Mohawks Questioned in Killing 2 St. Regis Police Officers, 2 Others Held in Canada," *The Post Standard*, May 14, 1990; CP, "Election Seen as End of Reserve War," *The Toronto Star*, May 21, 1990.

[519] CP, "Election Seen as End of Reserve War."

[520] Barbara Stith, "4 Mohawks Questioned in Killing 2 St."

[521] "In Québec, anyone convicted of 2nd degree murder gets an automatic life sentence and is not eligible for parole until 10 years have been served." AP, "Mohawk Editor Held in Killing," *The New York Times*, May 15, 1990.

Edwards. It was known that he was an avid anti-gambler, editorializing in the two newspapers he edited, and helping at the barricades.[522]

On May 14, all five Mohawks were arraigned at the court in Salaberry-De-Valleyfield, Québec. Andre Blanchette, a Sûreté du Québec officer, said that the charges could include complicity in the murder of Edwards or, at the very least, conspiracy. Doug George, the editor who turned himself in, said the five of them "were taken to Montreal on suspicion of murder, or some such stupid thing." While blaming the violence on the Warriors, George continued, "What happened was done in the defense of our lives which are threatened as a direct result of attacks by the Warriors."[523] John Boots, Warriors spokesman, commented that it was interesting to learn that two Mohawk Police officers were arrested. He said it supported the Warriors' contention that the police were involved with the problems.[524]

Beginning on May 17, Tom Sullivan, a Mohawk living in Syracuse, New York, went on a hunger-fast to raise attention to the plight of those living on the reservation and for peace. Two other local Mohawks, Wayne Oaks and Lee Snyder, joined him on May 20. Since the violence had begun and the reservation sealed off, food and money had begun to run out. Food deliveries to stores had been delayed or non-existent at times. In

---

[522] Ibid.
[523] CP, "Five Charged in Gun Killing at Akwesasne," *The Toronto Star*, May 14, 1990.
[524] Ibid.

addition, local businesses were reluctant to take a chance on having their vehicles damaged or possibly commandeered. Getting on and off the reservation was time-consuming, and lost time meant lost money.

Money was the other concern. Without traffic to and through the reservation there was a reduction of income across the economic spectrum. The loss of traffic hurt the casinos and all of the other businesses, including the non-Native companies on the outskirts of Akwesasne. Casinos and gambling had been on the reservation for years. During this time, many prospered from employment with the gambling industry. Along with the casinos, the tourist trade increased. While the Bear's Den had slot machines at one point, it has operated as store, gas station, and gift shop, which still exist today. Business supplies companies, travel agents; building suppliers, etc. were affected. With the closing of the roads into the reservation, came the closing of the valve on money coming into the community.

On May 24, the New York State Police allowed cars to pass the roadblocks and to drive freely on Route 37 across the reservation. The State Police continued to keep a presence on and off the main highways. Norman Treptow, who owned a lumber business within the barricaded area, said, "Everybody that I've talked to is very happy. The other businesses are ecstatic, I'm sure."[525] Francis

---

[525] Barbara Stith, "Lift Roadblock, but Vow to Remain on Reservation," *The Post-Standard*, May 26, 1990.

Boots, a Warrior, said, "It's convenient for the white folks, but the bottom line is we're [Mohawks] still under siege."[526]

When the roads across the reservation reopened came the state promised to spend $2.5 million to resurface roads in St. Lawrence and Franklin County. Many of the roads had been damaged because of the detours.[527] However, along with the promise of money, came the acknowledgement that the State Police would be on the reservation for the near future. Cuomo, in discussing an indigenous police force, said, "Getting to that point will be difficult."[528] The chiefs on the American side of the reservation agreed that the NYSP would have to patrol until their own force could be constituted.[529]

On June 2, elections were held at Akwesasne on the American side of the border, with Norman Tarbell and Russell Lazore running against the anti-gambling faction. Norman Tarbell won with 637 votes to Harold Tarbell, the incumbent's 538 votes. This was in reality a referendum on gambling since Norman Tarbell was a pro-gambling Chief. The election had its problems and challenges. Prior to the election, the Grand Council of the Iroquois Confederacy requested the election be postponed and that the other two chiefs, Jacobs and White, be investigated for their connection to smuggling.[530]

---

[526] Ibid.

[527] Thomas Fine, "St. Regis Policing Priced at $630,000," *The Post-Standard*, May 30, 1990.

[528] Stith, "Lift Roadblock, but Vow to Remain on Reservation."

[529] Ibid.

[530] Sean Kirst, "Iroquois Body Seeks Probe of Mohawk Chiefs," *The Post-Standard*, May 26, 1990.

Harold Tarbell was going to contest the election because Chiefs Jacobs and White used tribal rules to exclude 500 US Indians on the Canadian side of the border from voting. Harold Tarbell contended that these were anti-gambling Mohawks who were excluded unfairly.[531] On June 27, Cuomo submitted two bills to the New York State legislature. One was to allow Mohawks and eight other territories to plan and implement a Native police force.[532] The other was to give the governor permission to negotiate and approve gambling compacts with the various reservations and tribes in New York State. Cuomo thought that he already had the power of negotiation because he was the chief executive of the state. Just as the US president negotiates treaties with foreign countries Cuomo felt he was in the same position in the state. Not everyone was supportive of this legislation. Mohawk leaders were opposed to a bill that had no Native input. Chief Tom Porter, said, "The Indian Nations in the State of New York have not had time to read or understand the implication of this." Henrik Dullea, Cuomo's representative, indicated that the tribes in New York State had been kept fully informed of the negotiation. Dullea said, "copies of a draft bill were sent to New York tribes and an aide to Cuomo discussed the bill in detail with traditional council

---

[531] AP, "Gambling Supporter Wins Election as Chief of Embattled Mohawk Tribe," *The Toronto Star*, June 3, 1990.
[532] Barbara Stith, "Bill Would Authorize Tribal Police Forces," *The Post-Standard*, June 28, 1990.

member Ron LaFrance before its release."⁵³³

Oka and the Warriors

In July, the concerns of Mohawks were drawn across the border to another reserve, the Kanehsatake Mohawks, near Oka, Québec.⁵³⁴ The

---

⁵³³ Matthew Cox, "Mohawks Oppose Bills on Gaming, Police," *The Post-Standard*, June 30, 1990.

⁵³⁴ "March 1989: Oka Mayor Jean Ouellette announces his municipality's plans to build a luxury housing development and expand a private golf course into bordering lands which are part of the Mohawk Nation.

August 1989: Kanehsatake Mohawks call for a moratorium on development.

May 1990: Despite an injunction to prevent protesting, the Mohawks build a barricade.

July 5 1990: Indian Affairs Minister Tom Siddon starts negotiations with the Mohawk band council. Pressure to remove the barricades increases as Québec Minister of Public Security Sam Elkas threatens government action.

July 11, 1990: Corporal Marcel Lemay is killed when 100 Sûreté du Québec officers raid an area known as the Pines. Another 900 officers move into the bordering town of Oka. Mohawks build additional barricades and seize the Mercier Bridge.

July 12, 1990: By this time, a police blockade has been set up a few miles before the.

July 13, 1990: Journalists complain that they are unable to get inside to get the story. The police give accreditations to some

Aug. 20, 1990: The Canadian Armed Forces replace the Sûreté du Québec. Supplies, including film and sound stock, cannot be exchanged.

Aug. 28, 1990: Negotiations break down, and the army is ordered to dismantle the barricades. The Red Cross brings in emergency supplies as well as stretchers and body bags. Seventy-five residents from the village of Kahnawake evacuate and their vehicles are

town of Oka, Québec, wanted to extend its public golf course into traditional Mohawk land that was considered sacred. A Sûreté du Québec officer was killed over this conflict about sovereignty and the possession of sacred land. Corporal Marcel Lemay of the Sûreté du Québec was participating in a raid on July 11, 1990, when a 100-other riot-equipped officers attacked the Mohawk barricades. With a plan to dislodge them from the 'Pines.'[535] What connected Oka and Akwesasne were the Warriors. (See Figure 12. Famous stand-off during the Oka Crisis between Pte. Patrick Cloutier, a perimeter sentry, and Anishinaabe warrior Brad "Freddy Krueger" Larocque. Page 130)

Reports stated that of the 150-armed Warriors at Oka, up to 40 of them were from Akwesasne and had been involved with the recent uprising there.[536] The Mohawk Nation Council of Chiefs at Akwesasne condemned the Warriors for trying to stop progress for peace. It was their council's contention the Warriors destroyed the possibility of

---

attacked by a waiting mob. CBC management, thinking there may be a massacre, removes all its journalists.

Sept. 1, 1990: As the army advances, the Mohawks barricade themselves into the Kanehsatake Treatment Centre. Fifty-Eight Natives and 11 journalists remain behind the lines.

Sept. 25: 1990: The Mohawks have decided to walk out and return to Montreal."

Karen Mazurkewich, "Kanehsatake 270 Years of Resistance," *Playback*, September 13, 1993.

[535] Reuters, "Officer Dies as Mohawk Indians, Québec Police Fight Fierce Battle," *St Petersburg Times*, July 12, 1990.

[536] John F. Burns, "Canada Proposes Settlement in Mohawk Standoff," *The New York Times*, July 29, 1990.

succeeding in a peaceful negotiation with the Kanesatake Mohawks.[537] The Oka situation ended in September of 1990. This episode showed the extensiveness of the Warrior's influence and their willingness to become involved over sovereignty and land claims. As at Akwesasne, the Warriors enjoyed support from a portion of the community.

In August 1990, Art Montour was sentenced to a ten-month prison term for the blockade at Akwesasne during the raid. During the same month, NYSP Superintendent Thomas Constantine testified in front of a US Senate Committee in Washington DC, that the Warriors at Akwesasne had initiated much of violence during the uprising. Constantine said they were well armed; their weaponry included AR-15 assault rifles, Mini-14s, Chinese AK-47s, and 50 caliber machine guns. In addition, the Warriors had hundreds of other weapons and small arms and thousands of rounds of ammunition. Constantine said that the core was comprised of a handful of people who were distributed between the Ganienkeh, Akwesasne, and Kahnawake territories.[538] Not everybody agreed. Leon Shenandoah, Chief of the Onondaga nation, thought the Warriors should have been arrested and had been allowed to cause unrest. Shenandoah believed that when the Warriors became involved Mohawks

---

[537] Staff, "Indian Chiefs, Warriors Split over Oka Land," *The Toronto Star*, July 27, 1990.

[538] Darcy Henton, "The Oka Standoff: Mohawk Warriors - Self-Described Freedom Fighters - Have Taken Control. Heroes to Some, Others Call Them a Brainwashing Cult," *The Toronto Star*, August 19, 1990.

as a group were weakened internally and easier to control.[539]

Over time things improved, however, there were bumpy periods. In September 1990, a fight broke out on Route 37 between 30 state police officers and a large number of Mohawks. During the incident, three Mohawks were arrested, and three police officers were injured.[540] The fight stemmed from a charge that the police were harassing Mohawks as they were walking down the road. Many complained that the (See Figure 13. Map of Kanesatake, Oka, Québec. Page 131) police asked for identification and generally stopped anyone they saw.[541] There were times, as in October 1990, when casinos would reopen and the state would crack back down on them. Dullea, Cuomo's aide, said that the state had investigated the casinos and was not going to allow the casinos that operated on the reservations prior to state gaming negotiations to operate.[542]

Sovereignty was always part of the equation. At times, Mohawk leaders were pulled apart by outside forces appealing to particular needs. One example was when Steven Sanders, New York Legislative Committee Chairman, and his eight-member committee made a number of recommendations

---

[539] Laurie Watson, "Iroquois Confederacy to Meet over Warrior Society," *United Press International*, August 24, 1990.

[540] Rebecca James, "Police, Indians Injured in Fight at St. Regis," *The Post-Standard*, September 16, 1990.

[541] James, "Police, Indians Injured in Fight at St. Regis."

[542] Staff, "Police Raid Possible to Stop Renewed Gambling on Reserve." *The Toronto Star*, October 22, 1990.

concerning the governing of the Reservation.[543] Chief Tom Porter, Traditionalist, thought that the state committee should at least listen to the needs of the community. Ex-Chief Harold Tarbell thought that some of the recommendations were sound. Yet Head Chief, L. Davis Jacobs, believed they were paternalistic at best. Despite reports that Sanders had the Mohawks' best interest in mind his recommendations served to be divisive.[544]

On November 2, anti-gambling Mohawk Doug George was cleared of second-degree murder charges. Provincial Court Judge Pierre Laberge said, "After reviewing the evidence, it is my ultimate conviction that if the same evidence is brought before a judge and jury, [George] would be acquitted."[545]

During this period, Cuomo had other things on his mind that were at least as important as dealing with the aftermath of Akwesasne. He was coming up for reelection as governor in 1990 and a possible candidacy in the 1992 presidential election was speculated. Just a month after the horrific events at

---

[543] "1) Stop its negotiations with the St. Regis tribal council to establish legalized casino gambling on the reserve. 2) Continue indefinite policing of the reserve by New York state police. 3) Establish a permanent police station closer to the reserve with its own personnel to reduce policing costs. 4) Appoint a special prosecutor to handle illegal gambling and smuggling prosecutions on the reserve. 5) Intensify efforts to create employment opportunities and economic development at Akwesasne and other reserves." Darcy Henton, "Single Government Urged for Akwesasne Reserve," *The Toronto Star*, October 17, 1990.

[544] Ibid.

[545] CP, "Mohawk Editor Cleared of Murder Charge," *The Toronto Star*, November 2, 1990.

Akwesasne, Cuomo's campaign for governor was seen as a "warm-up to the main event."[546] Although Cuomo's third term as governor was assured because of the inadequacies of his republican opponent, the state was in poor shape. In 1990, the state had a "slumping economy, a soaring crime rate and $3 billion in new taxes."[547] One of the Governor's major problems was the crime rate. Cuomo's opponents at the time could have pointed to a 20 percent increase in violent crimes during his tenure and an increase in the size of the state prison system.[548]

Cuomo's seemed to spread the blame for problems to the federal government and other political parties and away from his role as governor. He then would bring the problem to the news media's attention and put forth his solution(s). In this way, Cuomo could appear to be acting on the problem while having no real effect on it.[549] Commenting on this strategy, one reporter said that the majority of voters did not think that Governor Cuomo had a magic bullet to stop the soaring crime rate or away to prop up the sagging economy. "What they do demand from him is that he offer the reassurance that he is concerned about the situation and has it under control. And creating the perception of caring and control is, most political

---

[546] Johnathan D. Salant, "Mario Cuomo for Governor -- or President?" *The Post Standard*, June 10, 1990.

[547] Jay Gallagher, "Campaign '90; Cuomo Cruising toward a 3rd Term," *USA Today*, November 2, 1990.

[548] Elizabeth Kolbert, "Cuomo's Campaign: Crime? Taxes? Look Elsewhere," *The New York Times*, September 5, 1990.

[549] Ibid.

strategists agree, what Governor Cuomo does best."[550]

This is certainly the strategy Cuomo used with the situation at Akwesasne. He framed the problems there as local and then sent the state police to the area to control situational 'spillage' into the rest of the state with abject police enforcement. Through this process, he supported the abolishment of illegal gambling that satisfied state law and negotiated with the recognized Akwesasne government for federally sanctioned legal gambling creating the "perception of caring and control."[551]

In a written communication from Dan White, Ph.D., White speculated that his possible presidential campaign might have been a reason for the way Cuomo handled the violence and illegal gambling at Akwesasne. The situation seen as criminal and it also addressed Native American rights. Because of federal law, the reservation could offer some forms of legal gambling. It would be important strategy for a possible presidential run to advance a positive profile of Native American rights and to downplay the violence being experienced there without making any commitments.[552]

By the beginning of 1991, Cuomo's proposed budget included 72 New York State Police Officers assigned to the reservation, although a sub-station on the reservation was not proposed in the budget. Joseph Grey, a spokesman for the American Tribal

---

[550] Ibid.
[551] Ibid.
[552] Dan White. Ph.D., to Ernest R. Rugenstein, April 26, 2008.

Council, said a permanent assignment of officers might ease some of the community tensions.[553] Doug George, who had been the editor of local newspapers at Akwesasne, was cleared of his charges and decided to move to the Oneida nation. As of April 1991, he was still strong in his anti-gambling convictions.

Violence was threatened during preparations for the elections on the Canadian side of the reservation. Elections were held on June 22, 1991, and Mike Mitchell won re-election. Robert Skidder made a good showing in a field of 44 candidates for 13 positions. Of the other 12 positions, one-half of them went to pro-gambling members.[554] On January 9, 1992, Akwesasne Grand Chief Mike Mitchell and Mohawk Warrior Leader Francis Boots agreed to work together for Mohawk sovereignty. Although they were on opposite sides of the gambling issue, they now agreed, "that we never want to fight each other again."[555] Chief Mitchell also said, "We also agreed that the enemy is not among ourselves. It's out there. What threatens our very existence is somewhere out there. That's what we gave to fight for."[556] The governor's proposal on January 22, 1992, did not foresee any end in sight to the costly

---

[553] Barbara Stith, "Troopers to Stay Cuomo Wants to Station 72 at St. Regis," *The Post-Standard*, February 1, 1991.

[554] Dan Karon, "Mohawks Threaten Blockade; Bridge Congestion Prompts Renewed Threat at Cornwall," *The Ottawa Citizen*, August 29, 1991; Barbara Stith, "Troopers Find Slot Machines at St. Regis," *The Post-Standard*, September 12, 1991.

[555] CP, "Akwesasne Mohawks Finally Bury the Hatchet," *Toronto Star*, January 9, 1992.

[556] Ibid.

police presence on Akwesasne. It predicted their presence would last until 1993.[557]

Epilogue of the Troubles

Between, January 1989 and January 1991, the Mohawks were torn apart by inter-cultural differences. In an area, the size of Brooklyn, with the population of a small college campus - five jurisdictions governed its inhabitants and the Mohawks had no control over it. On the American side, especially in the Eastern United States, reservations are *Domestic Dependent Nations*, similar to the homelands in South Africa.[558] Their external interactions and defense positions are under the jurisdiction of the federal government, but they have a great deal of latitude in the regulation of their internal affairs. The United States also has a

---

[557] Staff, "St. Regis Expense Persists," *The Post-Standard*, January 22, 1992.

[558] "In 1831 the US Supreme Court issued a decision that defined Native Americans as "domestic dependent nations" instead of foreign nations. This re-designation allowed states, such as Georgia, to disenfranchise Native American tribes of their lands. The Supreme Court refused to intervene stating that the Cherokee Nation didn't have control of their lands, because they were not a foreign nation with sovereignty rights. The "Cherokee Tribe is a state in the sense that it is a "distinct political society," but is not a foreign state within the meaning of Article III of the Constitution. It is more like a "domestic dependent nation" with the relation of the tribe to the Federal government like that of "ward to guardian." The tribes are separate nations within a nation." U.S. Department of the Interior, Bureau of Indian Affairs, "Supreme Court Decisions: Cherokee Nation v. Georgia, 1831," US Department of the Interior, http://www.classbrain.com/artteenst/publish/article_132.shtml (accessed September 14, 2007).

"'Major Crimes Act' specifically applying to Indians, which allows state authorities to intervene in cases of murder, kidnapping," etc.[559] The Canadian side of the reservation is controlled differently. Unlike the US, where states have jurisdiction, in Canada, the criminal code is federal. The Mohawks have less autonomy than those in the US, which allows the Canadian government to react more quickly to any situation.[560]

In Canada, gambling was illegal and was not tolerated. The Mohawks in Canada were divided on the issue, but the reservation government followed the federal government's position on gambling. In return, Canadian Mohawks enjoyed the same rights as other Canadian citizens including the right to vote and universal health care. Another cultural difference between the Canadian and US Mohawks are that there is more commerce on the Canadian side of the reservation. The majority of the Canadian population, commerce, finance, industry, and education, are along the southern border of the country. Ottawa, the capital of Canada and all of its major cities, except for those of Newfoundland and Labrador, is within one hour of the US-Canadian border.

A different set of circumstances existed on the American side of the reservation. Gambling is legal on Indian reservations within a prescribed set of provisions enacted between the individual tribes and the state, and then sanctioned by the federal

---

[559] John Godfrey, "Mohawk Unrest Obscures Native Entrepreneurship," *The Financial*, May 4. 1990.
[560] Ibid.

government. Gambling has brought a great deal of economic growth to the US side of the reservation. This was important because it is located in what is known as the rustbelt.[561] Northern New York is sparsely populated and has few jobs. In recent years, the most lucrative employment was working for the New York State Corrections Department. If a Mohawk did not work in corrections or work off the reservation, there were few economic possibilities on the reservation. The casinos bridged this gap with well-paying jobs.

Casinos and gambling caused major divisions between the people of the reservations. The casino owners and employees saw it as a solution to the economic depression of the reservations. The Warriors officially had no opinion on gambling *per se*. Their main focus was that they did not want outside entities controlling what was permitted on Mohawk territory. Most of the Warriors were pro-gaming. They saw practical, economic reasons for having casinos on the reservation. Pollution had destroyed the traditional trades of dairy farming and fishing, and with building of the Seaway, hunting and trapping disappeared. The Warriors saw gambling offered a new way. The anti-gambling faction saw casinos and gaming as a dissipating habit that destroyed lives and ruined families. The anti-gambling faction wanted to see the economy turn around but wanted to find another way to build economic security other than by gambling and

---

[561] Janis Barth, "Ogdensburg Waits for Next Boom - History of St. Lawrence River City Has Been Economic Roller Coaster," *The Post-Standard*, January 29, 1988.

smuggling.

When the factions became violent, when the official tribal governments asked for help, those who could have stepped up to their jurisdictional duty did not act. The tribal governments from both sides of the border, the Canadian federal and provincial governments along with the US federal government made repeated requests to Governor Cuomo to send the NYSP onto the reservation to diffuse the situation on the US side of the border.[562] When he did not, violence continued.

---

[562] Verhovek, "Mohawks Ask Cuomo to Join a Peace Effort;" Lichfield. "Mohawks Go to War over Bingo;" Lorch. "Behind Violence, Tensions Roil Mohawks."

CHAPTER 7

A System Analysis of Cultures and the Uprising

When analyzing the Uprising at Akwesasne, it was caused by the incongruity of the cultures involved interacting in a crisis situation. It must be acknowledged that there was an ongoing animosity with the tribal and traditional governments versus the federal, state, and provincial governments. This animosity between the different cultures was primarily over sovereignty.[563] Additionally, there have always been differences between the Tribalists, and the Traditionalist Mohawks. Both sides struggle for Mohawk autonomy within their philosophical framework. Their differences were typically concerned with how sovereignty would be achieved, and what it would look like in its final form. But these are not the aspects of the situation that were driving the violence. They were merely pre-loading the tension and anxiety. The actual cultural causes of the uprising fall into two categories, internal and external. Although the internal causes are important to the events which

---

[563] "Sovereignty is the claim to be the ultimate political authority, subject to no higher power as regards the making and enforcing of political decisions . . . Sovereignty should not be confused with freedom of action: sovereign actors may find themselves exercising freedom of decision within circumstances that are highly constrained by relations of unequal power." Buzan, Barry. The Concise Oxford Dictionary of Politics. New York, N.Y.: Oxford University Press (OUP-USA Dictionaries Program), 2003.

transpired it was the external causes that tipped the scale and drove the situation to deadly violence.

There was an ongoing animosity between the tribal and traditional governments and the federal, state, and provincial governments. This animosity between the different cultures was primarily over native sovereignty.[564] The Tribalists and the Traditionalist Mohawks have long held differences concerning the conceptualization of sovereignty. Both sides struggled for Mohawk autonomy within their own philosophical framework. Their differences were usually over how sovereignty would be achieved and what it would look like in its final form. However, these are not the aspects of the situation that drove the violence. The true cultural causes of the uprising fall into two categories, internal and external. Although the internal causes play a role in the events that transpired, the external causes tipped the scale and drove the situation to deadly violence.

A Look at the Internal System

Internally, there were two additions to the cultural landscape that provided fuel for the eventual violence in the Mohawk community. While there are official jurisdictional and political boundaries, there are few cultural ones. When

---

[564] "Sovereignty is the claim to be the ultimate political authority, subject to no higher power as regards the making and enforcing of political decisions . . . Sovereignty should not be confused with freedom of action: sovereign actors may find themselves exercising freedom of decision within circumstances that are highly constrained by relations of unequal power." *The Concise Oxford Dictionary of Politics*, s.v. "Sovereignty."

something affects Akwesasne on one side of the St. Lawrence River, it affects the other side too. This is what happened with the introduction of high stakes casino gambling and the rise of the Warriors as a quasi-pro-gambling entity.

The Warriors were a self-appointed group of traditionalists that believed in sovereignty and the belief that there needed to be peacekeepers in the community. They became a problem by adopting more than just the traditionalist slant on sovereignty. Their concept of sovereignty included crossing the border without paying duty or taxes, and crossing with untaxed cigarettes and fuel to reselling to non-Natives living off the reservation. This type of thinking about sovereignty began to encompass many economic schemes and, with them, problems began to occur.

These Warriors firmly believed that the US and Canadian governments and their associated secondary entities had no jurisdiction over any part of Akwesasne. To them, it was Mohawk land, and anything the Mohawks wanted to do was beyond state or provincial control. The Warriors interpreted Mohawk relationship with the federal governments as having diplomatic equivalency. They viewed the elected tribal governments as extensions of and controlled by the 'white' government. They believed that the elected chiefs on both sides of the border were ineffectual, and moving away from sovereignty and towards complicity with 'white' government. Further, the Warriors regarded the elected councils request for the New York State Police's presence on the American side of the reservation as an invitation to bring foreign forces onto sovereign territory. On the Canadian side, the council had the use of the (St. Regis) Mohawk Police Force, who were trained by the OPP. The Warriors saw both of these entities as extensions of 'white' government.

Although the traditionalists and the Warriors shared similarities between their concepts of sovereignty, the Warriors saw the traditionalists as tainted. The Warriors thought that the traditional chiefs had compromised excessively with the elected chiefs and had condoned the use of outside forces on the reservation. Further, the Warriors felt that the traditionalists had lost sight of the wisdom of *The Great Law of Peace*.[565]

The traditionalists follow the teachings of Handsome Lake (Ganioda'yo) that are formalized in *The Code of Handsome Lake*.[566] The code was

---

[565] Constitution of the Iroquois: The Great Binding Law, Gayanashagowa.

[566] "In 1799, Handsome Lake (Ganioda'yo) had the first in a series of visions while lying in his bed deathly ill. A messenger from the Creator appeared to him, giving him instructions for the Iroquois. Handsome Lake recovered and preached these messages to the Seneca in what became known as the Code of Handsome Lake. Iroquois people traveled many miles to hear his message, and every year the prophet traveled to other Iroquois settlements teaching his code.

After Handsome Lake's death in 1815, his teachings continued to spread and became the foundation for the Longhouse religion. Still a vital force, this religion plays an important role in preserving the Iroquois' sacred and cultural heritage."
The Alcoa Foundation Hall of American Indians, "Handsome Lake," Carnegie Museum of Natural History, http://www.carnegiemnh.org/exhibits/north-south-east-west/iroquois/handsome_lake.html (accessed October 5, 2007).

given to the Iroquois to restore their pride and reinvigorate their morality. Its intent was to teach them how to live with their traditions and to accept parts of the colonial culture so that their own culture could survive and stay healthy.[567] Conversely the Warriors followed the teachings of Louis Hall.[568] Hall, in his reinterpretation of the *Great Law of the Peace,* challenged the Traditionalists. He refuted what he saw as the peace-loving, dovish approach of the traditional chiefs, and advocated the use of force to back up the legitimate claims of the Mohawks. Hall thought threats could be made to force concessions and to correct long-held grievances and the collective dispossession of Natives.[569] This increased the cultural animosity in the community. The animosity increased further with introduction of gambling.

When gambling was added into the culture, the members of the community predictably reacted in two ways. Some accepted it for of financial and economic reasons, while others rejected it for financial, economic, moral, and religious reasons. Gambling-centered high-stakes casinos contributed to the cultural conflict and created tension on the reservation.[570] Many Mohawks believed that the profits from the reservation casinos and bingo halls went exclusively to hall owners and their non-

---

[567] Phil Preston, "A Note on Education," Indian Time, http://members.aol.com/miketben1/cc9.htm (accessed July 15, 2006).

[568] Louis Hall is also known as Karoniaktajeh

[569] Preston, "A Note on Education."

[570] Appleby, "Tensions Simmer."

Indian management teams."[571] This challenged the control of the tribal managers.[572] There had been low stakes bingo on the reservation for years; some games had operated in local churches. The community radio station used radio bingo to raise their revenues. Low stake games seemed acceptable with the majority of the reservation, and in May 1985, the Tribal Council became a fifty percent partner in the Mohawk Bingo Palace, a high stakes bingo establishment that started advertising off the reservation.[573] While this caused some dissension with accusations of outside influence, most accepted it. Over time, other private high stakes gambling establishments opened, and some of these added casino gaming. (See Figure 14. Mohawk Bingo Palace Akwesasne. Page 131)

With the Supreme Court ruling in 1987 and Congress' passing of the *Indian Gaming Regulatory Act* (1988), casino gambling increased. Eventually, slot machines were added to many of the private halls, and changed the factions on the reservation once again. Casino gambling shifted traditional alliances and caused increased tensions. This brought the charge of outside influence and control.[574] The reservation took corrective measures at times. In 1987, a referendum decided that casino gaming was not allowed. This was unacceptable to those who were directly involved with casinos.

---

[571] Stuart, "A Crisis of Hegemony."

[572] Ibid., 27.

[573] Rudy Platiel, "Reserve Reaps High Stakes Indians Hit Jackpot on Bingo," *The Globe and Mail*, July 25 1985.

[574] Appleby, "Tensions Simmer."

They continued to promote them and defy both tribal and state warnings and raids.

As discussed earlier, the Canadian section of the reservation, gambling was illegal despite the desires of community members. There was a sizable portion on the Canadian side that did not like casinos, including the council leadership, and a majority of the Native Canadian government. These anti-gambling proponents made their feeling known across the entire reservation. On the American side of the reservation, both the US government and the tribal council allowed gambling. New York allowed it through a special compact with the Mohawks. The residents of the American side of the reservation were split in their feelings over the casinos. The majority of the US tribal council was willing to have an agreement with the state government, and a large portion of the people were grateful for the economic upturn that casino gambling brought to the community.

Gambling opponents saw it as a community-wide cultural problem. They saw gambling as a dissipating habit that hurt people emotionally, spiritually, morally, economically and, at times, physically. Gambling was not allowed on one part of the reservation, and they were going to do everything they could to control it or keep it out off the reservation. The proponents of casino gambling saw gambling as something that only concerned the US part of the reservation. As such, they did not think they needed to respond to the wishes of the Canadians Mohawks. Because of the proponents' concept of sovereignty, they felt that New York State government had no jurisdiction over the issue.

The proponents received support from the Warriors, who initially did not take sides on gambling but became supporters of the casinos because of their similar stance on sovereignty. These conflicting points of view created pressure on the societal structure of Akwesasne.

Cultural lines shifted between tribalizes and traditionalists. Tribalists, also known as Contemporary Mohawks or Christian Indians, were in favor of elected forms of government. They wanted the benefits and accepted obligations of citizenship, and they recognized a special relationship that the Tribalists had with the state and federal governments and their suzerainty. Traditionalists, and to a great extent the Warriors, do not believe in paying taxes, voting, or joining the armed forces. They usually take their children out of government schools and believe in absolute sovereignty of Mohawk people and Mohawk lands.[575]

With gambling, the previously well-defined characteristics of each group became mixed, with each side showing traits of the other. Gambling is the type of issue that cuts across socio-political lines in its support. Issues like gambling, abortion, or the environment, and pollution can bring together large, eclectic groups of people who work together on one issue. This is what gambling did on the reservation. Gambling caused people who would be on different sides of most issues to come together in ways that would not unlikely.

---

[575] Alan Richman, "15 Traditionalists Serving 3-Year Terms," *New York Times*, August 31, 1979.

For example, the pro-gambling side connected with the Tribalist and legal viewpoint that the American side of the reservation was distinct and separate from the Canadian side despite their otherwise cultural similarities. They accepted that US federal policies and laws controlling that portion of Akwesasne. If there were a referendum or any sort of vote on gambling, only those registered in the US were allowed to vote. However, their viewpoint on traditional sovereignty was that New York State, and to some extent the federal government did not have control over their casino operations. Additionally, many on the pro-gambling side were also involved in the smuggling of cigarettes. Here again their definition of sovereignty becomes skewed. They did not see bringing cigarettes across the border as smuggling because they did not recognize the border because they saw it as a 'white' political boundary and not one of their own making. They saw the reservation on both sides of the border as a single entity, contradicting the political viewpoint they had on gambling. Smuggling additionally put a twist in the sovereignty stance of bringing items across the border such as household goods and appliances. The federal governments did not necessarily have to discriminate between the two acts and regard both as smuggling if duty was not paid.

The anti-gambling also crossed over and had mixed characteristics. However, their mixture was different order. The problem of having casinos on the Canadian side of the border was not open for discussion because the federal government in Canada prohibited it. So, while the anti-gambling faction that had the support of the Canadian Mohawk government, the tribal police force had no fear of casinos in Canada. Yet, the Canadian Mohawk government and police force crossed the border as both cultural and political entities to try to prohibit gambling in a section of the reservation over which they had no jurisdiction. Although there were anti-gambling proponents on the US side, they were in the minority and did not receive the same government support. The majority of the Mohawk government on the US section of the reservation supported gambling, as did the Warriors who were, for all practical purposes, acting as the constabulary on the US portion.

At one point during this situation, an interesting juxtaposition is found. The majority of the Mohawk government on the US side of the reservation and the Warriors who were acting and recognized externally as the acting constabulary, did not want outside police forces interference. In contrast, the Canadian Mohawk government and police force, although neither had jurisdiction on the American side, encouraged the involvement of New York State Police. In this case, the anti-gambling faction displayed an odd mixture of characteristics.

With the addition of gambling and the rise of the Warriors to a cultural landscape that was already crowded by jurisdictional and environmental problems, there was a rise in the anxiety of the community. Because the Mohawks could not achieve a collaborative political atmosphere in their territory, they were unable to reach an intra-cultural solution to the gambling question. This inability forced them to rely on external input to find a solution to their situation. They had entered into a cultural and political purgatory.

The External Pressure on the System

It was difficult for a people who feel they are a homogeneous group, sharing the same customs, language, and history to be split governing themselves. Leaders from different parts of the reservation were trying to serve their people but were hindered by imposed artificial barriers across their land. They were trying to bring about change and reclamation of their land with the ultimate goal of sovereignty. For the Mohawks of Akwesasne, this was impossible. Their land was under the control of outside agencies and institutions. In the eyes of the federal, state and provincial governments, the tribal governments were seen as a county or town. Although, the tribal governments and reservation had peculiar rights and expectations but, they were still legally subordinate to the hierarchy of the federal, state and provincial governments of the US and Canada.

As much as they may have wanted to control their own destiny, the Mohawks had very little ability to do so. Recall the thoughts of Seneca Henry Lickers. He had lived at Akwesasne since 1975, working on environmental problems. Lickers pointed out that it was not uncommon to hear about gambling, casinos, and smuggling. He said those living off the reservation accused them of the problems and did not understand why the Mohawks "do such things?" Lickers continued, saying that the destruction of the land and water was what that led to many of the Mohawks' social and economic problems. "Through all of this, we've tried to maintain our traditional ways and found we couldn't. When you destroy a man's environment, you destroy the man. Akwesasne can very much be the example."[576]

Mohawks on the Canadian side of the reservation were well aware of their subordinate position. There was no illusion as to who was ultimately in charge. True, the Mohawks would challenge their perceived treaty rights, but overall the federal and provincial governments could enter the reservation at any time to enforce the law. In Canada, gambling was illegal and would not be tolerated. The Mohawks in Canada were divided on the issue, but the reservation government followed the federal government's position on gambling.

The American side was more complicated, with the state and the federal governments having jurisdiction. The US Mohawks did have some authority over their own territory; however, they were seen as domestic dependent nation and still inferior to the federal and state governments.[577] In

---

[576] Barbara Stith, "St. Regis Mohawks Find Environment a Unifying Issue," *The Post-Standard*, February 25, 1990.

[577] "In the words of 19th century Supreme Court Chief Justice John Marshall, tribal nations are considered "domestic, dependent nations" *(Cherokee Nation v. Georgia,* 1831). In other words, since Indians are accorded recognition as nations in the U.S. constitution, they retain that status; and since they are within the borders of the United States, they are domestic. Because they are not entirely independent, however, they are considered dependent." Dr. Donald Beck, Professor and Acting Chair of Native American Studies at the University of Montana.

Donald Beck, *Technical Assistance on Native American Culture:*

most instances the BIA controlled, rather than facilitated the Mohawks interaction with the federal government. In New York, the State Police discharged the Governor's instructions and dictates. The NYSP's jurisdiction included the roads and highways on the reservations.[578]

During 1989-1990, the reservation was paralyzed over internal animosity. The Canadian Mohawks had no legal right to interfere in the workings of the American Mohawk government or institutions; however, they had an intrinsic cultural right to do so. The traditionalist council, although respected and influential, was legally impotent because, other than culturally, they were not legally recognized as a government on either side of the border. The Warriors held an unusual role. They were pro-sovereignty and it seems that would have made them *de facto* pro-gambling. As far as the US or Canadian law was concerned, they should have held no legal status and were more akin to a citizen action group. Legally, only the St. Regis Mohawk Tribal Council was recognized to care for the concerns of the Mohawks on the US side of the border. Both New York State and the US Federal Government interacted only with this council.

Throughout the 1970s and 1980s, both federal and state governments officially responded to the needs of the US Mohawks. The NYSP responded to

---

Improving W.I.P.A. Services to Native American S.S.A. Beneficiaries with Disabilities (Missoula, Montana: American Indian Disability Technical Assistance Center, 2007).

[578] New York State Police, "Overview: New York State Police," New York State Police, http://www.troopers.state.ny.us/ (accessed June 5, 2007).

road accidents, emergencies, and to apprehend criminals. Additionally, they conducted criminal investigations and conducted raids on the reservation when called upon by the tribal council or out of necessity. However, this policy began changing in June 1989. The NYSP started to encounter a different set of circumstances, the Warriors Society had become much more vocal, militant, and xenophobic. The elected tribal government did not recognize the Warriors. They could have been considered a rogue element regardless of the virtues of their stance on gambling. The Warriors had a following and were supported financially by a number of elements that included smuggling.

When things began to fall apart on the reservation, the US tribal government, although divided on many issues, called for NYS intervention. The response received seemed to be the result of non-sequitur thinking. Prior to June 1989, the NYSP would raid the casinos and try to put them out of business. They kept the roads open and the motorist safe. Even after the Indian Gaming Regulatory Act (1988) was passed, the casinos had to be approved by the reservation community and elected government, after which they had to meet state standards. The state decided what types of gambling it would permit and would collect, along with the federal government, payroll taxes, FICA, and any other fees.

After June 1989, New York State seemed to take a different approach. The NYSP closed the reservation a number of times to outside traffic. What is interesting is that they allowed other groups on the reservation to blockade major highways. Another change was the way New York State enforced law on the reservation. Instead of working with the elected council, state officials chose to interact with the Warriors. Ostensibly, the reason was so that New York State did not make waves and worsen the situation. However, by doing this, the state gave a tremendous of amount of power to a group that, while they might have been popular they did not have the sanction of the tribal government recognized by New York. The state sent mixed message when they chose to deal with the Warriors. Those who opposed gambling had a voice in the elected government up until the June 1990 election now felt ignored. There were those on the anti-gambling side that became frustrated and started to take the law into their own hands. With every action, there was a reaction that became the catalyst for further action.

The Mohawks were dissatisfied with New York but also with the Canadian government and its associated provinces. Even after repeated requests from Ottawa through Washington DC, and later directly by Washington DC, New York's Governor Cuomo refused to act. His refusal to become involved allowed the violence worsen, with homes being fired upon by automatic weapons and even burned-down. Yet, even while the request for help was ignored, New York State was attempting to negotiate with the tribal council and allow casinos on the reservation. Anxiety was high, and the only institution that had the legal responsibility to act in this situation was not acting, but watching.

The problem was a non-enforcement of the laws that were set in place over the reservation. If the state authorities had let the Mohawks govern themselves then at the very least, they should have allowed them the right to conduct their own internal affairs. Essentially two governments were set in place to govern one people. The plight of the Mohawks is similar to that of East and West Berliners during the Cold War. Although the Mohawks do not have a wall to cross, they have the St. Lawrence River; both federal governments patrol a watery no man's land. Unlike the Berlin wall, no Mohawk was shot because they crossed the border, but they could be arrested and their belongings confiscated. At the very least, they could be detained and searched simply because they wanted to visit the other side.

What emerged was a clash between the different cultures within the Mohawks, and the cultures of the US, Canada, Ontario, Québec, and New York. Governments, laws, and traditions internally fractured the Mohawks, who saw themselves as a distinct people. The Mohawks lacked the sovereignty and the self-determination to handle the problems that had befallen them. They did not lack the ability to work out a solution; they were not given the chance to do so. Solutions were imposed on them. While gambling and smuggling, were the issues, gambling had heated the atmosphere to an explosive point on the reservation. Canada and the US had different cultural views on gambling. Force and overwhelming numbers were eyed as the solution by both governments. It seemed to be the only option to stop the violence and prevent further bloodshed on the reservation. After two died New York State acted in conjunction with the Canadian forces to stop the violence. New York State said the issue was sovereignty. Cuomo viewed the situation as one that the Mohawks had to solve, and then the state would become involved. He had consistently framed the problem as a delicate balance of state and federal jurisdiction and Mohawk sovereignty. However, Cuomo also thought there were other problems besides gambling at Akwesasne. One was the Indian concept of sovereignty. Many of the Mohawks he said "regard themselves as a part of a nation. They are a nation. They're a conquered nation. And they, some of them, will not accept that you obliterate their existence as a nation just because you're more powerful than them.[579] With New York State refusing to take action the other external governments also refused to act.

The violence erupted in the early morning of May 1, 1990, with a firefight between pro- and anti-gambling forces. Probably as much out of fear as conviction, the two sides fired on each other for hours. After it was over two men were dead, shot during the exchange. It was only then that the external powers acted, rushing troops and police into a community that had been battered and torn apart. The US portion of the reservation had slipped through anarchy into chaos.

---

[579] Sam Howe Verhovek, "Whose Law Applies When Lawlessness Rules on Indian Land?" *New York Times*, May 6, 1990.

A System Analysis of the Uprising

A review of the situation makes it apparent which cultures are involved. The Mohawk culture, unified in some aspects, and not in others, is overpowered by not one but two dominate powers that discharge a portion of their jurisdiction through three subordinate powers. The Mohawks at Akwesasne feel the brunt of this. Both sides of the border suffer. The increase of stress and anxiety caused by the different cultures interacting in non-collaborative, non-productive ways created a volatile condition that led to violence and eventually murder. The reservation already saturated with anxiety over gambling was pushed to a point of violence from the external pressures put upon it.

There is evidence that supports the observation that external forces can cause violence and even death within an affected culture. This is especially found to be true when referring to stress and anxiety. Viewing the situation at Akwesasne in an anthropological and historical paradigm brings forth evidence of similar outcomes to other failed cultural interactions. One investigation, that had a similar outcome as Akwesasne, is a prehistoric culture in San Pedro se Atacama, Chile.[580] Christina Torres-Rouff, and Marìa Antonietta Costa Junqueira went to Dan Pedro to investigate the prehistoric population there. Their study analyzed the:

---

[580] Torres-Rouff, Christina, and Marìa Antonietta Costa Junqueira. " Interpersonal Violence in Prehistoric San Pedro De Atacama, Chile: Behavioral Implications of Environmental Stress." *American Journal of Physical Anthropology* 130, no. 1 (2006): 60-70.

periods marked by prosperity and interregional interaction, as well as times of
severe drought, social stress, and widespread poverty. A sample of 682 crania was
analyzed for evidence of cranial trauma in order to assess changing patterns of
interpersonal violence during the occupation of the oases.[581]

Torres-Rouff, and Junqueira found, from their investigation, that "cranial trauma" in the population fluctuated in relation to the availability of resources and societal stress. The higher number of cranial fractures corresponds to the most severe, "social disruptions and resource unpredictability."[582] Their study, also shows, that with, re-stabilization of society, and more predictable food supply, the violence subsided. Further, it demonstrates how environmental, and social disruptions can have a cumulative effect on local populations.[583]

When examining the result of the investigation at San Pedro De Atacama, Chile a number of similarities are found with Akwesasne. First, both populations are indigenous, and although not identical, there would be similar attitude to nature, reverence to wide life, and to the earth. Additionally, the communities would be tribal in government. We find Akwesasne very similar although a thousand years apart. Outside stresses

---

[581] *Ibid.*, 60.
[582] *Ibid.*, 66.
[583] *Ibid.*

on San Pedro De Atacama, that could not be affected by the community, created internal stresses on the population. As stress rose, so did anxiety, and the population became prone to violence. When the stress and anxiety, reached a critical point, death within the community occurred.

The community at Akwesasne found itself in a similar circumstance. There were internal issues these were magnified with the stress created by the outside agencies. The fact, that those who should have responded to the pleas of Tribal government on the reservation, but did not respond, increased the stress and anxiety on a community already at a dangerously high stress level. As violence, in the form of gunfire and arson, got worse, fear and stress rose even higher in the community. The fact, that the Canadians, and the Americans, did not work together, was from cultural differences on their view of Indians. New York State did not work in harmony with other government agencies because of a cultural difference in the political viewpoint of the situation. Cuomo was of the opinion that the Mohawks should settle the problem, and Washington felt Cuomo should, The Mohawks of Akwesasne, as a whole, had cultural differences with the other groups. Eventually these differences raised the stress and anxiety level on the reservation to the critical point with the outcomes of violence and death.

A psychological example of stress and anxiety causing violence is seen in the socialization of children. Psychologist, Dr. Aletha Solter, in her book *Tears and Tantrums*[584] states, one condition that produces violence in children, is when they have been hurt. Solter says that this includes, not only physical violence, such as beatings, or sexual abuse, but also emotional abuse. Interestingly enough the author said, "the accumulation of minor hurts (stress) can lead to violent behavior as well."[585] That, "anxieties, disappointments, and frustrations" can cause children to act out, and strike others.[586]

Another condition for violence, Solter wrote, was children who had been hurt or stressed and could not find a way to release. They had no voice, to talk it out, and release the pressure. When someone is the victim of violence and they repress those emotions "violence toward self or others is almost an inevitable outcome."[587]

Solter's analysis of how stress in children can cause a violent outcome has some interesting parallels to the situation with the Mohawks at Akwesasne. The Mohawks of Akwesasne are not children, howeer, in the situation that has been described, they are the minor culture between two major ones. In this position, the Mohawks, are subordinate to the other two cultures. Further when studying the similarities between the Mohawks and Solter's scenario it is found there is a correlation in how the Mohawks suffered from anxieties,

---

[584] Solter, Aletha, Ph.D. *Tears and Tantrums: What to Do When Babies and Children Cry*. Goleta, CA.: Shining Star Press, 1998.
[585] *Ibid.*
[586] *Ibid.*
[587] *Ibid.*

disappointments, and frustrations, and have accumulated small stresses over time. It seems that this aspect alone would breed violence. When you include the other condition concerning, how the repression of emotions, and the inability to release them, can cause violence the uprising at Akwesasne was almost inevitable.

Another viewpoint that supports the observation that a clash of cultures caused the uprising at Akwesasne is Bowen Systems Theory.[588] When investigating the Akwesasne community, in its simplest form, it is found that its functioning is affected by the behavior of its people. In other words, the Akwesasne community, is considered a cultural 'system.' As a cultural system, it interacts with other cultural systems. All of these systems are open, or closed,[589] to a certain degree.

---

[588] "Dr. Murray Bowen, a psychiatrist, originated this theory and its eight interlocking concepts. He formulated the theory by using systems thinking to integrate knowledge of the human species as a product of evolution and knowledge from family research. . . Bowen family systems theory is a theory of human behavior that views the family as an emotional unit and uses systems thinking to describe the complex interactions in the unit. It is the nature of a family that its members are intensely connected emotionally. . . The connectedness and reactivity make the functioning of family members interdependent. A change in one person's functioning is predictably followed by reciprocal changes in the functioning of others."
Bowen Theory. Bowen Center for the Study of the Family: Georgetown Family Center, 2004. Accessed August 18, 2007. Available from http://www.thebowencenter.org/theory.html.

[589] ". . . systems are open or closed depending on the degree to which they are organized and interact with the outside environment. An open system receives input such as matter, energy, and information from its surroundings and discharges output in the environment. Theoretically, closed systems are rarely, if ever,

No system, or very few systems, are truly closed, however they can be technically closed, or at least partially closed, when compared to other systems.[590] It would have to be noted that Akwesasne was culturally closed in many aspects. Although, there were factions on the reservation, and in some instances, actually a fractured community, there was always a spirit of what it meant to be a Mohawk. The people of Akwesasne always knew they had a different history than the surrounding communities and their own peculiar cultures. The other cultural systems were open. The interaction between the three major cultural systems, Canadian, American, and Mohawk, is in itself a system and operates in balance following the legal precepts agreed upon between the three cultural systems. When imbalances occur within this system measures, that have been agreed upon, are implemented, to regain the balance of the larger system.[591] These measures would include acts such as, responding to requests

---

completely isolated or closed off from the outside. . . to be truly operating in a closed system, all outside transactions and communications would have to cease to exist which is highly improbable."
Andreae, Dan. "System Theory and Social Work Treatment." In *Social Work Treatment*, ed. Francis J. Turner. New York, N.Y.: The Free Press a Division of Simon and Schuster Inc., 1996, 609.

[590] *Ibid*,

[591] Kerr, Kathleen B., M.S.N., M.A. "An Overview of Bowens Theory." In *Understanding Organizations: Application of Bowen Family Systems Theory*, ed. Ruth Riley Sagar and Kathleen Klaus Wiseman. Washington D.C.: Georgetown University Family Center, 1982, 1-2.

for help, patrolling roadways, enforcing laws, and honoring treaties and agreements,

When measures are not taken to restore balance, then the system will react in predictable ways in order to regain balance. If this fails, then symptoms occur which are an indication of anxiety driven by the imbalance. In systems theory, every part of the system touches every other part. Not only is there interdependence between people in a system but also an emotional interaction. When the system breaks down it affects everyone in the system, and that can change the behavior of people in the system. Their behavior "is not necessarily a characteristic of them alone but indeed is also determined to a certain extent by the functional position that person occupies in the system."[592] So the actions of the Mohawks, the NYSP, and the Canadian forces were reacting to the overall breakdown in the system. Dr. Edwin H Friedman in his book. *A Failure of Nerve: Leadership in the Age of the Quick Fix,* would have identified part of the breakdown in the system coming from New York State's reaction to the situation. Friedman believes that there is a "widespread misunderstanding about the relational nature of destructive process in . . . institutions that leads leaders to believe that" problems can be solved with a reasonable approach to them or through some form of role modeling.[593] Following along Friedman's line of thought, New

---

[592] *Ibid.*, 2-3.
[593] Friedman, Edwin H., Dr. *A Failure of Nerve: Leadership in the Age of the Quick Fix*. Bethesda, Maryland: The Edwin Friedman Estate/Trust, 1999, 11.

York State should have taken a stand to set limits to the situation at hand. But that did not occur, and imbalance increased within the larger system and all of the component (cultural) systems. The Mohawks, operating as a closed system, had no way to release the stress that resulted from the outside forces on their system. This in turn affected the individuals within Akwesasne.

The Mohawks were suffering two factors that were creating an inability for them to contend with the situation. The people were being overwhelmed by the increasing anxiety in the situation and it became "critically stressful and destabilizing."[594] Additionally, the Mohawks found that blaming the old scapegoats, the Warriors and gambling, did not relieve the anxiety and stress that was affecting the reservation, but aggravated it. The situation had grown larger than the sum of its parts. When each of these factors is found within a system, it suggests, the leaders of the society have lost their capacity to lead. They "find themselves on a treadmill of efforts to get free, unable to gain the distance that could shift their orientation and polarized on anxiety driven issues."[595]

Akwesasne was suffering from chronic anxiety. Chronic anxiety is an all-encompassing regressive emotional process that can envelope and connects an entire community. It is not angst, or community nervousness, but is deeper. It is not dependent on events or a particular time. It concerns more about the Mohawks' focus on anxiety than its cause.

---

[594] *Ibid.*, 78.
[595] *Ibid.*, 79.

Chronic anxiety is similar to the atmosphere of a room filled with natural gas. One spark and the whole room would explode. Akwesasne had no way to dispense the fumes, so it remained volatile, susceptible to external stress and pressure. As for the Mohawks, there was no one single entity that could speak for, or lead the community out of the situation. The external system had broken down, and the cultural systems were not responding, and the Mohawks suffered the consequences. It could be said that New York State struck a match and the Mohawk cultural system exploded violently.[596]

In analyzing the uprising at Akwesasne, it is found that external forces acting upon an already stressful reservation caused violence to occur between Mohawks, and eventually led to the deaths of two individuals and the damage and destruction of a great deal of infrastructure. The conclusion that external stress caused the violence is supported historically and anthropologically with the results at the prehistoric site of San Pedro De Atacama, Chile. It was found that as external, and environmental stresses, increased the society became more violent and the death rate increased. It can be concluded that just as the external stresses caused violence at the Chile site the same response is seen at Akwesasne. As outside stresses and anxiety increased at Akwesasne the acts became more violent. These acts included barricades, arson, destruction of property, firing and wounding others and finally the death of two individuals.

---

[596] *Ibid.*, 78-80.

When examining the events at Akwesasne psychologically, the facts of the event are compared to a situation where stress causes children to act out, and become violent. As the stress and anxiety increases with children it becomes more prevalent that a child could act violently and strike out at others. The Mohawks at Akwesasne were put in a similar psychological situation because of their position as a minor culture being over powered by two major cultures. This scenario created stress that resulted in the Mohawks acted out in a predictable manner.

Finally, the events at Akwesasne were viewed through the lens of Bowens System Theory. The analysis found, that as the various systems involved broke down, stress and anxiety increased through all of the systems. The more open cultural systems could respond to this stress by interacting with other systems. The Mohawk's cultural system was closed culturally, and politically it was mixed,[597] and could not react in a healthy way. As the Mohawk system broke down, it affected the individuals in the system, and eventually brought about violence and death.

CONCLUSION:

An Event that Changed the Course of History

---

[597] The Mohawks were culturally closed because to be a Mohawk you had to be born a Mohawk. It was politically mixed because different factions had different opinions. The Warriors wanted a closed system while others were willing to cooperate have an open system in one degree or another.

The events that transpired between June 6, 1989 and May 1, 1990 changed the course of the Mohawk people, and the land of Akwesasne. The uprising had been called a Civil War, the violent response to a political question between the Mohawks. It was a way to settle old scores and to muscle in a new political reality, where money was king and sovereignty was cheap.

Others felt that this was the same old business as before, cops and robbers, cowboys and Indians, squabbling over ancient treaties, *Manifest Destiny*, and modern political realities. They see it as the act of fighting for the right to cross over the border, to visit relatives, and to smuggle contraband with impunity. All of it getting out of hand with people's lives affected, community friendships strained, and the death of two innocent bystanders.

What happened at Akwesasne started when their land was taken, and their wells were polluted. It was when a nation was divided into multiple zones so that land that was once a single entity, was split five ways jurisdictionally. The Mohawk culture was fractured not by their own doing, but because of outside entities. In the 1980s, gambling came to the reservation in minor ways, and evolved over time to where it was big business. It was not sanctioned by the state, or by referendum. It was decided by the community that casino style gambling had to go. Even in early1989, the owners of the casinos had contacted the State Police about a peaceful raid when the time came.

On June 6, 1989 fights broke out that ended up at Tony's Vegas International. The police responded, but instead of breaking up what had become a riot, they arrested Tony Laughing on gambling charges and left his casino to the crowd. It was the same course of action when they arrested the owner of Josie's bar. When they took her away, they left the crowd to riot and burn the establishment down. Based on this earlier incident in May 1984[598] the police must have suspected this, or something similar would occur under these similar circumstances. The State Police left, and the crown destroyed the interior. This gave licensed to violence and was the beginning of the cultural schism. The Mohawks do not have, a cohesive, fully recognized, government to represent and protect the community. They are splintered, and have to rely on outside forces for protection, especially on the American side. The American Tribal government was powerless to stop the violence, and New York State refused to act. The

---

[598] On May 9 1984 two people were killed on a motorcycle after leaving Josie's Bar. On May 10th, New York State Police took the owner of Josie's, Josephine White, into custody in connection with the accident. There were about 250 to 300 protesters surrounding the building as the State Police took White away. The police did not disperse the crowd and around 9PM about 50 men pushed through the front of the crowd, broke into the bar and started it on fire. As the fire department responded 300 protesters on foot and in automobiles blocked them. Even though they were close by they were not allowed to put out the fire. When the State Police did return, they intervened in the situation, however Josie's was totally destroyed.

Boorstin, Robert O. "A Tavern Is Burned to the Ground on an Indian Reservation Upstate." *New York Times*, May 11, 1986, 29. and Fein, Esther B. "Indians' Rage at Illegal Bar Fuels Upstate Fire." *New York Times*, May 12, 1986, A1.

Canadian side of the reservation was under the power and the protection of the Canadian and provincial governments except for a small piece of the reservation that was part of Québec, but attached to the US mainland. It is here that the violence took its heaviest toll. Canadian police could not reach this small part of Québec unless by boat. To reach this area by car either the Sûreté du Québec, or the Ontario Provincial Police, would have to get permission from the US government, and New York State to enter the country. It was not until after the two men died that Canadian forces were given an escort to go investigate. These cultural interactions between Ottawa, Washington D.C, Albany, Cornwall, and Hogansburg began to seem more like cultural clashing than diplomacy. As these cultures interacted the Mohawk government was powerless to stop the violence, the Canadian forces could not reach the area, and New York State refused to act. Out of a sense of frustration, on both sides, a firefight commenced after a boat crossing the St. Lawrence River was fired upon. At the end of it two people were dead because of an uprising caused by a clash of cultures.

APPENDIX 1: RESEARCH

Document Research

The literature connected to this time period and the events at Akwesasne fit into three major categories. These are sources that concern the uprising in 1989 and 1990, those that deal with tribal/Indian sovereignty and gambling, and works concerning the American Indian Movement (AIM). These sources provide a background for the interpretation and investigation of events during the uprising.

Uprising Resources

A number of sources reviewed deal with the uprising during 1989 through 1990 include a number of books. *Life and Death in Mohawk Country* by Bruce E. Johansen is a well-researched work that brings an interesting light to the events that occurred.[599] Johansen, using primary sources, including oral interviews, demonstrates how the uprising was the result of ongoing long-term "white" disregard for the environment and how it affected the Mohawks. Another component that the author brings into the discussion is how the various governments did not take appropriate action in a timely fashion when problems arose. Because of

---

[599] Bruce E. Johansen, *Life and Death in Mohawk Country* (Golden, Colorado: North American Press, 1993).

the degradation of the land, the hopelessness of the situation, and the scarcity of jobs around the reservation, people turned to the gambling trade. With gambling, there was quick return on the money, and many jobs were created; however, the author depicts how gambling broke down the society and the internal structure of the reservation. When the internal structure fell apart and civilian authority could not keep the peace, chaos followed. Unchecked chaos broke the society into factions resulting in death and the destruction of infrastructure. Johansen demonstrated the situation as more of the same feud between the majority governments and the tribal governments.[600]

Another work reviewed was *Lasagna,* written by Ronald Cross and Héléne Sévigny.[601] The book details Ronald Cross (Lasagna), his life, his acceptance of Mohawk traditions, and his time behind the barriers at Kanesatake, his trial, and its result. It also looks at the impact of media on the situation and how the government used it to their advantage. Although the book examines how this event affected Cross, it also points to the problems at Kanesatake and Akwesasne and government interaction. It explores how the uprising and death at Oka was a continuation of non-indigenous governments taking land from the Mohawks.[602] Cross and Sévigny claimed that various governments used the tactics of manipulation and obfuscation of the press to misrepresent the

---

[600] Ibid.

[601] Ronald Cross and Héléne Sévigny, *Lasagna: The Man Behind the Mask.* (Vancouver: Talon Books, 1994).

[602] Ibid.,126-127.

situation and hide the Canadian and Québec governments' agendas. These tactics went beyond just influencing the press; they affected everything from treaties to legal decisions. Recently, indigenous peoples have regained some of their rights, but the government continues the process of taking them. Cross and Sévigny state multiple times that the action taken by the government was a repeat of the past.[603] However, their book does not examine the entire situation, but rather centers on Cross (Lasagna) and his interaction with the government.

People of the Pines: The Warriors and the Legacy of Oka, written by Geoffrey York and Loreen Pindera is another book that was investigated.[604] York and Pindera were reporters covering the violence at Oka (Kanesatake). They discuss the background behind the 1990 situation and describe it as a 270-year ongoing conflict. The authors also tie Akwesasne into the situation through the Warrior Society, which was very active during the uprising at Akwesasne, and later shifted to Oka (Kanesatake) when the problem surfaced there.[605] Overall, the book is well researched and brings a unique perspective on the Oka conflict and the Warrior Society.

Another source produced about the uprising is Rick Hornung's first person account entitled *One*

---

[603] Ibid., 178-179.
[604] Geoffrey York and Loreen Pindera, *People of the Pines: The Warriors and the Legacy of Oka* (Boston: Little Brown Company, 1991).
[605] Ibid.

Nation Under the Gun.⁶⁰⁶ Hornung covered the events at Akwesasne as a regular contributor to the *Village Voice*.⁶⁰⁷ His work brings a personal viewpoint to the situation. Originally, the material was presented as an article in the *Village Voice* on May 15, 1990.⁶⁰⁸ The book is described by Hornumg as, "reporting on the fly, running between interviews, shootouts, car ramming, standoffs, troop deployments, and press conferences," beginning in September 1989.⁶⁰⁹ The work includes a number of interviews and conversations as well as a narrative timeline of the event. Hornung's book has been a center of controversy. The Superior Court, on July 25, 1991, imposed an injunction on the distribution of Hornung's book, citing that two Mohawks, Ellen Gabriel and Denise Tolley, challenged their interviews. Both said Hornung had never interviewed them; however, the Superior Court of Canada lifted the injunction on August 2, 1991 for lack of evidence.⁶¹⁰ The book acknowledges the influence that outside cultures had on the reservation during this time. Hornung's work is considered a primary source since a great deal of his writing is personal accounts of events.

Other sources that cover various aspects of this uprising include *Warrior Societies in Contemporary*

---

⁶⁰⁶ Rick Hornung, *One Nation under the Gun: Inside the Mohawk Civil War* (New York: Pantheon, 1991).

⁶⁰⁷ The Village Voice is a weekly New York City tabloid that features investigative articles and current affairs.

⁶⁰⁸ Hornung, *One Nation under the Gun*, ix.

⁶⁰⁹ Ibid.

⁶¹⁰ Dan Burke, "The Mohawks' War; One Nation under the Gun: Inside the Mohawk Civil War by Rick Hornung (Stoddart, 304 Pages)," *Maclean's*, August 19, 1991, 40.

Indigenous Communities, written by Dr. Alfred Taiaiake and Lana Lowe,[611] and Charles Stuart's, *A Crisis of Hegemony: An Analysis of Media Discourse*.[612] Both of these works depict the uprising as a symptom of a simmering long-term problem. Each source views the violence as a result of continual injustices against the Mohawks. Taiaiake and Lowe felt the Warriors and their actions were a response to these situations. They assert, "There is broad support among traditional indigenous people across the country for action, even militant action, against the continuing unjust dispossession of indigenous peoples from their lands."[613] Stuart's work looks at how the media was used to shape the conflict. He wrote, "within this theoretical framework the media are viewed as an ideological mechanism perpetuating the existing hegemonic relationship."[614] Each of these sources is minimally biased and shows their scholarship and research of the events that took place.

The Native American Entrepreneur and the Mohawk Civil War, written by Sandra Busatta, depicts the situation at Akwesasne as a civil war.[615] Busatta wrote that, "The hot issue in the brief civil

---

[611] Alfred Taiaiake and Lana Lowe, *Warrior Societies in Contemporary Indigenous Communities* (Victoria, BC: University of Victoria, 2005).

[612] Charles Stuart, *A Crisis of Hegemony: An Analysis of Media Discourse* (Ottawa, Ont.: University of Ottawa, 1993).

[613] Taiaiake and Lowe, *Warrior Societies*, 55.

[614] Stuart, *A Crisis of Hegemony*, 5.

[615] Sandra Busatta, *The Native American Entrepreneur and the Mohawk Civil War* (Padova, Italy: Università degli Studi di Padova, 2005).

war in Akwesasne was that profits from the seven reservation casinos[616] and bingo halls were going exclusively to hall owners and their non-Indian management teams."[617] She adds that the "factional civil war" at Akwesasne and later at Kanesatake and Kahnawake challenged the corporate tribal managers' control.[618] Although biased in some aspects, Bursatta's work is vibrant and expressive in support of her thesis.

Sovereignty and Gambling Resources

The second category explored dealt with tribal an Indian sovereignty and gambling. A major work that investigates this aspect is Steven Light and Kathryn Rand's work *Indian Gaming and Tribal Sovereignty: The Casino Compromise*.[619] The authors analyze the effect of gambling on tribal sovereignty. In general, they felt that it had a positive effect on the tribe's economy as well as Native society. Light and Rand discuss how gaming on an Indian reservation is basically different than Las Vegas or Atlantic City gambling because the tribal government owns it. The authors state that the main reason for this difference involves the tribe's political autonomy, which is

---

[616] An illegal casino usually has more than high stakes bingo or card games but typically includes roulette and slot machines. At Akwesasne it could further mean a casino that is not approved by the tribal government.
[617] Stuart, *A Crisis of Hegemony*, 19.
[618] Ibid., 27.
[619] Andrew Steven Light and Kathryn R. L. Rand, *Indian Gaming & Tribal Sovereignty: The Casino Compromise* (Lawrence: University Press of Kansas, 2005),17-20.

legally protected by federal Indian law.[620] Their exploration of this subject, although complete, does not exactly echo the situation found at Akwesasne. The situation at Akwesasne involved private casinos where this source is discussing tribal casinos.

W. Dale Mason's book *Indian Gaming: Tribal Sovereignty and American Politics*[621] echoes Light and Rand's analysis of tribal sovereignty. Mason centers on New Mexico and Oklahoma and predicts that tribal self-government may approach equity with states' sovereignty within the federal government. The author writes, "Legalized gambling on Indian lands and reservations is an increasingly important component of tribal economics and political life."[622] "It is a new source of tribal-state conflict and the debates will continue well into the twenty-first century."[623] Mason, although writing about the history of gambling on reservations, treats the concept of tribal sovereignty very well. The author's further investigation of the financial aspects of this collaboration between Tribal government and gaming is informative to those researching this field. Another source written by Light and Rand is *Indian Gaming Law: Cases and Materials*. This casebook details how policies and laws dealing with Indian gaming have gradually changed over time. The authors give a complete

---

[620] Ibid.

[621] Walter Dale Mason, *Indian Gaming: Tribal Sovereignty and American Politics* (Norman, OK: University of Oklahoma Press, 2000).

[622] Ibid., Jacket.

[623] Ibid.

treatment of the history of gaming and deal with the important court decisions. Further, they show how the federal government's policies on casino gambling impacted the conduct of tribal government and its impact on decision-making.[624] *Indian Gaming Law: Cases and Materials* is an excellent source on the subject and should be consulted in research of this nature. A source that deals with tribal-state interaction is Jeffery S. Ashley and Secody J. Hubbard's book *Negotiated Sovereignty: Working to Improve Tribal-State Relations*.[625] The authors believe that to have good relations between the federal government, state governments, and with the various tribes there has to be recognition of how tribal sovereignty fits in the federal system. They state that these relationships will not evolve and grow if the government tries to hamper and impede tribal sovereignty and refuses to negotiate with Indian governments.[626] The authors take a bold and thorough look into the subject of tribal and state relations and do fairly well dealing with a difficult topic.

Erin Fouberg's book *Tribal Territory, Sovereignty, and Governance: A Study of the Cheyenne River and Lake Traverse Indian Reservations* discusses that although the physical territory and level of sovereignty direct the course

---

[624] Ibid.

[625] Jeffery S. Ashley and Secody J Hubbard, *Negotiated Sovereignty: Working to Improve Tribal-State Relations* (Westport: Praeger Publishers, 2004).

[626] Ibid.

of tribal government, these factors are not conclusive.[627] Fouberg states that other aspects that affect tribal government include a reservation's economy and the available leadership. His book tells of the changes that occurred to the Cheyenne River and Lake Traverse Indian Reservations and how they were affected by changes in physical territory, which in turn impacted economic resources and leadership.[628] Fouberg's book is an informative investigation into this subject. Even though some of the findings expressed would apply to Akwesasne, the book delves more into the Lake Traverse and Cheyenne River Indian Reservations and the events at those locations.

Lane gives an excellent review of the history of the Cabazon tribe of California that fought for the right to have gambling casinos in his book *Return of the Buffalo: The Story Behind America's Indian Gaming Explosion*.[629] The author describes how the tribe fought against the state of California, the county of Riverside, and the city of Indio that led to the Supreme Court decision concerning their right to have gambling on their reservation.[630] In their book *Keeping Promises: What Is Sovereignty and Other Questions About Indian Country,* Reid, Winton, and Cates write about the complex

---

[627] Erin Fouberg, *Tribal Territory, Sovereignty, and Governance: A Study of the Cheyenne River and Lake Traverse Indian Reservations* (New York: Routledge, 2000).

[628] Ibid.

[629] Ambrose I. Lane, *Return of the Buffalo: The Story Behind America's Indian Gaming Explosion* (Westport, Conn.: Bergin & Garvey Paperback, 1995).

[630] Ibid.

interrelationship between the Indian tribes and the federal government.[631] Their work details the various treaties and pledges made by the government and how these have affected sovereignty.[632] The book contains a wealth of information and should be considered a research source for Native American sovereignty.

Kevin Bruyeel's book *The Third Space of Sovereignty: The Postcolonial Politics of US-Indigenous Relations* discusses the effect of treaties and the changes that occurred after the US government ended making treaties in the 1870s.[633] The authors relate how Indian status and how tribal sovereignty has been affected since then.[634] The source gives a fair, but limited, discussion of US-Indian relationships. Another book that deals with similar aspects of sovereignty and government interaction is *The Politics of Hallowed Ground: Wounded Knee and the Struggle for Indian Sovereignty*[635] written by Mario Gonzalez and Elizabeth Cook Lynn. The authors explore with the controversy involved with the massacre at Wounded Knee and the related history of the Wounded Knee

---

[631] Betty Reid, Ben Winton and Gwendolen Cates, *Keeping Promises: What Is Sovereignty and Other Questions About Indian Country* (Tucson, AZ: Western National Parks Association, 2004).

[632] Ibid.

[633] Kevin Bruyneel, *The Third Space of Sovereignty: The Postcolonial Politics of U.S.-Indigenous Relations* (Minneapolis, MN: University of Minnesota Press, 2007).

[634] Ibid.

[635] Elizabeth Cook-Lynn and Mario Gonzalez, *The Politics of Hallowed Ground: Wounded Knee and the Struggle for Indian Sovereignty* (Champaign, IL: University of Illinois Press, 1998).

Survivors Association. They detail the bias affecting the association in trying to address the legal ramifications of the massacre.[636] This is a significant source concerning the events at Wounded Knee and is a valid source for detailed research.

Gail H. Landsman in her book *Sovereignty and Symbol: Indian-White Conflict at Ganienkeh* examines the events that occurred at Moss Lake, New York.[637] In her work, Landsman investigates the motives of the state and the Mohawks that were involved in the takeover of the Girl Scout Camp. The author discusses how the New York State government refused to negotiate in good faith with the Indians who were looking for a peaceful solution to the situation. Her work explores the problems of tribal sovereignty and the non-responsive interaction that caused the deaths of two people.[638] Although her work has met with critical reviews, I felt it was an informative exposé on the experience of the Mohawks at Moss Lake. She draws out a number of points that enlighten the reader about the root causes of the Mohawk movement for sovereignty.

Laurence M. Hauptman has written a number of books that deal with Indian, in particular Iroquoian, tribal-governmental relationships. Hauptman is considered by many to be an exquisite

---

[636] Ibid.

[637] Gail H. Landsman, *Sovereignty and Symbol: Indian-White Conflict at Ganienkeh* (Albuquerque, NM: University of New Mexico Press, 1988).

[638] Ibid.

historian on Mohawk history and culture. Each of his works mentioned here are well researched and should be considered good source material. In his book *Formulating American Indian Policy in New York State, 1970-1986* Hauptman investigates how various New York State agencies handled Iroquoian land claims, and how these agencies failed in the process, and how these failures affected the Iroquoian government.[639] Another work by Hauptman is *The Iroquois Struggle for Survival: World War II to Red Power*.[640] In this work, the author produces an in-depth review and analysis of the history of the Iroquois since World War Two and the problems they have experience with land claims, tribal sovereignty, and adjusting to federal policies. He shows how the problems of the Iroquois are typical of other tribes in their struggle with the federal government.[641] Continuing in his analysis of the Iroquois and their situation, Hauptman's book *The Iroquois and the New Deal* adds important information.[642] He details how the Iroquois were both helped and hindered by the New Deal, and how the Indian Reorganization Act added more government control. However, New Deal legislation did provide a number of programs and

---

[639] Laurence M. Hauptman, *Formulating American Indian Policy in New York State 1970-1986* (Albany, NY: State University of New York Press, 1988).

[640] Laurence M. Hauptman, *The Iroquois Struggle for Survival: World War II to Red Power* (Syracuse: Syracuse University Press, 1986).

[641] Ibid.

[642] Laurence M. Hauptman, *The Iroquois and the New Deal* (Syracuse: Syracuse University Press, 1988).

opportunities for tribes and individual Tribal members.⁶⁴³

Hauptman's writings are also found in *Iroquois Land Claims* edited by William A. Starna and Christopher Veesey.⁶⁴⁴ The book looks at both the Iroquoian and New York State sides of the land claims issue. It is well written and brings forth a large and varied historiography. The series of essays were originally presented at a Colgate University symposium in April 1986.⁶⁴⁵ *Iroquois Land Claims* investigates not only the land claims and the impact they had on individual tribes and on the homeowners who lived in the surrounding areas. It points out the complexities of the situation and how none of the participants will be completely satisfied.⁶⁴⁶ One of Hauptman's essays is entitled *Iroquois Land Issues*.⁶⁴⁷ It investigates how the land issues affect the relationship between New York State and the various Iroquoian tribes. He explains how state government responds inadequately to tribal problems when violence is threatened.⁶⁴⁸ Another essay Hauptman wrote was *The Historical Background to the Present-Day Seneca Nation-*

---

⁶⁴³ Ibid.

⁶⁴⁴ Christopher Veesey and William A Starna, eds., *Iroquois Land Claims* (Syracuse: Syracuse University Press, 1988), 1.

⁶⁴⁵ Ibid.

⁶⁴⁶ Ibid.

⁶⁴⁷ Laurence M. Hauptman, "Iroquois Land Issues: At Odds with the "Family of New York,"" in *Iroquois Land Claims*, eds. Christopher Vecsey and William A Starna (Syracuse: Syracuse University Press, 1988), 67-86.

⁶⁴⁸ Ibid.

Salamanca Lease Controversy.[649] In this, Hauptman deals with the controversy concerning ninety-nine-year leases from the Seneca Nation to the City of Salamanca. The author takes a historical look at how the authority of New York State compromised tribal sovereignty. Hauptman demonstrates why the Iroquois have negative perceptions of the state and its dealings.[650]

In their book *Uneven Ground: American Indian Sovereignty and Federal Law* written by David Wilkins and K. Tsianina Lomawaima, the authors discuss how Federal law interacts with Indian legal issues.[651] The authors show how the government treats tribal sovereignty unfairly and the laws make justice for Indians nearly impossible and unpredictable.[652] In a work by Wilkins entitled *American Indian Sovereignty and the US Supreme Court: The Making of Justice*, the author analyzes fifteen court cases to prove that the Court has limited or extinguished Indian rights.[653] Wilkins details, through the court cases, that the courts ignore tribal rights and sovereignty acting in ways

---

[649] Laurence M. Hauptman, "The Historical Background to the Present-Day Seneca Nation-Salamanca Lease Controversy," in *Iroquois Land Claims*, eds. Christopher Vecsey and William A Starna (Syracuse: Syracuse University Press, 1988), 101-122.

[650] Ibid.

[651] David E. Wilkins and K. Tsianina Lomawaima, *Uneven Ground: American Indian Sovereignty and Federal Law* (Norman, OK: University of Oklahoma Press, 2002).

[652] Ibid.

[653] David E. Wilkins, *American Indian Sovereignty and the U.S. Supreme Court: The Masking of Justice* (Austin, TX: University of Texas Press, 1997).

that significantly limit a tribe's prerogatives, and at times, take tribal land.[654] Both of these works takes an unsympathetic view of the federal government's stance on Indian rights and tribal sovereignty. Each of these works should be considered necessary reading when investigating the relationship between government and tribes.

In *The Nations Within: The Past and Future of American Indian Sovereignty* Authors Vine Deloria Jr. and Clifford M. Lytle begin with the history of Indian treatment by the federal and state governments.[655] They analyze the conflict in Congress over Indian rights; explore house hearings and the Indian Reorganization Act. Deloria and Lytle also look at the beginning of Native nationalism and the eventual outcome of tribal sovereignty.[656] The book was a good analysis; however, it was the exploration of the US House of Representatives transcripts that begins to tell the story of Indian rights and the government.

Joanne Barker, the editor of the book of essays *Sovereignty Matters: Locations of Contestation and the Possibility in Indigenous Struggles for Self-Determination* that deal with indigenous problems throughout the US, from the East Coast to Hawaii, discussing sovereignty and tribal cultural self-

---

[654] Ibid.

[655] Vine Deloria, Jr. and Clifford M. Lytle, *The Nations Within: The Past and Future of American Indian Sovereignty* (Austin, TX: University of Texas Press, 1998).

[656] Ibid.

determination.[657] The essays discuss the real purpose of the treaties made with Indians and how the international community views them. Additionally, the writings investigate how the spiritual side of sovereignty affects indigenous perceptions of tribal government and land ownership.[658] Although an interesting book, it supplied minimal information on the research topic. I felt that it was worthy source material regardless of its usefulness to this investigation. Another book that opposes current government regulations and discusses the need for a new outlook on tribal sovereignty is Pommersheim's, *Braid of Feathers: American Indian law and Contemporary Tribal Life*.[659] The author conducts an excellent examination of the "historical, legal and cultural elements [that are] embedded" into the reservation and how they affect tribal life and outlook on sovereignty.[660] Further, Pommersheim adequately conducts an extensive review of US Supreme Court decisions where there was little concern over human welfare, and where racism and inadequate historiography were used to further the government's decisions.[661] The book *Tribes, Treaties, and Constitutional Tribulations* by Vine

---

[657] Joanne Baker, ed., *Sovereignty Matters: Locations of Contestation and Possibility in Indigenous Struggles for Self-Determination* (Evanston, Illinois: John Gordon Burke, 2004).

[658] Ibid.

[659] Frank Pommersheim, *Braid of Feathers: American Indian Law and Contemporary Tribal Life* (Berkeley, CA: University of California Press, 1997), 8.

[660] Ibid.

[661] Ibid, 8-9.

Deloria Jr. and David E. Wilkins examines the US Constitution with respect to Indians and tribal sovereignty.[662] The authors show how the Constitution deals with Indians and tribal sovereignty, and how Indian tribes are not truly included in the constitutional framework and should be dealt with through treaties.[663] Their look at this topic is well thought out and fully supported in their documentation. The authors addressed a difficult topic well by using a great deal of research acumen.

Earl L. Grinols wrote an excellent book entitled *Gambling in America: Costs and Benefits.*[664] Within it, he demonstrates how the government and society in general have drawn the wrong conclusions concerning casino gambling. Grinols writes that most see gambling as a boon to local economies, especially for tribal communities however he presents data to the opposite. He states that communities with casinos have a greater number of compulsive gamblers and exposes gambling to an even larger population. The author states gambling gives reservations a false sense of sovereignty that in reality does not exist.[665] Although there is scholarship that disagrees with the author's findings, his argument is compelling. It is a well-researched and persuasive document.

---

[662] Vine Deloria, Jr. and David E. Wilkins, *Tribes, Treaties, and Constitutional Tribulations* (Austin, TX: University of Texas Press, 1999).

[663] Ibid.

[664] Earl L. Grinols, *Gambling in America: Costs and Benefits* (New York, NY: Cambridge University Press, 2004).

[665] Ibid.

Resources on the American Indian Movement

Included in this group is Paul Chaat Smith and Robert Allen Warrior's book *Like a Hurricane: The Indian Movement from Alcatraz to Wounded Knee*.[666] The authors write about the period from the 1969 occupation of Alcatraz to the occupation of the Bureau of Indian Affairs building in Washington in 1972 to the two-month uprising at Wounded Knee in 1973. Smith and Warrior's book shows both sides of the issues and exploration of this source contributes to a well-balanced investigation of these topics.[667]

One of the best-known treatments of events at Wounded Knee is Peter Matthiessen's *In the Spirit of Crazy Horse*.[668] His work is split into three internal books. In the first book, the author looks at the history of the Oglala Lakota from 1835 to 1965 and the beginnings of the American Indian Movement (AIM) from 1968 to 1975. The second book details the shoot-out on the Pine Ridge Indian Reservation, the investigation, trial, conviction of Leonard Peltier and his time as a fugitive. It also examines the trials at Cedar Rapids and at Fargo. In the third book, the author ties the pieces together,

---

[666] Paul Chaat Smith and Robert Allen Warrior, *Like a Hurricane: The Indian Movement from Alcatraz to Wounded Knee* (New York, NY: New Press, 1997).

[667] Ibid.

[668] Peter Matthiessen, *In the Spirit of Crazy Horse* (New York, NY: Penguin, 1992).

covering the time period from 1976 to 1981.[669] Matthiessen's book gets to the crux of many of the problems associated with Indian sovereignty, rights, and what Wounded Knee represents to the Native American struggle. While biased it brings the Native side to the table.

Another examination of the Wounded Knee take-over is Joseph H. Trimbach's *American Indian Mafia: An FBI Agent's True Story about Wounded Knee, Leonard Peltier, and the American Indian Movement (AIM)*.[670] Trimbach gives an opposite viewpoint to Matthiessen's book. Trimback finds that the FBI had been maligned, and gives a timeline of the events. Additionally, he presents evidence that Leonard Peltier had not been falsely accused and was guilty of the charges brought again him. The author uses interviews and photographs to document his claims, and sees himself as bringing closure to a misrepresented event.[671] As with the previous work by Matthiessen, Trimbach's book is biased. However, it does courageously bring to light aspects of the events that have been previously under explored. Trimbach's book is a necessary resource for any investigation of AIM and the events at Wounded Knee.

The American Indian Movement (AIM) is also explored in the autobiography titled *Ojibwa Warrior: Dennis Banks and The Rise of The*

---

[669] Ibid.

[670] Joseph H. Trimbach, *American Indian Mafia: An FBI Agent's True Story About Wounded Knee, Leonard Peltier, and the American Indian Movement* (Parker, CO: Outskirts Press, 2007).

[671] Ibid.

American Indian Movement by Dennis Banks and Richard Erdoes.[672] The book begins on May 8, 1972, with a description of the atmosphere at Wounded Knee and movements of the Indians. Throughout Banks and Erdoes' work they detail the life of Banks from his early youth, to his time of forced assimilation at a government boarding school to his outlook of life when he returned to his homeland. The authors discuss Banks' time in the Air Force and the experiences he had when he returned from service. Banks became instrumental in founding the American Indian Movement because of what he saw on the reservation when he returned from the Air Force and the way his cohorts were treated by white Americans.[673] As with most autobiographies one needs to read the work with reservations. The author is fairly impartial, although his biases filter through, such as, the light in which author casts himself during various events and his interpretation of events. The autobiography is a good source but one that needs to be used in conjunction with other sources.

Kenneth S. Stern's book, *Loud Hawk: The United States Versus the American Indian Movement* details the arrest and thirteen-year trial of Dennis Banks, KaMook, Kenny Loud Hawk, Russell Redner, Anna Mae Aquash, and Leonard Peltier.[674] His book explores the US government's

---

[672] Denis Banks and Richard Erdoes, *Ojibwa Warrior: Dennis Banks and the Rise of the American Indian Movement* (Norman, OK: University of Oklahoma Press, 2005).

[673] Ibid.

[674] Kenneth S. Stern, *Loud Hawk: The United States Versus the American Indian Movement* (Norman, OK: University of

opposition to the American Indian Movement that eventually created Wounded Knee conflict. Stern describes the case from the time he was a law student to when he argued the case in front of the Supreme Court as lead council.[675] The book shows the personalities of those who were involved at Wounded Knee well, and brings to light certain insights into the case.

A source that deals with Indian politics and the abuse of their culture by the US is edited by Daniel M. Cobb and Loretta Fowle and is entitled *Beyond Red Power: American Indian Politics and Activism Since 1900*.[676] The essays cover Indian activism, tribal policy, foundations of federal Indian law, and termination of tribes, along with historical and contemporary evaluation. The text includes the Seminoles, Miamis, Choctaws, Lakotas, and the Ojibwes.[677] The strength of this work is the varied historiography brought together. It is a good addition to the source material for AIM.

Another source, edited by Troy R. Johnson, Joane Nagel, and Duane Champagne is *American Indian Activism: Alcatraz to the Longest Walk*.[678]

Oklahoma Press, 2002).

[675] Ibid.

[676] Daniel M. and Loretta Fowle Cobb, eds., *Beyond Red Power: American Indian Politics and Activism since 1900* (Santa Fe, NM: School for Advanced Research Press, 2007).

[677] Ibid.

[678] Troy R Johnson, Joane Nagel, and Duane Champagne, eds., *American Indian Activism: Alcatraz to the Longest Walk* (Champaign, IL: University of Illinois Press, 1997).

The book is a compilation of articles that are reminiscences of Alcatraz and American Indian activism. Subjects include tribal sovereignty, struggles for liberation and the influence of the federal government. The editors see the occupation of Alcatraz as the beginning of a nine-year period of Red Power and challenges on to the US government.[679] It is filled with excellent sources that give readers a base on which to do further research on the topics of this examination.

There have been long-term effects on tribal sovereignty because of the application of federal and state laws. There have been attacks, not just on sovereignty, but also on cultural distinctives and economic resources. Federal and state laws have caused groups, such as AIM and various Warrior Societies to push back against the prejudice and injustices of the system. These struggles have caused economic deprivation, the occupation of federal land, and even death.

Gaming was one solution to the economic problems on reservations. Originally prevented by federal, state, and local laws, the US Supreme Court sanctioned gambling was sanctioned in 1988 by the US Supreme Court as a product of the recognition tribal sovereignty and economic disadvantages.

The Akwesasne uprising had some similar elements to the AIM struggle and unique in its own way. At Akwesasne, the differences included multiple interactions between the US and Canadian federal governments, state and provincial governments, and the tribal governments. The

---

[679] Ibid.

situation intensified and eventually influenced the Warrior Society and the gaming factions. Circumstances rose to a level that led to violence and deaths during 1989 and 1990.

APPENDIX 2: OTHER SOURCES

This is a list of other sources that can provide a further information on the events before and after 1990 on Akwesasne. This list is by no means exhaustive however it provides a place to do further research.

One Nation under the Gun: Inside the Mohawk Civil War
April 14, 1992
by Rick Hornung

Life and Death in Mohawk Country
May 1, 1993
by Bruce E. Johansen (Author), John Kahionhes Fadden (Illustrator)

History of The St. Regis Akwesasne Mohawks
1947
by Aren [Ray Fadden] Akweks (Author)

St. Regis Tribe of Mohawk Indians, Petitioner, v. State of New York. U.S. Supreme Court Transcript of Record with Supporting Pleadings
October 28, 2011
by Paul F Myers (Author) and Paxton, Blair (Author)

Conflict, Confrontation, and Social Change on the St. Regis Indian Reserve (Applied Anthropology Documentation Project)
1971
by Jack A Frisch (Author)

Mohawk Interruptus: Political Life Across the Border of Settler States
May 9, 2014
By Audra Simpson(Author)

Oka
August 23, 2011
by Harry Swain (Author)

Lasagna: The Man Behind the Mask
2009
Ronald Cross (Author) and Helene Seigny (Author)

BIBLIOGRAPHY

Adams, Jim. "Canadian Supreme Court Reverses Decisions on Duty-Free Mohawk Border Crossing." *Indian Country Today*, June 11, 2001.

Adansun, Lyn and Mary Jo Pellerin. "No Treaties Mentioned in Dispute." *The Globe and Mail*, June 21, 1980, Canada.

Adler, Margo. "Notes from NPR: Akwesasne." ed. Iroquois Museum. Cobleskill, NY, August 6,1980.

Alfred, Taiaiake, Ph.D. and Lana Lowe, M.A. "Warrior Societies in Contemporary Indigenous Communities." A Background Paper Prepared for the Ipperwash Inquiry, University of Victoria, 2005.

Andreae, Dan. "System Theory and Social Work Treatment." In *Social Work Treatment*, ed. Francis J. Turner. New York, N.Y.: The Free Press a Division of Simon and Schuster Inc., 1996.

Anonymous. "Conversation Concerning Smuggling across the St. Lawrence River." ed. E.R. Rugenstein. Knapps Station, Norwood, NY, 2006.

AP. "Mohawk Factions End Tense Armed Face-Off after Arrival of Police." *The New York Times*, June 15, 1980, 1.

"Mohawk Business Call for Resignation of Tribe's Chiefs." *The Post-Standard*, September 26, 1987, 81.

"Slot Machines Seized at Indian Reservation." *The New York Times*, December 17, 1987, 17.

"St. Regis Mohawks, Canadian Guards Clash at Border." *The Post-Standard*, July 24, 1987, B1.

"Indians Block Bridge to U.S. In Dispute over Reservation Raid." *The Associated Press*, October 15, 1988.

"Turtle Symbolizes Tribes' Past and Its Troubled Future." *Journal of Commerce*, February 3, 1988, 1A.

"Bingo Buses Attacked at Indian Reservation." *New York Times*, October 10, 1989, B2.

"Fight on Indian Reservation as Casinos Divide Mohawks." *New York Times*, September 3, 1989, 40.

"Gambling Raids on Indian Land Divide a Tribe." *The New York Times*, July 21, 1989, B1.

"Mohawk Pleads Guilty in Illegal Casino Case." *New York Times*, December 19, 1989, B2.

"Mohawks Insulted by Offer Land Talks Break Down." *The Post Standard*, April 28, 1989, B1.

"Mohawks Protest Reservation Roadblocks." *New York Times*, July 30, 1989, 30.

"Mohawks Vote for Resuming of Gambling at Reservation." *The New York Times*, August 10, 1989, B3.

"Police Removing Roadblocks at Reservation." *The New York Times*, August 1, 1989, B4.

"Reservation Gambling Protest." *New York Times*, September 11, 1989, B4.

"Troopers Back Off, Mohawk Chief Says." *The Post-Standard*, June 4, 1989, D1.

"Casino Supporter Wins Mohawk Council Vote." *New York Times*, June 3, 1990, 36.

"Casino War Foes Agree to Hold Public Meeting." *The Toronto Star*, May 9, 1990, A14.

"Factions Blame Each Other for Bloodshed." *The Post-Standard*, July 12, 1990, A1.

"Gambling Pact Sought for Akwesasne Reserve." *The Toronto Star*, June 29, 1990, A11.

"Gambling Supporter Wins Election as Chief of Embattled Mohawk Tribe." *The Toronto Star*, June 3, 1990, A2.

"Indians Stand Off Troopers after Copter Hit by Shot." *New York Times*, April 1, 1990, 31.

"Mohawk Blames Governor for Strife Suspect Says Tensions Remain High." *The Post-Standard*, September 27, 1990, B1.

"Mohawk Editor Held in Killing." *The New York Times*, May 15, 1990, B4.

"Mulroney Hints at Force against Mohawks." *New York Times*, August 27, 1990, 7.

"N. Y Troopers, 3 Mohawks Hurt in Brawl." *The Toronto Star*, September 16, 1990, A21.

"New York's Official Statement." *The Post-Standard*, May 2, 1990, A6.

"Officer Dies as Mohawks and Quebec Police Clash." *New York Times*, July 12, 1990, A1.

"Police Move onto Mohawk Reservation Cornwall, Ontario." *Hobart Mercury*, May 3, 1990.

"Pro-Gambling Chief Sworn In." *The Toronto Star*, July 3, 1990, A9.

"Quebec Mohawks Keep up Bridge Blockade." *New York Times*, July 16, 1990, 3.

"School Opens after Standoff." *The Buffalo News*, September 17, 1996, A6.

"History of Conflict." *The Associated Press State & Local Wire*, June 5, 2003.

AP-CP. "Mohawks Maintain Blockade at Reserve." *The Toronto Star*, July 22, 1989, A12.

"New Mohawk Police Force Proposed for Reserve." *The Toronto Star*, May 8, 1990, A8.

Appelman, Hilary. "Dispute over Gambling Splits Traditional Mohawk Society." *The Associated Press*, May 5, 1990.

Appleby, Timothy. "Mohawks Want Cuomo to Act in Dispute." *The Globe and Mail*, January 16, 1990.

Armstrong, Jane. "Mohawks Wait out Strife in Government Barracks." *The Toronto Star*, May 6, 1990, A21.

"Police 'Hijack' Oka Talks." *The Toronto Star*, July 22, 1990, A1.

Aubry, Jack. "Court Rejects Native Smuggling Argument; Ruling Sets Precedent: Natives Have No Special Privilege to Bring Cigarettes across Border." *The Ottawa Citizen*, January 26, 1993, A1.

"Mohawk Self-Rule on the Table." *The Ottawa Citizen*, April 7, 1994, A4.

Austen, Ian. "Indians Meet State Envoy as Reserve Tension Eases." *The Globe and Mail*, June 17, 1980, Canada.

"Tribal Ways Rip Indian Family Apart on Reserve." *The Globe and Mail*, June 23, 1980.

"Troopers Keep Peace in Mohawk Dispute." *The Globe and Mail*, June 16, 1980, Canada.

Baker, Geoff. "Native Attack at Akwesasne Leaves Two Policemen Injured." *The Gazette*, November 1, 1991, A1/Front.

Barnsley, Paul. "The Indian Act - Serious Internal Error: Discontinue Use." *Windspeaker* 2003.

Barth, Janis. "Mohawk Land Raided Slot Machines Seized." *The Post Standard*, December 17, 1987, A1.

"Conference to Discuss River Pollution." *The Post-Standard*, March 29, 1988, B3.

"Greenpeace Plan St. Lawrence Pollution Protest." *The Post-Standard*, May 13, 1988, B3.

"Mohawk Chief Arrested During Protest at Canadian Border." *The Post Standard*, March 23, 1988, B1.

"Ogdensburg Waits for Next Boom - History of St. Lawrence River City Has Been Economic Roller Coaster." *The Post Standard*, January 29, 1988, B1.

"Remembering the Days When the St. Lawrence River Was Pure." *Post-Standard*, July 10, 1988, C1.

"Tests Show Akwesasne Laced with PCBs." *The Post-Standard*, May 24. 1988, B1.

"B.I.A. Claims Referendum Has No Clout Lt." *The Post-Standard*, August 9, 1989, B2.

"Mohawk Council Urges Reservation Curfew." *The Post-Standard*, November 29, 1989, B1.

"Reservation Violence Targets Police Patrols." *The Post-Standard*, November 28, 1989, B1.

"Toxic Lesson Taught at Freedom School Mohawks Building New School House Far from Gm Dump." *The Post-Standard*, September 10, 1989, C1.

"A Land Lost, a People in Agony." *The Post-Standard*, April 15, 1990, A11.

Barth, Janis and Elizabeth C. Petros. "Gambling Foes Boycott St. Regis Election 'We're Considering This an Illegal Vote'." *The Post-Standard*, August 8, 1989, B1.

"Pact Would Let Police Resume St. Regis Patrol." *The Post-Standard*, August 8, 1989, B1.

"Indians, Police in Standoff Gambling Raid Met with Force." *The Post-Standard*, July 21, 1989, A1.

Beauchamp, W.M. "Mohawk Notes." *The Journal of American Folklore* 8, no. 30 (1895): 217-221.

"Iroquois Games." *The Journal of American Folklore* 9, no. 35 (1896): 269-277.

"Indian Corn Stories and Customs." *The Journal of American Folklore* 11, no. 42 (1898): 195-202.

Beck, Dr. Donald, Professor and Acting Chair of Native American Studies at the University of Montana. *Technical Assistance on Native American Culture: Improving W.I.P.A. Services to Native American S.S.A. Beneficiaries with Disabilities*. Missoula, Montana: American Indian Disability Technical Assistance Center, 2007, Issues Brief #5.

Belsie, Laurent. "Mohawk Warriors Make Some Native Leaders Uneasy." *Christian Science Monitor*, October 18, 1990, 10.

Benedict, A. L. "Has the Indian Been Misjudged? - a Study of Indian Character." *International Journal of Ethics* 12, no. 1 (1901): 99-113.

Bergman, Brian. "A Book under the Gun: Two Mohawks Attack Retrospective on Oka." *Maclean's*, August 5, 1991, 50.

Biolsi, Thomas. "Bringing the Law Back In: Legal Rights and the Regulation of Indian-White Relations on Rosebud Reservation." *Current Anthropology* 36, no. 4 (1995): 543-571.

Blake, Michael. "Dances with Wolves." ed. Kevin Costner. Los Angeles: Orion, 1990.

Block, Irwin. "Mohawk Activist Hall Dead at 77; Writer Was Considered Warrior Society's 'Ideological Father'." *The Gazette*, December 11, 1993, A8.

Bonaparte, Darren. "Millions of Communist Can't Be Wrong." *The Indian Times*, June 15, 1990, 2.

"Border Crossing Rights." *The Wampum Chronicles: A Website of Mohawk History* 2002, http://www.wampumchronicles.com/bordercrossing.html .

Bond, P. and Timothy Pickering. *Explanatory Article to Article 3 of the Jay Treaty, Signed at Philadelphia May 5, 1796*. Vol. 2 Treaties and Other International Acts of the United States of America: Documents 1-40: 1776-1818, ed. Hunter Miller. Washington: Government Printing Office, 1931.

Bonvillain, Nancy. *Ethnographic Exploratory Research: The Census Process at St. Regis Reservation*. Albany, NY: Research Foundation of the State University of New York at Stonybrook, Sponsored by: Center for Survey Methods Research, 1989, Report # 3.

Boorstin, Robert O. "A Tavern Is Burned to the Ground on an Indian Reservation Upstate." *New York Times*, May 11, 1986, 29.

Boucher, Richard. "State Department Regular Briefing." *Federal Information Systems Corporation, Federal News Service*, May 2, 1990.

Bowen Theory. Bowen Center for the Study of the Family: Georgetown Family Center, 2004. Accessed August 18, 2007. Available from http://www.thebowencenter.org/theory.html.

Bramstedt, Connie. "Chief Says State Exploits St. Regis Gambling Issue." *The Post-Standard*, July 30, 1989, A1.

Brandao, J.A. and William A. Starna. "The Treaties of 1701: A Triumph of Iroquois Diplomacy." *Ethnohistory* 43, no. 2 (1996): 209-244.

Braun, Liz. "Onomsawin at Sundance Filmmaker's Fourth Oka Crisis Film Draws attention." *The Toronto Sun*, January 17, 2001, 5.

Brazao, Dale. "Customs Officers Work under 'Siege' as Indians Linger." *The Toronto Star*, October 16, 1988, A2.

"Outraged Mohawks Block Bridge." *The Toronto Star*, October 15, 1988, A1.

"Dead Man Was on 'Hit List,' Chiefs Claim." *The Toronto Star*, May 4, 1990, A12.

"Give Peace a Chance, Mourners Chant." *The Toronto Star*, May 5, 1990, A3.

"Warriors' Smuggling, Gambling Key to Oka Dispute, Chief Says." *The Toronto Star*, August 24, 1990, A2.

Bremner, Charles and. "Police Step in as Red Indian Feud Kills Two." *The Times*, May 3, 1990.

A Brief History of the O.P.P. Government of Ontario, Canada, 2006. Accessed June 6, 2007. Available from http://www.opp.ca/Recruitment/opp_000580.html.

Brook, Ray. "Troopers Say They Won't Allow Blockades by Casino Opponents." *The Post-Standard*, November 3, 1993, B1.

Bryden, Joan. "Akwesasne Reserve: MP Demands Action on 'Rambo-Style' Military Equipment." *The Ottawa Citizen*, April 28, 1992, A4.

Buckie, Catherine. "Judge Erred, Crown Says in Appealing Mohawks' Acquittal." *The Gazette*, February 25, 1992, A4.

"Warriors Appeal Conviction, Say Judge Misdirected Jury." *The Gazette*, February 21, 1992, A4.

Bureau of American Ethnology, Handbook of American Indians North of Mexico. *Caughnawaga [Now Called Kahnawake]*. L'Encyclopédie de l'histoire du Québec, 2004. Accessed January 31, 2007. Internet. Available from
http://www2.marianopolis.edu/quebechistory/encyclopedia/Caughnawagekahnawake.htm.

Bureau of Indian Affairs. The Columbia Electronic Encyclopedia. © 2000–2007 Pearson Education, publishing as Infoplease.com, 2007. Accessed September 5, 2007. Internet. Available from http://www.infoplease.com/ce6/history/A0825102.html.

Bureau of Indian Affairs: Answers to Frequently Asked Questions.
Bureau of Indian Affairs: Department of the Interior, October 24, 2001. Accessed July 25, 2007. Available from http://usinfo.state.gov/russki/infousa/society/bia.pdf.

Burke, Dan. "An Ancient Warrior Code." *Macleans*, August 6, 1990, 22.

"The Mohawks' War; One Nation under the Gun: Inside the Mohawk Civil War by Rick Hornung (Stoddart, 304 Pages)." *Maclean's*, August 19, 1991, 40.

Burke, Paul. *Treaty with the Seven Nations of Canada*. First People of America and First People of Canada: Turtle Island, Accessed February 9, 2007. Available from http://www.firstpeople.us/FP-Html Treaties/TreatyWithTheSevenNationsOfCanada1796.html.

Burns, John F. "Canada Proposes Settlement in Mohawk Standoff." *The New York Times*, July 29, 1990, 6.

"Mohawks Make a Point: They Are Distinct, Too." *New York Times*, July 14, 1990, 2.

Burns, M.C. "Iroquois Leaders Back Mohawks During UN Meeting in Switzerland." *The Post-Standard*, July 31, 1990, B1.

"Warrior's Words Call for Execution." *The Post Standard*, July 4, 1990, A1.

"Mohawks Open European Office Warrior Society Raises Money in The Hague. Traditional Chiefs Disapprove." *The Post-Standard*, February 3, 1992, C2.

"Once Accused of Murder, an Activist Forges a New Life." *The Post-Standard*, April 2, 1992, B1.

Busatta, Sandra. "The Native American Entrepreneur and the Mohawk Civil War." Università degli Studi di Padova,

Buzan, Barry. *The Concise Oxford Dictionary of Politics*.
New York, N.Y.: Oxford University Press (OUP-USA Dictionaries Program), 2003.

Byrnne, Caroline. "Mohawks May Get Visit by Mandela, Official Says." *The Toronto Star*, July 16 1990, A5.

Callison, James P. *The Iroquois Constitution*. The University of Oklahoma Law Center, 1999. Accessed 2003. Available from www.law.ou.edu.

Calloway, Colin G. *The American Revolution in Indian Country: Crisis and Diversity in Native American Communities*. First ed. Cambridge: Cambridge University Press, 1995.

Came, Barry. "Lasagna Unmasked." *Maclean's*, March 29, 1993, 14.

Canada, Government of. *Canadian Indian Act R.S. 1985 C 1-5*. 2001. Accessed December 31, 2001. Available from http://laws.justice.gc.ca/en/I-5/text.html.

Canada, Minister of Public Works and Government Services. *Indian Populations Projections for Canada and Regions 1998-2008*. Ottawa: Minister of Indian Affairs and Northern Development, 2000, QS-3618-000-BB-A1.

Northern Indicators 2000. Ottawa: Minister of Indian Affairs and Northern Development, 2000, QS-3564-010-BB-A1.

Canadian, Press. "Akwesasne at a Glance." *The Toronto Star*, April 28, 1990, A12.

Canby Jr., William C. *American Indian Law in a Nutshell*. Second ed. St. Paul, Minn.: West Publishing Co., 1981. Reprint, 1988.

Cardozo, Christopher. *Native Nations: First Americans as Seen by Edward S. Curtis*. Boston: Little, Brown and Company, 1993.

Carnegie, Thomas. "Where Have We Failed with Native Peoples?" *The Toronto Star*, October 19, 1988, A26.

"Carrol V. U.S., 267 U.S. 132 (1925)." United States Supreme Court, 1925.

Chamberlain, Alexander F. "American Indian Names of White Men and Women." *The Journal of American Folklore* 12, no. 44 (1899): 24-31.

Champagne, Linda. *Under Fire at Akwesasne*. The Mohawk Nation: New York State Martin Luther King, Jr., Institute for Nonviolence, 1990.

"Cherokee Nation V. The State of Georgia." 30 US 1: US Supreme Court, 1831.

Chiefs, The Onondaga Council of. "We Have Witnessed the Corruption of Young People by These Business." *The Post-Standard*, July 28, 1989, B3.

Chronology of Events During the Oka Crisis. GlobalTV.com Montreal, 2001. Accessed 4 April 2003. Available from http://www.geocities.com/av_team2001/oka.html.

Citizen, News Service. "Around the Nation." *The Ottawa Citizen*, January 7, 1992, A3.

"New York Governor Oks Mohawk Casinos." *The Ottawa Citizen*, October 16, 1993, C2.

Claiborne, William. "Gambling Dispute Makes Reservation a War Zone; Mohawks Battle at U.S.-Canadian Border." *The Washington Post*, April 27, 1990, A37.

"U.S. And Canadian Police Bring Calm to Warring Mohawk Reservation." *The Washington Post*, May 3, 1990, A36.

Clark, Marc and Brenda O'Farrell. "Casinos and Bingo Games Divide Indian Bands." *Maclean's*, September 18, 1989, 21.

"Gambling and Guns." *Maclean's*, September 18, 1989, 21.

Colden, Cadwallader. *The History of the Five Indian Nations of Canada Which Are Dependent on the Province of New York in America*. Second ed. New York: New Amsterdam Book Company, 1902. Reprint, Ithaca: Cornell University Press, 1964.

"The Constitution Act." 1982.

Contenta, Sandro. "Peace Role at Oka Blamed for Loss of Job." *The Toronto Star*, September 15, 1990, A12.

"Single Native Governing Body May Be Solution Officials Say." *The Toronto Star*, May 4, 1990, A12.

"Along for a Ride into Dangerous Waters - Cigarettes from Indian Reserve Smuggled out on Speeding Boats." *The Toronto Star*, August 29, 1992, A2.

"Oka Flare-up Sparks Session on Self-Rule." *Toronto Star*, August 22, 1992, A9.

Countryman, Edward. "Indians, the Colonial Order, and the Social Significance of the American Revolution." *William and Mary Quarterly, Third Series* 53, no. 2 (1996): 342-362.

Cox, Matthew. "Cuomo Willing to Meet with St. Regis Factions." *The Post Standard*, December 21, 1989, B1.

"Federal Mediator Agrees to Help Resolve Tensions at Ganienkeh." *The Post-Standard*, April 4, 1990, B1.

"In St. Regis Strife, Echoes of History." *The Post Standard*, July 10, 1990, A1.

"Mediator Shocked as "Big Bluff" Turns into Deadly Gun Battle." *The Post-Standard*, July 12, 1990, A1.

"Mohawks Oppose Bills on Gaming, Police." *The Post-Standard*, June 30, 1990, B1.

Cox, Matthew and Tom Foster. "Crime Figure Questions Have Followed Munley Operator of Mohawk Bingo Accused of $1.2m Ripoff." *The Post-Standard*, September 26, 1989, A1.

"State, Mohawks Try to Set House Rules for Gambling." *The Post-Standard*, October 25, 1989, A1.

Cox, Matthew, Sean Kirst, and Todd Lighty. "Cuomo Top Aid Ready to Talk with Mohawks." *The Post Standard*, May 8, 1990, B3.

CP. "Cornwall Island Band Files Suit against U.S. Aluminum Firms." *The Globe and Mail*, February 21, 1980, Canada.

"Ottawa Backs Study of St. Regis Band." *The Globe and Mail*, October 31, 1980, Across Canada.

"Band Seeks to Block Reynolds Expansion." *The Globe and Mail*, May 6, 1981.

"Indians Concerned About PCB Threat." *The Globe and Mail*, December 24, 1981, Across Canada.

"Harassment Cited Indians Seek Own Force to Police 3 Communities." *The Globe and Mail*, October 6, 1986, A11.

"Mohawk Band Council Wants OPP Kept Off the Reserve." *The Toronto Star*, October 6, 1986, A7.

"Mohawk Chief Fights for Right to Shop on U.S. Side of Reserve." *The Toronto Star*, November 12, 1987, A7.

"Border Reserve Called Smugglers' Den up to $250 Million of Cigarettes Handled a Year, Newspaper Says." *The Toronto Star*, January 19 1988, G13.

"Border Trial for Mohawk Delayed 1 Year." *The Toronto Star*, April 28. 1988, A7.

"Chief Accuses Customs Officers of Making Racist T-Shirt." *The Toronto Star*, September 18, 1988, A7.

"Customs Wants Probe of Alleged Smugglers." *The Toronto Star*, January 22, 1988, H8.

"Judge Acquits Four Charged in Smuggling." *The Toronto Star*, January 8, 1988, A7.

"Native Tax Row Sparks Threat to Take over Island Bridges." *The Toronto Star*, September 19, 1988, A7.

"Anti-Casino Natives Want to Impeachment of Two Chiefs." *The Toronto Star*, September 8, 1989, H16.

"Armed Indians Blockade New York Highway." *The Toronto Star*, July 21, 1989, A10.

"Customs Officers Threaten Walkout." *The Toronto Star*, October 20, 1989, A12.

"Emergency Declared as Police Leave Reserve." *The Toronto Star*, November 18, 1989, A13.

"Freed Mohawk Casino Owner Must Stay Off Cornwall Reserve." *The Toronto Star*, October 19, 1989, B23.

"Gamblers Boycott Mohawk Meeting." *The Toronto Star*, August 31, 1989, A15.

"Gambling Foes Stage Peaceful Protest." *The Toronto Star*, September 10, 1989, A17.

"Gunshots Cut Power to Mohawk Casinos." *The Toronto Star*, September 11, 1989, A13.

"Indians Take Trailer from Customs Site." *The Toronto Star*, May 10, 1989, A9.

"Mohawk Gambling Row Flares as Gunshots Cut Casinos' Power." *The Toronto*, September 11, 1989, A13.

"Mohawk Indians Battle State Police." *The Toronto Star*, July 25, 1989, A4.

"Mohawk Tribe, NY State Suing Three Us Firms over Pollution." *The Toronto Star*, June 1, 1989, A7.

"Mohawks Oppose Golf Course Plan." *The Toronto Star*, July 31, 1989, A9.

"Mohawks Repel 8 Bingo Buses." *The Toronto Star*, October 16, 1989, A12.

"Mohawks Take Down Roadblocks." *The Toronto Star*, July 24, 1989, A4.

"Mohawks Threaten Fight in Dispute over Gambling." *The Toronto Star*, August 29, 1989, A12.

"Mohawks, Quebec Crees to Sign 'Free-Trade Deal'." *The Toronto Star*, January 5, 1989, A7.

"Mounties Man Border near Reserve." *The Toronto Star*, October 30, 1989, A22.

"Police Leave Mohawk Reserve." *The Toronto Star*, November 17, 1989, A26.

"RCMP Forced from Reserve." *The Toronto Star*, May 25, 1989, A7.

"Residents Vote in Support of Gambling on Reserve." *The Globe and Mail*, August 10, 1989.

"Band Ordered to Remove Barricades Blocking Road." *The Toronto Star*, July 3, 1990, A9.

"Consultants Hired to Heal Mohawks' Deep Splits." *The Record*, October 26, 1990, D6.

"Controversial Mohawk Leader Surrenders to RCMP." *The Toronto Star*, October 2, 1990, A13.

"Election Seen as End of Reserve War." *The Toronto Star*, May 21, 1990, A8.

"Families Flee Reserve under 'Rain of Rocks'." *The Toronto Star*, August 29, 1990, A1.

"Five Charged in Gun Killing at Akwesasne." *The Toronto Star*, May 14, 1990, A5.

"Grenade Wounds Three." *The Toronto Star*, April 24 1990, A2.

"Gunman Opens Fire in Casino on Reserve." *The Toronto Star*, January 14, 1990, A26.

"Gunshots Trigger Akwesasne Fears." *The Toronto Star*, October 24, 1990, D26.

"Kahnawake Tense as Police, Mounties Set to Replace Army." *The Toronto Star*, October 16, 1990, A9.

"Mohawk Editor Cleared of Murder Charge." *The Toronto Star*, November 2, 1990, A15.

"Mohawk Murder Charge Laid Staunch Opponent of Reserve Casinos Pleads Not Guilty." *The Toronto Star*, May 15, 1990, A12.

"Mohawk Victim Was Innocent Bystander." *The Toronto Star*, May 7, 1990, A8.

"Mohawk Warriors Vow They'll Oust Chiefs." *The Toronto Star*, May 9, 1990, A14.

"Mohawks Blockade Casino Roads." *The Toronto Star*, March 25, 1990, A11.

"Mohawks Refused to End Blockade." *The Globe and Mail*, July 9, 1990.

"Murder Charge Laid in Reserve Shooting." *The Toronto Star*, May 15, 1990, A4.

"Pro-Gambler Faces Weapons Charge." *The Toronto Star*, May 27, 1990, A7.

"Quebec Offers to Reopen Talks with Mohawks." *The Toronto Star*, July 24, 1990, A9.

"Shootout Heightens Tensions on Reserve." *The Toronto Star*, January 15, 1990, A2.

"Talk Begin with Mohawks as Barricade Tensions Grow." *The Toronto Star*, July 10, 1990, G10.

"Who's Who in Native Fort." *The Toronto Star*, September 11, 1990, A8.

"Akwesasne Re-Elects Anti-Gambling Chief." *The record*, June 24, 1991, B3.

"Armed RCMP Accused of Terrorizing Children." *The Toronto Star*, April 30, 1991, A26.

"Mohawks Set to Negotiate Self-Government." *Toronto Star*, December 15, 1991, A12.

"Rae 'Determined' to Push for Self-Rule at Akwesasne." *The Toronto Star*, January 21, 1991, A10.

"Warriors Tried to Provoke Attack, Oka Report Says." *The Toronto Star*, June 23, 1991, A8.

"Akwesasne Mohawks Finally Bury the Hatchet." *Toronto Star*, January 9, 1992, A9.

"Mohawks to Boycott Constitutional Vote." *The Toronto Star*, September 25, 1992, A14.

"$1.5 Million for Oka Mohawks." *Hamilton Spectator*, March 30, 1993, A2.

"Mohawk Chief Assails Mayor of Cornwall." *The Financial Post*, November 26, 1993, 39.

"Mohawks Threaten to Sue Cuomo." *The Financial Post*, August 12, 1993, 5.

"Mohawks Set up Police Force at Oka, Defy Provincial Police (Chiefs from Kahnawake, Akwesasne and Kanasatake)." *Canadian Business and Current Affairs*, November 18, 1994.

"Pollution Changes Mohawk Way of Life." *Canadian Business and Current Affairs*, July 5, 1994.

"St. Lawrence Cleanup to Begin This Month." *The Record*, September 12, 1994, A9.

"Concern Raised over St Lawrence River Cleanup." *Canadian Business and Current Affairs* 1995.

"RCMP Beefs up Quebec Border Patrol." *Canadian Business and Current Affairs*, June 12, 1995.

"Court Backs Quebec Native Rights (at Akwesasne Reserve and Maniwaki)." *Canadian Business and Current Affairs*, October 3, 1996.

"Mohawks Go to Court for Right to Cross Border without Paying Duty." *Canadian Business and Current Affairs*, September 29, 1996.

"Three Mohawk Bands Sign Policing Deal (at Kanesatake)." *Canadian Business and Current Affairs*, June 13. 1996.

"Courts Grants Akwesasne Mohawks Duty-Free Status [Federal Court of Appeal]." *Canadian Business and Current Affairs*, July 1, 1997.

"RCMP Aids Us Authorities in Smuggling Investigation [Operation Orienteer]." *Canadian Business and Current Affairs*, July 20, 1997.

"High Court to Hear Border Crossing Case." *Canadian Business and Current Affairs*, October 16, 1999.

CP-AP. "Power Cut, Mohawks Say Reserve 'Lawless'." *The Toronto Star*, August 29, 1989, E20.

CP-Staff. "Indians Vow Revenge after Massive Raid on Mohawk Reserve." *The Toronto Star*, October 14, 1988, A5.

"Police Arrest 7, Seize $200,000 in Illegal Goods in Reserve Raid." *The Toronto, Star*, October 14, 1988, A7.

"Mohawk Indians Trash Casino in Bid to Eliminate Gambling." *The Toronto Star*, June 7, 1989, A31.

"Emergency Talks Set to Quell Native Violence." *The Toronto Star*, May 2, 1990, A3.

"Police Officer Is Shot Dead in Gun Battle with Mohawks." *The Toronto Star*, July 11, 1990, A1.

Craig, Jon. "St. Regis Fracas Cost Taxpayers $630,000 State's Expense Will Go Higher When Troopers' Salaries Are Added In." *The Post-Standard*, May 29, 1990, A1.

Crawford, Neta C. "A Security Regime among Democracies: Cooperation among the Iroquois Nations." *International Organization* 48, no. 3 (1994): 345-385.

Cross, Ronald and Héléne Sévigny. *Lasagna: The Man Behind the Mask*. Vancouver: Talon books, 1994.

Cross, Whitney R. *The Burn-over District: The Social and Intellectual History of Enthusiastic Religion, 1800-1850*. Ithaca: Cornell University Press, 1982. Reprint, First Paperback edition.

Curran, Peggy, and Michelle LaLonde."Governments Fear Warriors Tory MP Says." *The Gazette*, November 26, 1991, A7.

D'Arcy, McNickle Center for the History of the American Indian. *The History and Culture of Iroquois Diplomacy: An Interdisciplinary Guide to the Treaties of the Six Nations and Their League*, ed. Francis Jennings, William N. Fenton, Mary A. Druke, and David R. Miller. Syracuse, NY: Syracuse University Press, 1995.

Davis, Barbara A. *Edward S. Curtis: The Life and Times of a Shadow Catcher*. San Francisco: Chronicle Books, 1985.

Davis, Matt. "Indians Buy Assault Rifles: "They're Having a War Down There"." *The Post-Standard*, May 3, 1990, A8.

Deloria, Jr., Vine. *American Indian Policy in the Twentieth Century*. Norman, OK: University of Oklahoma, 1992.

Derfel, Aaron. "Mohawk Sues Surete for His Murder Arrest after Akwesasne War; Anti-Gambling Editor Says Police Went after Him Because of Tip from Warriors." *The Gazette*, March 8, 1995, A4.

Derfel, Aaron, and Elizabeth Thompson. "No Raid Coming, Edgy Mohawks Told; Kanesatake Chief Says He Fears Army Invasion in a Few Days." *The Gazette*, February 16, 1994, A1/Front.

Dickson-Gilmore, E. Jane. ""This Is My History, I Know Who I Am": History, Factionalist, Competition, and the Assumption of Imposition in the Kahnawake Mohawk Nation." *Ethnohistory* 46, no. 3 (1999): 429-450.

Dimmock, Gary. "Running Human Cargo: Akwesasne Indian Reserve, Which Straddles the St. Lawrence and the Canada-U.S. Border, Has Long Been a Smuggler's Paradise for Moving Guns and Drugs. Nowadays, However, Smugglers Are Cashing in on a New Trade: Migrants from China and Pakistan." *The Ottawa, Citizen*, September 18, 1999, B4.

Dippie, Brian W. *The Frederic Remington Art Museum Collection*. Ogdensburg, NY: Frederic Remington Art Museum, 2000.

Dixon, Alan. *Barricades at Akwesasne*. Peace and Environment News, May 1990. Accessed April 6, 2003. Available from http://www.perc.ca/PEN/1990-05/dixon.html.

Doran, Kwinn H. "Ganienkeh: Haudenosaunee Labor-Culture and Conflict Resolution." *The American Indian Quarterly* vol. 26, no. 1 (2002`): 1-23.

Doyle, Patrick. "Mob Protesting Native Blockade Battles Police." *The Toronto Star*, August 13, 1990, A1.

"Mohawks Bury Dead but Not the Hatchet." *The Independent*, May 8, 1990, 12.

"Mohawks Wait in Fear 'Sure We're Scared,' Warriors Say." *The Toronto Star*, July 13, 1990, A1.

"PM Wants Probe of 'Disgraceful' Riot 'Racism at Any Time Is an Evil,' He Says." *The Toronto Star*, August 30, 1990, A2.

"RCMP Defends Officers' Action at Mercier Riot." *The Toronto Star*, November 8, 1990, A13.

"Tear Gas Fired Again in Skirmish at Bridge." *The Toronto Star*, August 14, 1990, A8.

"Tensions Boil over at Mercier Barricades." *The Toronto Star*, July, 18 1990, A1.

Duffy, Lori. "Trooper Hit with Lead Pipe at St. Regis." *The Post-Standard*, November 10, 1992, A5.

Dunn, Kate. "Tensions Have Eased in Kanesatake: Chief; He Says Surete Patrols Are Keeping Away from Two Sensitive Areas." *The Gazette*, August 24, 1992, A3.

Dunn, Shirley W. *The Mohicans and Their Land 1609-1730*. Fleischmanns: Purple Mountain Press, 1994. Reprint, 1995.

Editor. "Natives Simmer on the Backburner." *The Toronto Star*, October 19, 1988, A26.

"Mohawk Standoff Sovereignty Not a Sometime Thing." *The Post-Standard*, July 27, 1989, A10.

"Akwesasne." *The Toronto Star*, May 3, 1990, A26.

"The Mohawk Defense of Kanasetake (Aka Oka, Quebec, Canada)." *The Edmonton Journal*, May 6, 1991, Editorial.

"Mohawk Unease If the State Gives Them a Chance, the St. Regis Population Will Have a Big Decision to Make." *The Post-Standard*, May 13, 1991, Editorial Page.

"Mohawks Were Protecting Selves." *The Gazette*, December 12, 1993, B3.

"One Law - for All!" *The Toronto Star*, February 6, 1994, C1.

Editorial, Windsor Star. "Supreme Court Ruling a Victory for Fairness and Equality Among All Canadians." *The Guardian*, May 30, 2001, A7.

Egan, Kelly. "Akwesasne's Economic Savior: Casinos Used to Cause Fighting in the Streets. Now Mohawks Are Counting on a New Casino to Bring Prosperity." *The Ottawa Citizen*, January 18, 1999, A5.

Engelbrecht, William. "The Iroquois: Archaeological Patterning on the Tribal Level." *World Archaeology* 6, no. 1, Political System (1974): 52-65.

Esch, Mary. "The Mohawks Call Their Homeland Akwesasne, "Land Where the Partridge Drums." It's a 25-Square-Mile Reservation Spanning the St. Lawrence River, a Place Where They Once Could Hunt and Fish for Food. Today the White Man's Chemicals Have Poisoned Akwesasne and the Mohawk Way of Life Is in Peril." *From the Associated Press News features*, January 24, 1988.

Faber, Harold. "New York Returning Wampum Belts to Onondagas." *New York Times*, August 13, 1989, 39.

Fadden, John. *Divisiveness at Akwesasne: Legacy of 19th Century Colonialism*. The Mohawk Nation of Akwesasne, 2002. Accessed 28 August 2002. Available from http://www.peacetree.com/akwesasne/division.htm.

Farnsworth, Clyde H. "Cornwall Journal: In Dodge City East, Cigarette Wars and Shootouts." *The New York Times*, January 1, 1994, 4.

Fein, Esther B. "Indians' Rage at Illegal Bar Fuels Upstate Fire." *New York Times*, May 12, 1986, A1.

Felson, Richard B. ""Kick'em When They're Down": Explanations of the Relationship between Stress and Interpersonal Aggression and Violence." *The Sociological Quarterly* 33, no. 1 (1992): 1-16.

Ferguson, Jonathan. "Mohawk Reserve Perfect Global Banking Centre MP Proposes." *The Toronto Star*, December 2, 1987, F1.

and David Vienneau. "Leaders to Discuss Joint Police Force." *The Toronto Star*, May 3, 1990, A14.

Fine, Thomas. "Canada Pressures Cuomo on St. Regis." *The Post-Standard*, April 27, 1990, A1.

"Chief: Troopers Ignoring St. Regis Gunplay." *The Post-Standard*, January 30, 1990, B1.

"Driver Runs into Trooper. Flees to Reservation." *The Post-Standard*, April 3,
1990, B1.

"Police Seal Off St. Regis after 2 Mohawks Slain, Troopers Search for Snipers." *The Post-Standard*, May 2, 1990, A1.

"Reservation Quiet, Open to Traffic During Weekend." *The Post Standard*, March 12 1990, B1.

"St. Regis Head Chief Asks Buh for Help." *The Post Standard*, March 13, 1990, A1.

"St. Regis Policing Priced at $630,000." *The Post-Standard*, May 30, 1990, B1.

"Threats, Tensions, Escalate on Reservation Gambling Issue Puts St. Regis on 'Red Alert'." *The Post Standard*, March 27, 1990, B1.

and Sean Kirsst. "2 Victims Differed in Views of Dispute." *The Post-Standard*, May 2, 1990, A4.

Fiss, Tanis. *Analysis of the First Nations Fiscal and Statistical Management Act*. Victoria, BC: Center for Aboriginal Policy Change, 2003.

Ford, Tom. "Power Smokescreen: The Fight over Cigarette Smuggling Is a Fight over Sovereignty." *The Record*, February 15, 1994, A7.

Foster, Tom. "Firm Sues State for Seizing Slots." *The Post-Standard*, September 27, 1989, B1.

"Police Car Hit by Shots at Regis." *The Post-Standard*, November 3, 1989, B1.

"I.R.S. Slaps $2.4m Tax Lien on Casino Owner." *The Post Standard*, February 6, 1990, B1.

"Warrior Society's Militant Message Splits Iroquois Traditionalists." *The Post-Standard*, July 9. 1990, A1.

Frechette, Wayne C. "Action at Cornwall Features Cigarettes, Cocaine and Guns." *Canadian Business and Current Affairs*, January 1994, 32-33.

Friedman, Edwin H., Dr. *A Failure of Nerve: Leadership in the Age of the Quick Fix*. Bethesda, Maryland: The Edwin Friedman Estate/Trust, 1999.

From Revolution to Reconstruction - an .HTML project. *The Jay Treaty, 1794: Treaty of Amity, Commerce, and Navigation*. The Solon Law Archive-Canadian Constitutional Documents, April 18, 2003. Accessed December 12, 2006. Available from http://odur.let.rug.nl/~usa/D/1776-1800/foreignpolicy/jay.htm#IIIexp.

Gaines, Judith. "Lure of Wealth Divides Mohawks." *The Boston Globe*, August 16, 1989, 3.

GAM. "Troopers Leave Reservation." *The Globe and Mail*, August 29, 1979.

Gamble, David. "Send in Troops, Hanger Urges." *The Toronto Sun*, October 5, 1996, 2.

Garnnett, Henry. "The Mapping of New York State." *Journal of the American Geographic Society of New York* 27, no. 1 (1895): 21-29.

Gaudette, Michel. "Wrong to Depict Quebec as Anti-Native." *The Toronto Star*, September 25, 1991, A24.

George-Kanentiio, Doug. "How Much Land Did the Iroquois Possess?" *Akwesasne Notes New Series*, Fall - October/November/December 1995, 60.

"First of May Stirs Powerful Memories for Mohawk People." *The Post-Standard*, May 5, 1996, Editorial.

Aim: Make Peace with the Spirits. News From Indian Country, 2002. Accessed January 31, 2007. Internet. Available from http://www.indiancountrynews.com/aim.cfm.

George-Kanentiio, Douglas M. "Struggle at Akwesasne Mohawks Need Time to Heal Wounds." *The Post-Standard*, April 23, 1990, A9.

George-Kanentilo, Doug. "Dispute Simmers as Mohawks Oppose Gaming Compact." *The Post-Standard*, November 21, 1993, AA5.

Gerew, Gary. "Mohawk Freed after 11 Days without Bail Judge Finds No Evidence of Danger." *The Post-Standard*, August 1, 1989, B1.

Getches, David H., Daniel M. Rosenfelt, and Charles F. Wilkinson. *Cases and Materials on Federal Indian Law,* American Casebook Series. St. Paul, Minn: West Publishing Company, 1979.

Ghobahy, Omar Z. *The Caughnawaga Indians and the St Lawrence Seaway*. New York: The Devin-Adair Company, 1961.

Goad, G. Pierre. "Gambling Dispute Take Violent Turn at Indian Reserve." *Wall Street Journal*, September 15, 1989, 8.

Godfrey, John. "Mohawk Unrest Obscures Native Entrepreneurship." *The Financial*, May 4. 1990, 9.

Goldstein, Lorrie. "Warriors? No Thugs." *Toronto Sun*, February 8, 1994, 12.

Gordon, Bernard and Julian Hulevy. "Custer of the West." ed. Robert Siodmak. Bruxelles: Cinerama International, 1968.

Gormley, Michael. "Mohawks Find Peace, Wonder If It's for Real." *The Times Union*, April 23. 1995, A1.

Gorrie, Peter. "Mohawk Fishing Policy Sparks Anger in Cornwall." *The Toronto Star*, July 24, 1991, A10.

Gras, Joseph. *The Catholic Encyclopedia*. Vol. III. New York: Robert Appleton Company, 1908.

Graymont, Barbara. *The Iroquois in the American Revolution*. First Paperback ed. Syracuse, NY: Syracuse University Press, 1972.

Great Lakes Water Quality Agreement. Environmental Canada, December 12, 2006. Accessed January 31, 2007. Available fromhttp://www.on.ec.gc.ca/greatlakes/default.asp?lang=En&n=FD65DFE5-1.

Grey, Zane. "Fighting Caravan." ed. Otto Brewer, David Burton. Hollywood: Paramount, 1931.

Grey, Zane, Ethel Doherty, and Lucien Hubbard. "The Vanishing American." ed. George B. Seitz. Hollywood: Paramount, 1926.

Grinde, Jr., Donald A. and Bruce F. Johnson. "Sauce for the Goose: Demand and Definitions for 'Proof' Regarding the Iroquois and Democracy." *William and Mary Quarterly* 53, no. 3, Indian and Others in Early America (1996): 621-636.

Haan, Richard. "The Problem of Iroquois Neutrality: Suggestions for Revision." *Ethnohistory* 27, no. 4, Special Iroquois Issue (1980): 317-330.

Hall, Louise. *Biography: Louis Karoniaktajeh Hall*. Hall, Louise, August 1, 2003. Accessed January 20, 2007. Available from http://louishall.com/bio/hisstory.html.

Hall, Tex. "Opposition to Department of Interior Proposed Legislation That Provides an Offer of Total Settlement to Individual Tribal Members Regarding Mismanagement of Individual Indian Money Accounts by the United States: Resolution #Sd-02-069." In *National Conference of American Indians*, ed. Juana Majel. San Diego, California: Washington, D.C: NCAI Headquarters, 2002.

Hauptman, Laurence M. *The Iroquois Struggle for Survival: World War II to Red Power*. Syracuse: Syracuse University Press, 1986.

Formulating American Indian Policy in New York State 1970-1986. Albany, NY: State University of New York Press, 1988.

The Iroquois and the New Deal. Syracuse: Syracuse University Press, 1988.

"Iroquois Land Issues: At Odds with the "Family of New York"." In *Iroquois Land Claims*, ed. Christopher Vecsey and William A. Starna, 67-86. Syracuse: Syracuse University Press, 1988.

The Iroquois in the Civil War. Syracuse: Syracuse University Press, 1993.

Henson, C.L. *From War to Self-Determination: A History of the Bureau of Indian Affairs*. American Studies Resources Centre, Aldham Robarts Centre, Liverpool John Moores University, Mount Pleasant, Liverpool, United Kingdom, 1996. Accessed July 10, 2007. Internet. Available from
http://www.americansc.org.uk/Online/indians.htm.

Henton, Darcy. "4 Mohawks Hurt in Clash as Anger Boils Over." *The Toronto Star*, April 27, 1990, A1.

"500 Mohawks Waiting Off Reserve Amid Peace Talks in Casino War." *The Toronto Star*, May 1, 1990, A2.

"Akwesasne Wounds Won't Heal Soon." *The Toronto Star*, May 13, 1990, B1.

"Anti-Casino Mohawks Vow to Resolve Reserve War Alone Reserve Becomes War Zone over Gambling." *The Toronto Star*, April 29, 1990, A1.

"Border Reserve's Gambling Crisis Turning into War." *The Toronto Star*, January 16, 1990, A8.

"Don't Allow Casinos at Akwesasne, N.Y. State Warned." *The Toronto Star*, October 16, 1990, A9.

"Gambling Feud Puts Indians on Brink of War." *The Toronto Star*, January 20, 1990, A2.

"Guns Silent but the Fury Remains Mohawks' Gambling War About Power and Money." *The Toronto Star*, May 5, 1990, D7.

"Indians Reject Quebec's Offer for New Talks." *The Toronto Star*, July 24, 1990, A9.

"Indians Stake Their Claim to Quebec 'If They (Quebecers) Want to Pull out with 15 Per Cent of the Land, We'll Let Them Go'." *The Toronto Star*, July 21, 1990, D1.

"Mohawk Leaders Fear Deaths in Gambling Feud." *The Toronto Star*, January 17, 1990, A2.

"Mohawks Flee Border Reserve to Escape Gambling Showdown." *The Toronto star*, April 28, 1990, A1.

"Mohawks in 9-Hour Gunfight on Reserve." *The Toronto Star*, May 1, 1990, A1.

"The Oka Standoff: Mohawk Warriors - Self-Described Freedom Fighters – Have Taken Control. Heroes to Some, Others Call Them a Brainwashing Cult." *The Toronto Star*, August 19, 1990, B1.

"Police Enforce Uneasy Peace on Reserve." *The Toronto Star*, May 3, 1990, A14.

"Police Restore Calm on Mohawk Reserve." *The Toronto Star*, May 2, 1990, A1.

"Single Government Urged for Akwesasne Reserve." *The Toronto Star*, October 17, 1990, A12.

"Two Mohawks Shot Dead in Casino War on Reserve Police Asked to Stop Gun Battles." *The Toronto Star*, May 2, 1990, A1.

"Uneasy Calm Falls on Reserve." *The Toronto Star*, April 30, 1990, A9.

"War over Gambling Heats Up Elderly Mohawks Rescued by Boat." *The Toronto Star*, April 27, 1990, A4.

"Akwesasne Fears Violence over Crucial Ballot Today." *The Toronto Star*, July 22, 1991, A11.

"Mohawks Owe Millions in Tax U.S. Revenue Collector Claims." *The Toronto Star*, September 18, 1991, A2.

"Noble Savage Image Self-Serving and Naive." *The Toronto Star*, December 17, 1994, J20.
and Dale Brazao. "Show of Force Halts Gambling War." *The Toronto Star*, May 3, 1990, A1.

Hill, Mike. "Reservation Feud over Gambling Turns Deadly." *The Associated Press*, May 1, 1990.

Hoel, Helge, Kate Sparks, and Cary L. Cooper. *The Cost of Violence/Stress-Free Working Environment*. Geneva: University of Manchester Institute of Science and Technology.

Hopkins, Grant. "Anglers Caught up in Fish War." *The Ottawa Citizen*, August 4, 1991, E6.

Hornung, Rick. *One Nation under the Gun: Inside the Mohawk Civil War*. New York: Pantheon, 1991.

"How Iroquois Confederacy Chiefs Conspired against Mohawk During the Oka Crisis, 1990: Afterward." *Mohawk Nation News* 1997, mohawkns@cyberglobe.net.

Howard, Burt. "Draft of Testimony on the Crisis at Akwesasne for Public Hearing in Albany on 8/2/90." ed. Iroquois Museum. Cobleskill, NY, August 31,1990.

Indian Gaming Regulatory Act. Public Law 100-497. U.S. 100th Congress, October 17, 1988. Accessed September 25, 2007. Available from: http://www.nigc.gov/LawsRegulations/IndianGamingRegulatoryAct/tabid/605/Default.aspx.

IPN. "Akwesasne Notes Loses Office." *Daybreak*, Winter 1988.

"State Police Confiscate Slot Machines from Akwesasne." *Daybreak*, Winter 1988.

The Iroquois Constitution. The University of Oklahoma Law Center, 26 February 1999. Accessed 27 October 2002. web. Available from http://www.law.ou.edu.

James, Rebecca. "Police, Indians Injured in Fight at St. Regis." *The Post-Standard*, September 16, 1990, D1.

James, Robert P. "Amid High Hopes and Ice Flows, St. Lawrence Seaway Opens Season." *Traffic World*, April 6, 1992, 34.

Jay, John. *The Jay Treaty; November 19, 1794*. Vol. 2 Treaties and Other International Acts of the United States of America: Documents 1-40: 1776-1818, ed. Hunter Miller. Washington: Government Printing Office, 1931.

Jemisom, G. Peter. "Sovereignty and Treaty Rights – We Remember." *Akwesasne Notes New Series* 1995, 10-15.

Johansen, Bruce. *Akwesasne's Toxic Turteles*. Clear Light Publications, January 9, 2000. Accessed January 17, 2007. Available from http://www.tuscaroras.com/graydeer/pages/Toxicturtle1.htm.

Johansen, Bruce E. *Life and Death in Mohawk Country*. Golden, Colorado: North American Press, 1993.

"The Mohawks Still Face the Very Large Task of Healing the Wounds of Their Community: Akwesasne's Bitter Harvest." *The Ottawa Citizen*, May 5, 1993, A11.

Johnston, David. "Jury Duty Calls 2,500; Pool to Choose 12 for Mohawks' Trial Is Biggest in Country's History: Lawyer." *The Gazette*, January 13, 1992, A1/Front.

Jussim, Estelle. *Frederic Remington, the Camera & the Old West* Anne Burnett Tandy Lectures in American Civilization. No. 3. Fort Worth, Tex.: Amon Carter Museum, 1983.

Kane, Dan. "Casino Owner Gets 21 Months in Prison." *The Post Standard*, February 28, 1990, B3.

"Defender of Sovereignty Convicted Mohawk Activist Gracefully Accepts Federal Court Verdict." *The Post Standard*, April 11, 1990, B1.

"Mohawk Activist Goes to Trial." *The Post Standard*, February 15, 1990, B1.

and Elizabeth C. Petros. "Both Sides Say the Law Backs Them in Dispute." *The Post-Standard*, July 27. 1989, A8.

"Mohawks Claiming Brutality 11 Hurt in St. Regis Clash." *The Post-Standard*, July 25, 1989, A1.

Kappler, Charles J., ed. *United States V Mrs. P.L. Garrow (No. 4081)*. Vol. V Indian Affairs: Laws and Treaties, Part V: Important Court Decisions on Tribal Rights and Property. Washington: Government Printing Office, 1941.

Karon, Dan. "Akwesasne Casino May Re-Open; Large Establishment Was at Centre of 1990 Battle over Gambling." *The Ottawa Citizen*, July 9, 1991, C3.

"Mohawks Suspend Enforcement of Akwesasne Fishing Rules." *The Ottawa Citizen*, August 1, 1991, F3.

"Mohawks Threaten Blockade; Bridge Congestion Prompts Renewed Threat at Cornwall." *The Ottawa Citizen*, August 29, 1991, B4.

"Chief Seeks Probe by International Forces into Casino-War Slayings." *The Ottawa Citizen*, January 8, 1992, B2.

"Mohawk Refusal to Collect GST Delays Opening of Akwesasne Shopping Plaza." *The Ottawa Citizen*, July 16, 1992, B4.

Kates, William. "F.B.I. And State Police Raid Indian Gambling Casinos." *The Associated Press*, July 21, 1989.

"Government Says Warrior Leader Would Renew Reservation Tension If Released." *The Associated Press*, July 27, 1989.

"Violence Grows on Indian Nation Divided by Gambling." *The Associated Press*, September 2, 1989.

"As It Turns 40, St. Lawrence Seaway Now Just Part of the Neighborhood." *The Associated Press State & Local Wire*, April 4, 1999.

Kaufman, Michael T. "To the Mohawk Nation, Boundaries Do Not Exist." *The New York Times*, April 13, 1984, A2.

Kelsay, Isabel Thompson. *Joseph Brant 1743-1807: Man of Two Worlds*. First ed. Syracuse: Syracuse University Press, 1984. Reprint, 1986.

Kerr, Kathleen B., M.S.N., M.A. "An Overview of Bowens Theory." In *Understanding Organizations: Application of Bowen Family Systems Theory*, ed. Ruth Riley Sagar and Kathleen Klaus Wiseman. Washington D.C.: Georgetown University Family Center, 1982.

Killian, Michaell. "Cost of Indian Unrest Flares to $1.5 Million." *The Post-Standard*, September 21, 1989, B1.

"State Police Presence Debated." *The Post-Standard*, July 28, 1989, A8.

Kilpatrick, Jaquelyn. *Celluloid Indians: Native Americans and Films*. Lincoln: University of Nebraska Press, 1999.

Kirst, Sean. "Delicate Truce Is Threatened, Warriors Dislike Police Presence." *The Post-Standard*, May 9, 1990, B2.

"Delicate Truce Is Threatened Warriors Dislike Police Presence." *The Post-Standard*, May 9, 1990, B2.

"Iroquois Body Seeks Probe of Mohawk Chiefs." *The Post-Standard*, May 26, 1990, B1.

"Mohawks Negotiating Casino's Reopening." *The Post-Standard*, July 3, 1991, B1.

and Barbara Stith. "Gambling Factions Accused Each Other." *The Post-Standard*, May 2, 1990, A4.

Klein, Milton M. *The Empire State: A History of New York*. Ithaca: Cornell University Press, 2001.

Kopvillem, Peter, and Greg W. Taylor. "Tribal Warfare." *Mclean's*, May 14. 1990, 14.

Ann McLaughlin, and Dan Burke. "Fury in the Rank." *Maclean's*, August 6, 1990, 24.

Kotcheff, Tim. "CTV Report on Akwesasne Was Factual." *The Toronto Star*, May 6, 1990, B2.

Krims, Milton and Murice Geraghty. "Mohawk." ed. Kurt Neuman. Beverly Hills: Fox, 1956.

Kriss, Erik. "The Blockade's Other Cost." *The Post-Standard*, August 1, 1989, A4.

"Troopers' Overtime Soaring Violence Is Long over, but State Police Still at St. Regis." *The Post-Standard*, August 4, 1991, A1.

La Sûreté Du Québec: Organisation - Quatre Grandes Fonctions. La Sûreté du Québec, April 10, 2006. Accessed June 5, 2007. Available from http://www.suretequebec.gouv.qc.ca/.

LaLonde, Michelle. "Finances Far from Sound at Mohawk Radio Station." *The Gazette*, December 4, 1992, A1/Front.

"Man Might Have to Sue Minister to Get Full Information on Oka Cost." *The Gazette*, March 4, 1993, A4.

Landsman, Gail. "Ganienkeh: Symbol and Politics in an Indian/White Conflict." *American Anthropologist* 87, no. 4 (1985): 826-839.

and Sara Ciborski. "Representation and Politics: Contesting Histories of the Iroquois." *Cultural Anthropology* 7, no. 4 (1992):425-447.

Sovereignty and Symbol: Indian-White Conflict at Ganienkeh. Albuquerque: University of New Mexico Press, 1988.

Larrabee, John. "Mohawks Divided over Casinos; Debate Rages as Trial Starts; Details About Reservation." *USA Today*, December 15, 1989, 8A.

Lavigne, Yves. "Us Court Upholds Indian Band's Right to Sue Metals Firms." *The Globe and Mail*, April 17, 1981, Canada.

Laxer, James. *Protesters and Police at Akwesasne.* Web Accessed 6 April 2003. Available from http://www.jameslaxer.com/proteste.htm.

Lehman, J. David. "The End of the Iroquois Mystique: The Oneida Land Cession Treaties of the 1780s." *William and Mary Quarterly, Third Series* 47, no. 4 (1990): 523-547.

Lichfield, John. "Mohawks Go to War over Bingo." *The Independent*, April 29, 1990, 10.

Lighty, Todd. "Seizure of Camp Led to Ganienkeh Cuomo Negotiated End to Moss Lake Standoff." *The Post Standard*, March 31, 1990, A1.

Little Turtle, Jimmy, Tom Porter, and Barbara Barnes. "News Releases." Rooseveltown, NY: Akwesasne Notes, 1990.

Lloyd, T.G.B. "On the "Beothucs," a Tribe of Red Indians, Supposed to Be Extinct, Which Formerly Inhabited Newfoundland." *The Journal of the Anthropological Institute of Great Britain and Ireland* 4 (1875): 21-39.

Loewen, James Henry. *Lies across America: What Our History Sites Get Wrong*. New York: The New Press, 1999.

Lorch, Donatella. "Behind Violence, Tensions Roil Mohawks." *New York Times*, April 30, 1990, B1.

Ludtke, Jean E. "Mashpee: Town or Tribe? - Current Wampanoag Land Claims Suit." *American Anthropologist* 80, no. 2 (1978): 377-379.

Lyman, Christopher M. *The Vanishing Race and Other Illusions: Photographs of Indians By Edward S. Curtis*. New York: Pantheon Books, 1982.

Lyons, Oren, "Haudenosaunee Faithkeeper, Chief Oren Lyons Addressing Delegates to the United Nations Organization." In *the Year of the Indigenous Peoples*, 3. United Nations General Assembly Auditorium, United Nations Plaza, New York City: Craig Carpenter, Hoopa, CA, 1992.

Lyons, Oren, Vine Deloria, Jr. and Robert Venables. *Exiled in the Land of the Free – Democracy, Indian Nations, and the Us Constitution*: Clear Light Publishers, 1992.

MacDonald, Bob. "Problem Allowed to Fester." *The Toronto Star*, February 6, 1994, 8.

MacEachern, Rosalie. "Mohawk Council Angry with Ruling That Nullifies Last Summer's Election." *The Toronto Star*, May 8, 1987, A7.

"Mohawk Chief Faces Charge in Border Protest." *The Toronto Star*, March 23, 1988, A27.

Macleod, Ian. "Oka's Legacy; Two Years Later, Life Is Even Worse." *The Ottawa Citizen*, September 26, 1992, A1.

MacPherson, Don. "Police Role in La Salle Disgrace Chilling." *The Toronto Star*, August 31, 1990, A15.

Mann, Michael, Christopher Crowe, and Philip Dunne. "The Last of the Mohicans." ed. Michael Mann. Beverly Hills: Fox, 1992.

Map Data © 2007, NAVTEQ. *Ganienkeh*. Mapquest, 2007. Accessed September 21, 2007. internet.

Maraclle, Brian. "Sovereignty Is Solution to Strife at Akwesasne." *The Toronto Star*, May 7, 1990, A17.

"A Community's Slow Simmer." *Maclean's*, September 11, 1995, 32.

Marsden, William. "Tobacco Council Targeted in $1B Smuggling Case." *The Ottawa Citizen*, May 26, 2000, D1/Front.

Maser, Peter. "Mohawks Regret Bloodshed at Oka, Commission Told." *The Ottawa Citizen*, May 7, 1993, A14.

Mathur, Mary E. Fleming. "Iroquois Talk, Mr. Worth: A Reply to Sol Worth's Review of You're Are on Indian Land." *American Anthropologist* 75, no. 6 (1973): 2052-2053.

Maychak, Matt. "Cuomo Denies Blame in Native Deaths." *The Toronto Star*, May 3. 1990, A1.

Mazurkewich, Karen. "Kanehsatake 270 Years of Resistance." *Playback*, September 13, 1993, F8, F15.

McAndrew, Mike. "Mohawk Casino Owner to Appeal Sentence." *The Post Standard*, February 27, 1990, B2.

"Police: Mohawk Manned Barrier." *The Post-Standard*, March 30, 1990, B3.

McAndrew, Mike and Lori Duffy. "Group Promises Bail, Testimony for Leader of Indian Force." *The Post-Standard*, July 26, 1989, A4.

McQuillan, D. Aidan. "Creation of Indian Reserves on the Canadian Prairies 1870-1885." *Geographica Review* 70, no. 4 (1980).

Mennie, James. "Inquest Witness Won't Name People Standing near Her During Oka Raid." *The Gazette*, April 21, 1993, A4.

Merrell, James H. "Some Thoughts on Colonial Historians and American Indians." *William and Mary Quarterly* 46, no. 1 (1989): 94-119.

Mihesuah, Devon A. *American Indians: Stereotypes and Realities*. Atlanta: Clarity Press Inc., 1996.

Milius, John and Larry Gross. "Geronimo - An American Legend." ed. Walter Hill. Hollywood: Columbia Pictures, 1993.

Miller, Charles. "Mohawk Pleads Guilty Tarbell Admits Having Lots." *The Post-Standard*, November 28, 1989, B1.

Minister, of Indian Affairs and Northern Development. *You Wanted to Know: Federal Programs and Services for Registered Indians*. Ottawa, Ontario, Canada: Minister of Public Works and Government Services Canada, 1999.

Ministry, Indian and Northern Affairs. *Mandate, Roles and Responsibilities*. Minister of Public Works and Government Services Canada, September 12, 2007. Accessed October 1, 2007. Available from http://www.ainc-inac.gc.ca/ai/mrr-eng.asp#ft1a.

Miracle, Brian. "A Community's Slow Simmer." *Maclean's*, September 11, 1995, 32.

Mohawk, Council of Akwesasne. "Mohawk Governments of Akwesasne Position Paper for Environmental Protection Agency's Proposed Remedial Action for General Motors Corporation Central Foundry Division Superfund Site St Lawrence County, Massena, New York." *Indian Times*, June 22, 1990, 7.

Mohawk Council of Akwesasne, GIS/OVS. "Akwesasne and Surrounding Area." In *Portable Document Format*, 2005.

Mohawk Indian History. Access Genealogy: Indian Tribal Records, 2005 2004. Accessed July 27, 2005. Available from http://www.accessgenealogy.com/native/tribes/mohawk/mohawkhist.htm.

Mohawk, John C. "Sovereignty and Common-Sense Part Ii."

Indian Times, July 6, 1990, 3.

Morehouse III, Ward. "Feuding Mohawk Groups, NY Troopers in Standoff." *Christian Science Monitor*, June 24, 1980, 5.

Morgan, Lewis Henry. *League of the Haudenosaunee, Iroquois*. Rochester: Sage & Brother, Publisher, 1851. Reprint, New York: Corinth Books, 1962.

Morgan, Lewis Henry and Elisabeth Tooker. "The Structure of the Iroquois League: Lewis H. Morgan's Research and Observations." *Ethnohistory* 28, no. 3 (1983): 141-154.

Morgan, William Thomas. "The Five Nations and Queen Anne." *The Mississippi Valley Historical Review* 13, no. 2 (1926): 169-189.

Moriarty, Rick. "Fasting for Food on the Reservation Local Mohawk Seeks Supplies for St. Regis." *The Post-Standard*, May 21, 1990, B1.

Morin, Eloise. "Warrior Leader Appears in Court." *The Toronto Star*, October 4, 1990, A12.

"Warrior Leader to Appear in Court for Bail Hearing." *The Toronto Star*, October 4, 1990, A12.

Morton, Desmond. "We Need a Royal Commission to Examine Native Claim Issues." *The Toronto Star*, September 15, 1990, D2.

Nash, Douglas Roger. *Indian Gaming*. Find Law: For Legal Professionals, January 1, 1999. Accessed February 22, 2007. Available from http://library.findlaw.com/1999/Jan/1/241489.html.

NAVTEQ, Map Data © 2007. "Oka, Qc, Canada." Mountain View, CA: Google, 2007.

Naylor, Sue Weibzahl. "Casino Owner Arrested Laughing Caught Off Reservation." *The Post-Standard*, September 22, 1989, A1.

Neighbors, Cayuga. "Land Claim Award Should Be Fought by Landowners." *The Post-Standard* 2001, 15 (Letter to the Editor).

Nelis, Karen. "Iroquois, Jesuits Try to Heal Old Wounds." *The Post-Standard*, April 6, 1990, B1.

Nemerov, Alexander. *Frederic Remington & Turn-of-the-Century America* Yale Publications in the History of Art. New Haven: Yale University Press, 1995.

Newman, Peter C. "Haunted by History's Lively Ghosts." *Maclean's*, August 6, 1990, 40.

Nichols, Michael P. with Richard C. Schwartz. "Bowen Family Systems Theory." In *The Essentials of Family Therapy*, ed. Patricia Quinlin. Boston: Allyn and Bacon, 2001.

Nonvro, Lvceo. "The Long Fall of the Mohawk Warriors." *The Mackenzie Institute*, June 1996.

Norris, Alexander. "Slanted Story Account of 1990 Standoff in Quebec Is One-Sided Loo at Mohawk Nation." *The Post-Standard*, July 5, 1992, 13.

O'Hara, Jim. "Reservation Shootings Prompt Legal, Jurisdictional Questions." *The Post-Standard*, May 4, 1990, A4.

O'Neill, Terry. "Defeat of the Mohawks: The Supreme Court Sends a Strong Message to Natives Who Want to Base Claims on Oral Histories." *Canadian Business and Current Affairs*, June 25, 2001, 32-33.

O'Neil, Theresa D. "Telling About Whites, Talking About Indians: Oppression, Resistance, and Contemporary American Indian Identity." *Cultural Anthropology* 9, no. 1 (1994): 94-126.

Officer, Lawrence H. and Lawrence B. Smith. "The Canadian-American Reciprocity Treaty of 1855 to 1866." *The Journal of Economic History* 28, no. 4 (1968): 598-623.

Onondaga Nation: People of the Hill. Onondaga Nation, 2007. Accessed November 27, 2007. Available from http://www.onondaganation.org/gov/chiefs.html.

Ontario Provincial Police: Provincial Business Plan 2005. Orilla, Ontario, Canada: Ontario Provincial Police, 2005.

Osborn, William M. *The Wild Frontier: Atrocities During the American-Indian War from Jamestown Colony to Wounded Knee.* New York: Random House, 2000.

Overview: New York State Police. New York State Police, April 30, 2001. Accessed June 5, 2007. Available from http://www.troopers.state.ny.us/Introduction/Overview/.

Parker, Arthur C. *The Code of Handsome Lake, the Seneca Prophet.* sacred-text.com, 2001 1913. Accessed May 3 2003. Internet. Available from www.sacred-texts.com.

Parmenter, Jon William. "Pontiac's War: Forging New Links in the Anglo-Iroquois Covenant Chain, 1758-1766." *Ethnohistory* 44, no. 4 (1997): 617-654.

Parry, Thomas. "Shooting Worries Police on Reserve." *The Globe and Mail*, January 29, 1990.

Pellerin, Adamsun. Lyn and Mary Jo. "No Treaties Mentioned in Dispute." *The Globe and Mail*, June 21, 1980.

Perley, Warren. "Mohawks Threaten War over Cigarette Seizures." *United Press International*, October 14, 1988.

Peters, Margaret. "Letter to the Editor." *Indian Time*, June 22, 1990, 2.

(Konwakeri). "Dear Mrs. Sunday." *The Indian Times*, June 15, 1990, 2.

Peters, Theodore J. "What Is the Future of Akwesasne?" *Indian Time*, June 22, 1990, 2.

Peterson, Iver. "Cayugas Change Stance on Casinos." *New York Times*, May 9, 2003, New York/Region.

Petros, Elizabeth C. "Cops Would Enter Reservation, Ok or Not." *The Post-Standard*, September 8, 1989, A4.

"Cuomo Vows to Help End St. Regis Reservation Conflict." *The Post-Standard*, August 15, 1989, A5.

"Facing Camps Stick to Vigils Reservation Remains Quiet, Tense as Police, Mohawks Keep Distance." *The Post-Standard*, July 26, 1989, A1.

"Mohawks Forming Auxiliary Police Force." *The Post-Standard*, November 22, 1989, A9.

"Police Lift St. Regis Blockade." *The Post-Standard*, October 10, 1989, B1.

"Shots Fired at St. Regis Newspaper." *The Post-Standard*, November 14, 1989, B1.

"St. Regis Leaders Urge Restraint During Conflict." *The Post-Standard*, August 31, 1989, B1.

"State Police Facing $3.34 Million St. Regis Bill." *The Post-Standard*, November 27, 1989, B1.

"State Police Say Warriors Ok Not Needed Troopers Will Enter Reservation If Called." *The Post-Standard*, September 8, 1989, B1.

"State Searching for Ways to Offset St. Regis Expenses." *The Post-Standard*, November 26, 1989, C1.

"Warriors Denounce Weekend Violence at Reservation." *The Post-Standard*, October 12, 1989, B1.

Petros, Liz and Janis Barth. "St. Regis Reservation Sealed Off Following Gambling Raid Armed Indians Fend Off Troopers near Massena." *The Post-Standard*, July 21, 1989, B1.

Picard, Andre and Patricia Poirier. "Residents, Police Clash near Mercier Bridge More Tear Gas, Arrests Mark Second Night of Violence." *The Globe and Mail*, August 14, 1990.

Pitz, Henry C. *Frederic Remington: 173 Drawings and Illustrations*. New York: Dover Publications Inc., 1972.

Platiel, Rudy. "Reserve Reaps High Stakes Indians Hit Jackpot on Bingo." *Globe and Mail*, July 25 1985.

"Mohawks Reject Deal on Self-Rule Mercredi Told He Lacks Authority to Make Pact with Premiers on Native Rights." *The Globe and Mail*, August 22, 1992.

Preston, Phil. *A Note on Education*. Indian Time, April 1, 2004. Accessed July 15, 2006. Vol. 22, No. 13. Available from http://members.aol.com/miketben1/cc9.htm.

Priest, Lisa and Darcy Henton. "14 Mohawks Arrested in $1 Million Drug Raid." *The Toronto Star*, May 10, 1990, A1.

"Police Arrest 21 Mohawks, Seize Weapons in Drug Raid." *The Toronto Star*, May 11, 1990, A3.

Prince, J. Dyneley. "Some Forgotten Indian Place-Names in the Adirondacks." *The Journal of American Folklore* 13, no. 49 (1900): 123-128.

Raymo, Denise A. "St. Regis Mohawk Reservation - to Follow the Players Involved in Getting People over the American/Canadian Border for the Organization of the Americas Summit, You May Need a Scorecard and a Good Map." *The Associated Press State & Plattsburgh Press-Republican*, April 19, 2001, State and Region.

"Akwesasne Leaders Preach Involvement." *Plattsburgh Press-Republican*, July 2, 2003.

Reguly, Eric. "Military Metal Piling up on U.S. Side of Akwesasne." *The Financial Post*, April 24, 1992, 11.

Reilly, Jim. "Residents Flee Powder Keg St. Regis Still Calm, for Now." *The Post-Standard*, May 3, 1990, A1.

"A Mohawk Homecoming Indians from Akwesasne Start a New Life in Their Valley." *The Post-Standard*, November 7, 1993, A1.

Remington, Frederic. *The Collected Writings of Frederic Remington*, ed. Peggy and Harold Samuels. Garden City, New Jersey: Doubleday, 1979.

Reuters. "Canada's Military Prepares Move against Mohawks at Barricades." *New York Times*, August 29, 1990, 12.

"Officer Dies as Mohawk Indians, Quebec Police Fight Fierce Battle." *St Petersburg Times*, July 12, 1990, 20A.

Richman, Alan. "15 Traditionalists Serving 3-Year Terms," *New York Times*, August 31, 1979, 2.

"50 to 200 Upstate NYS Mohawk Indians, Traditionalists Who Refuse to Concede Sovereignty over Land to State." *New York Times*, August 29, 1979, 4.

Richter, Daniel K. "War and Culture: The Iroquois Experience." *William and Mary Quarterly* 40, no. 4 (1983): 528-559.

"Cultural Brokers and Intercultural Politics: New York - Iroquois Relations, 1664-1701." *Journal of American History* 75, no. 1 (1988): 40-67.

Rickard Sr., Joseph. *Sovereignty Undermined by Forced Citizenship and Restricted Passage Leads to Formation of Indian IDLA*. Niagara Falls, NY: Indian Defense League of America, 2001.

Roberts, Harold and Sean MacGregor. "Cry Blood, Apache." ed. Jack Starrett. Hollywood: Goldstone, 1970.

Rollins, Peter C. and John E. O'Connor eds. *Hollywood's Indian: The Portrayal of the Native American in Film*. Lexington: The University Press of Kentucky, 1998.

Rosenberger, Gary. "Armed Patrols Guard against Violence by Security Force." *United Press International*, August 30, 1989.

"Indian Editor Defies Threats." *UPI*, September 25, 1989.

Ross, Elizabeth. "Without Job Options, Mohawk Reservation Unstable." *Christian Science Monitor*, May 18, 1990, 8.

Roundpoint, Russel; Director. *Akwesasne.Ca*. Mohawk Council of Akwesasne, 2007. Accessed September 2007. Available from http://www.akwesasne.ca/.

Royal Canadian Mounted Police: Historical Highlights. Minister of Public Works and Government Services Canada, February 22, 2007. Accessed June 8, 2007. Available from http://www.rcmp-grc.gc.ca/history/highlights_e.htm#Expansion.

Rudolf, Alan and Robert Altman. "Buffalo Bill and the Indians or Sitting Bull's History Lesson." ed. Robert Altman. Hollywood: United Artist, 1976.

Rugenstein, Ernest R. "Remembering the Busloads from Rochester to Akwesasne." Troy, NY: Self-published, 2006.

Rushlo, Michelle. "Navajo Court Rules It Has Jurisdiction over Indians from All Tribes." *The Associated Press State & Local Wire*, May 13, 1999.

Sack, Kevin. "Cuomo Urges Internal Police for Mohawks." *New York Times*, May 8, 1990, B4.

Salant, Jonathan D. "Mohawk Chief Critical of Gm's Toxic Study." *The Post-Standard*, June 23, 1988, B1.

"St. Regis to Have Its Own Police, Courts If Senate, House Ok Funds." *The Post-Standard*, August 1, 1989, A4.

Samuel, Terence. "NY Mail Bombing Suspects Shared Cruel History." *Times-Picayune*, April 17, 1994, A14.

Sandefur, Gary D. "American Indian Migration and Economic Opportunities." *International Migration Review* 20, no. 1 (1986): 55-68.

Scanlon, Scott. "Troopers. Mohawks to Discuss Renewed Patrol Service." *The Post-Standard*, August 27, 1989, E1.

Schneider, Doug. "Police Report Quiet Night." *The Post-Standard*, May 5, 1990, A1.

Schneider, Keith. "Efforts Revive River but Not Mohawk Life." *The New York Times*, June 6, 1994, B1.

Sheremata, Davis. "Reserve Life Has Its Privileges: An Ontario Judge Rules That Mohawks Can Shop Duty-Free." *Canadian Business and Current Affairs*, July 28, 1997, 24-25.

"Reserve Life Has Its Privileges: An Ontario Judge Says Mohawks Can Shop Duty-Free." *Canadian Business and Current Affairs*, July 21, 1997, 31.

Shumway, J. Matthew and Richard H. Jackson. "Native American Population Patterns." *Geographical Review* 85, no. 2 (1995): 185-201.

Siblin, Eric. "Mohawks Warn They'll Resist Shipment: Vow to Use Every Means Possible to Stop Radioactive Material from Passing through Territory." *The Gazette*, October 2, 1999, A4.

Skdders, Margie. *Letter to Friends of the Akwesasne Freedom School*. Rooseveltown, NY: Akwesasne Freedom School, 1990.

Slowe, Peter M. "The Geography of Borderlands: The Case of the Québec-Us Borderlands." *Geographical Journal* 157, no. 2 (1991): 191-198.

Smith, Erminnie A. "The Customs and Language of the Iroquois." *The Journal of the Anthropological Institute of Great Britain and Ireland* 14 (1885): 244-253.

Smith, Robert L. "Iroquois Treasures Returning Home under Order of Congress, Museums Are Returning Sacred Objects Belonging to Native Americans." *The Post Standard*, July 5, 1996, C1.

Smothers, Ronald. "Bill Introduced." *New York Times*, March 17, 1976, 42.

"Bill Is Introduced in NYS Legis, for 9th Time in 9 Yrs, Aimed at Authorizing State to Return 5 Ceremonial Wampum Belts." *New York Times*, March 17, 1976, 42.

Solter, Aletha, Ph.D. *Tears and Tantrums: What to Do When Babies and Children Cry*. Goleta, CA.: Shining Star Press, 1998.

Southam, News. "Further Raid on Reserve Could Lead to Violence, Ottawa Told." *The Toronto Star*, October 18, 1988, A17.

"Wanted Warrior Reported Ready to Surrender." *The Toronto Star*, October 1, 1990, A9.

Southamstar, Network. "Mohawks Start Sign War on Roads through Reserve." *Toronto Star*, July, 23 1992, A10.

SPCL. "300 Indians Defy New York State Authority." *The Globe and Mail*, November 19, 1979.

Spencer, Gary. "State Police Cleared by Judge of Not Protecting Bar Owners." *New York Law Journal*, December 12, 1989, 1.

"Police Overtime Rejected in Mohawk Gunfight." *New York Law Journal*, August 19, 1992, 1.

"Seizure of Liquor Bound for Reservation Is Upheld." *New York Law Journal*, January 5, 1996, 1.

St. Regis, Mohawk Tribe. *Tribal History*. St. Regis, Mohawk Tribe, 2004. Accessed February 25, 2007. Available from http://srmt-nsn.gov/his.htm.

Staff. "Attempt to Settle Dispute between Mohawks and Canada over Customs Duties." *New York Times*, January 18, 1969, 15.

"Sheriff's Deputies Break Down Nailed up Doors." *New York Times*, February 23, 1969, 59.

"Trials Begin for 7 Mohawk Indians." *The New York Times*, March 26, 1969, 4.

"Iroquois Confed Leaders in Albany, NY." *New York Times*, April 17, 1970, 40.

"Tuscarora Indians Get Court Permit to Evict Non-Indian Families." *New York Times*, September 1, 1970, 24.

"Bill Signed for Wampum Belts to Be Returned." *New York Times*, July 2, 1971, 17.

"Series of Bills to Strengthen Treaty Rights of Reservation Indians." *New York Times*, March 11, 1971, 44.

"Iroquois Confederacy Grand Council Meeting Determines Bones Should Be Reinterred at Onondaga Reservation, NY." *New York Times*, August 6, 1972, 48.

"300 Indians Defy New York State Authority." *The Globe and Mail*, November 10, 1979, Canada.

"Armed Mohawk Factions Settle into Uneasy Peace." *New York Times*, June 16, 1980, B1.

"Besieged Mohawk Faction Resists Tribal Majority." *The New York Times*, June 2, 1980, B3.

"Saint Regis Reservation, N.Y., June 10 - Tension Remained High Today after a Series of Confrontations between Mohawk Indians and New York State Police Officers." *The New York Times*, June 11, 1980, B2.

"Ontario Mohawks Threaten to Seize Government Boat." *The Toronto Star*, June 3, 1988, A23.

"Anti-Casino Violence Breaks Out." *United Press International*, October 15, 1989.

"For the Record Tribe Files Suit." *The Globe and Mail*, May 31, 1989.

"Natives Fear Bloody War over Casinos." *The Toronto Star*, September 2, 1989, A1.

"Police Close Road as Mohawks Clash." *The Toronto Star*, September 3, 1989, A14.

"Reservation Violence." *The Washington Post*, October 10, 1989, A5.

"Signing of E.P.A.-Indian Agreement Slated." *United Press International*, March 27, 1989, Domestic News.

"We Have Witnessed the Corruption of Young People by These Businesses." *The Post-Standard*, July 28, 1989, B3.

"2 Men Arrested at Checkpoint." *The Post-Standard*, June 23, 1990, B1.

"3 Mohawks Plead Innocent to Assault." *The Post-Standard*, November 28, 1990, B1.

"11 More Hunted after Reserve Raids." *The Toronto Star*, May 11, 1990, A30.

"Bad Week for Warriors and Smugglers." *Indian Time*, June 22, 1990, 1.

"Barriers Are Down in Mohawk Dispute in Quebec." *New York Times*, August 30, 1990, 9.

"Canadian, U.S. Police Rush to Restore Peace in Indian Reserve." *The Xinhua News Agency*, May 2,

1990.

"The Cult of the MSSF: Tatics on Terrorism." *Indian Time*, June 22, 1990, 1.

"Drugs Seized on Reservation." *St. Petersburg Times*, May 11, 1990, 10A.

"Escalating U.S.-Canadian Indian Conflict Claims First Life." *The Xinhua General Overseas News Service*, May 1, 1990, Item No: 0501068.

"Evacuees Back to Canada-U.S. Indian Reserve as Violence Ends." *The Xinhua General Overseas News Service*, May 4. 1990.

"Gambling Fight Continues." *The Toronto Star*, March 26, 1990, A8.

"Indian Chiefs, Warriors Split over Oka Land." *The Toronto Star*, July 27, 1990, A11.

"Indian Missing since Gun Battle Found Alive." *United Press International*, April 28, 1990, Domestic News, BC Cycle.

"Indians Meet on Recent Violence." *The Post Standard*, March 8, 1990, B1.

"Man Accused of Phone Threats." *The Post-Standard*, April 23, 1990, B1.

"Many Chiefs, a Legal Maze." *USA Today*, May 3, 1990, 3A.

"Mohawk Editor Charged in Gambling War Slaying." *UPI*, May 14, 1990.

"Mohawk Gambling Dispute Erupts." *Facts on File World News Digest*, May 4, 1990, 330 B2.

"Mohawk Violence Escalates; Two Killed in Gun Battles." *United Press International*, May 1, 1990, Domestic News.

"Mohawks Reinforced Position at Disputed Site." *New York Times*, July 13, 1990, 4.

"Mohawks Stop Governor's Police and Gambling Bills." *Indian Time*, July 6, 1990, 1.

"Mohawks Vow to Blow Bridge If Any Natives Hurt by Police." *The Toronto Star*, July 12, 1990, A13.

"Murder Charges." *Maclean's*, May 28, 1990, 15.

"Native Charged with Murder in U.S.-Canada Indian Reserve." *The Xinhua News Agency*, May 15, 1990.

"New York - Hogansburg." *USA Today*, April 30, 1990, 7A.

"Ottawa Gesture to Mohawks." *New York Times*, July 28 1990, 2.

"Police Bring Calm to Embattled Canada-U.S. Indian Reserve." *The Xinhua News Agency*, May 3, 1990.

"Police Cars Overturned at Akwesasne." *The Toronto Star*, September 4, 1990, A3.

"Police Raid Possible to Stop Renewed Gambling on Reserve." *The Toronto Star*, October 22, 1990, A11.

"Police Say Man Rammed Officer." *The Post-Standard*, April 5, 1990, B1.

"Police Blockade Mohawk Territory after Helicopter Shooting." *The Associated Press*, March 31, 1990, Domestic News.

"Quebec Judge to Decide on Bail for 22 Warriors." *The Toronto Star*, October 5, 1990, A12.

"Raid." *Maclean's*, May 21, 1990, 17.

"Report: Mohawks Cornered by Army." *The Post-Standard*, September 8, 1990, B1.

"Several Shots Fired at Van." *The Post Standard*, February 3, 1990, B1`.

"Taking over the Nation: Tactics on Terrorism." *The Indian Times*, June 15, 1990, 1.

"Talks Await 24 Observers Taking Posts at Barricades." *The Toronto Star*, August 15, 1990, A2.

"Under Siege." *Maclean's*, July 23, 1990, 19.

"Warrior's Words Call for Execution." *Indian Times*, July 6, 1990, 1.

"Court Refuses to Uphold Election of Three Mohawks." *The Ottawa Citizen*, September 14, 1991, A18.

"European Criticism." *Maclean's*, January 28, 1991, 13.

"Mike Mitchell." *The Toronto Star*, May 10, 1991, A23.

"Mohawk Youths Attack Police Station." *The Associated Press*, October 31, 1991.

"Oka Recalled." *Maclean's*, July 22, 1991, 11.

"Slot Machine Owners Sought Police Discovered 20 Gambling Devices in a Van at the St. Regis Reservation." *The Post-Standard*, October 31, 1991, B1.

"Troopers Accuse Man of Smuggling Five Aliens across Border." *The Post-Standard*, November 19, 1991, B1.

"Bitterness on the Mohawk Reserve." *The Financial Post*, April 1, 1992, 38.

"Police Resume Searching for Man in Trooper Assault." *The Pot-standard*, November 11, 1992, B1.

"Retired State Trooper to Lead Independent Mohawk Police Force." *The Post-Standard*, June 12, 1992, B3.

"St. Regis Expense Persists." *The Post-Standard*, January 22, 1992, B2.

"Community-Driven Prevention: A Step in Process toward Native Self-Government." *Canadian Business and Current Affairs Journal*, April 2, 1993, 12.

"Smuggling Dividing Community of Akwesasne." *Canadian Business and Current Affairs*, November 21, 1993, 10.

"Speaker to Discuss Environmental Project at Mohawk Reservation." *The Post-Standard*, April 14, 1993, B2.

"Violence Mounts over Smuggling." *Canadian Business and Current Affairs*, November 7, 1993, 16.

"What Are SQ Officers Afraid Of?; Inquiry into Oka Crisis Should Proceed Unfettered." *The Gazette*, November 13, 1993, B4.

"Bloc Trying to Discredit Indians: Mohawks." *Canadian Business and Current Affairs*, March 13, 1994, 2.

"No Thanks for the Memories: Forgetful Mohawks Stymie an Oka Coroner's Inquest (Marcel Lemay Inquest)." *Canadian Business and Current Affairs*, February 14, 1994, 28-29.

"Patterns of Disease Prove Perplexing." *The Ottawa Citizen*, July 3, 1994, A7.

"Assigning the Blame." *Maclean's*, August 28, 1995, 23.

"Canada's Natives Get Bank of Their Own." *The Daily Record*, December 10, 1996, 2.

"Judges Consider Mohawks' Appeal Bid." *The Gazette*, September 14, 1996, A3.

"Oka-Crisis Mediator Dies." *The Gazette*, October 22, 1996, A3.

"Smuggling of Illegal Immigrants Rising, Us Cops Say." *Canadian Business and Current Affairs*, October 4, 1996.

"Road from Oka Finally Leads Mohawk 'Lasagna' Cross to Jail." *The Ottawa Citizen*, May 21, 1997, A3.

"Native Threats on Tobacco." *The Gazette*, June 18, 1998, B2.

"New York Military Operation Still in Effect: 'Gallant Piper' for Use against Indigenous Peoples." *Mohawk Nation News*, March 7, 1998, http://www.mohawknationnews.com/.

"Museum Returns Native Artifacts." *Associated Press*, November 12, 1999.

"Project Okidd - Akwesasne Mohawk Police Cornwall Regional Task Force (Federal Enforcement Unit)." *Canada Newswire*, June 9. 1999.

"Mohawk Tribal Council Takes Control of Casino." *The Buffalo News*, April 19, 2000, A8.

Montreal Gazette. "Road from Oka Finally Leads Mohawk 'Lasagna' Cross to Jail." *The Ottawa Citizen*, May 21, 1997, A3.

Stewart, Edison. "Natives, Unity Panel Wrangle over Self-Rule." *Toronto Star*, January 9, 1992, A9.

Stith, Barbara. "3 St. Regis Chiefs Agree to Trooper Presence." *The Post-Standard*, May 10, 1990, B4.

"4 Mohawks Questioned in Killing 2 St. Regis Police Officers, 2 Others Held in Canada." *The Post Standard*, May 14, 1990, A1.

"$78 Million Cleanup Unveiled for Gm." December 20, 1990, C1.

"Bill Would Authorize Tribal Police Forces." *The Post-Standard*, June 28, 1990, A1.

"Canadian Mohawks Close Council Office." *The Post Standard*, March 21, 1990, B1.

"Chief Claims Investigation Politically Motivated." *The Post Standard*, March 9, 1990, B1.

"Chronology: How Tensions Reached Boiling Point." *The Post-Standard*, May 2, 1990, A12.

"Indians Block Roads 3 Hurt." *The Post Standard*, March 24 1990, A3.

"Leaders Consider Closing Canadian Reservation." *The Post Standard*, March 7 1990, B1.

"Lift Roadblock, but Vow to Remain on Reservation." *The Post-Standard*, May 26, 1990, A3.

"Mohawks Situation Called Worst in Decades." *The Post Standard*, March 14, 1990, B1.

"Mohawks Want Vote to Resolve Conflicts." *The Post Standard*, March 17, 1990, B1.

"Non-Indians Erect Barrier to Protest Unrest at St. Regis." *The Post Standard*, April 20, 1990, B1.

"Possible St. Regis Closure Angers Merchants." *The Post Standard*, March 16, 1990, B1.

"Searchers. Police Find No Clues for Missing Man." *The Post-Standard*, April 27, 1990, B1.

"St. Regis Mohawks Find Environment a Unifying Issue." *The Post-Standard*, February 25, 1990, C1.

"Traffic Flows While Mohawks Discuss Proposed Blockade." *The Post Standard*, March 14, 1990, B1.

"Trooper Busy with Roadblocks." *The Post Standard*, April 19, 1990, B3.

"Trooper Accused of Brutality However, State Police Say Officer Was Hurt While Trying Make an Arrest at the St. Regis Reservation." *The Post-Standard*, November 22, 1991, B1.

"Troopers Find Slot Machines at St. Regis." *The Post-Standard*, September 12, 1991, B1.

"Troopers to Stay Cuomo Wants to Station 72 at St. Regis." *The Post-Standard*, February 1, 1991, B1.

Stockland, Peter. "Smoking Guns; Plan to Combat Smuggling on Reserves Will Lead to Violence, Native Leader Says." *The Toronto Sun*, February 4, 1994, 7.

Stuart, Charles. "A Crisis of Hegemony: An Analysis of Media Discourse." University of Ottawa, 1993.

Taiaiake Alfred, Ph.D. and Lana Lowe, M.A. "Warrior Societies in Contemporary Indigenous Communities." University of Victoria, 2005.

Taylor, Bill. "Heavily Armed Mohawks Overrun Cornwall Reserve." *The Toronto Star*, April 26, 1990, A2.

Terrell, Kenneth. "Duo Singing the Blues over Environment the Indigo Girls Say Native Americans Face Risks Caused by Environmental Racism." *The Post-Standard*, September 10, 1997, B5.

The Alcoa Foundation, Hall of American Indians. *Handsome Lake*. Carnegie Museum of Natural History, June 6, 1998. Accessed October 5, 2007. Available from http://www.carnegiemnh.org/exhibits/north-south-east-west/iroquois/handsome_lake.html.

The Lillian Goldman Law Library. *The Avalon Project*. Yale Law School, 2005 1996. Accessed March 3, 2006. Internet. Available from http://www.yale.edu/lawweb/avalon/avalon.htm.

Thompson, Elizabeth and Ann McLaughlin. "Warrior Leader Flees from Oka, Escapes to U.S." *The Toronto Star*, September 28, 1990, A12.

Thornton, Martin, Roy Todd, D.N. Collins, G. Mercer, H.N. Nicholson, and D.S. Wall. *Aboriginal People and Other Canadians: Shaping New Relationships*. Ottawa: University of Ottawa-Université D'Ottawa, 2001.

Thornton, Russell. "Aboriginal North American Population and Rates of Decline, Ca. A.D. 1500-1900." *Current Anthropology* 38, no. 2 (1997): 310-315.

Tierney, Christine. "Indians Battle Police Over Sacred Tribal Land." *The San Francisco Chronicle*, July 12, 1990, A1.

Tierney, John. "Mohawks Mourn Victim of Reservation Violence." *New York Times*, May 7, 1990, B2.

"Mohawks' Border World of Violence and Tradition." *The New York Times*, May, 5 1990, 1.

Tiller, Veronica E. Velarde. *Tillers Guide to Indian Country*.
Akwesasne Freedom School, 1996. Accessed October 12, 2004. Available from http://www.cradleboard.org/sites/akwesasn.html.

Tomsho, Robert. "Dumping Grounds: Indian Tribes Contend with Some of the Worst of America's Pollution." *Wall Street Journal*, November 29, 1990, A1.

Torres-Rouff, Christina, and Marìa Antonietta Costa Junqueira. " Interpersonal Violence in Prehistoric San Pedro De Atacama, Chile: Behavioral Implications of Environmental Stress." *American Journal of Physical Anthropology* 130, no. 1 (2006): 60-70.

Toulin, Alan. "MPs Block Bid to Make Reserve Bank Centre." *The Toronto Star*, December 3, 1987, A3.

Treaty of Ghent (1814). Vol. 2 Treaties and Other International Acts of the United States of America: Documents 1-40: 1776-1818, ed. Hunter Miller. Washington: Government Printing Office, 1931.

"Treaty with the Mohawk." In *7 Stat., 61.*, 1797.

"Treaty with the Seven Nations of Canada." In *7 Stat., 55*, 1796.

"Treaty with the Six Nations." In *7 Stat., 15*, 1784.

Trelease, Allen W. *Indian Affairs in Colonial New York: The Seventeenth Century.* Ithaca: Cornell University Press, 1960. Reprint, Lincoln: University of Nebraska Press, 1997.

"The Iroquois and the Western Fur Trade: A Problem in Interpretation." *The Mississippi Valley Historical Review* 49, no. 1 (1962): 32-51.

Trepanier, Nathalie. "Chief Predicts "War"." *The Ottawa Sun*, November 16, 2000, 5.

Trumbull, Mark. "News Currents." *Christian Science Monitor*, June 4, 1990, 2.

U.S. Customs and Border Protection: Securing America's Borders. U.S. Customs & Border Protection, July 15, 2003. Accessed 2007 June 8, Available from http://www.customs.gov/xp/cgov/border_security/border_patrol/border_patrol_ohs/history.xml.

"United States V. Mrs. P.L. Garrow (No. 4018)." In *Treasury Decisions*, 71, 421: United States Supreme Court, 1937.

Unknown. "Iroquois Conference - Notes." ed. Iroquois Museum. Cobleskill, NY, September 23, 1990.

US Department of the Interior, Bureau of Indian Affairs. *Supreme Court Decisions: Cherokee Nation V. Georgia, 1831*. US Department of the Interior, March 26, 2006. Accessed September 14, 2007. internet.

Bureau of Indian Affairs.
Famous Indians: a collection of biographies.
Washington, D.C.: US Government Printing Office, 2000.

American Indian population and labor force report 2001 ed. Office of Tribal Services. Washington, D.C.: US Government Printing Office, 2001.

Bureau of Indian Affairs. *Tribal Leaders Directory*, ed. Division of Tribal Government Services. Washington, D.C.: US Government Printing Office, 2003.

Usborne, David. "Self-Rule Offer Fails to Win over All Aboriginals." *The Independent*, October 26, 1992, 12.

Vaughan, Alden T. "From White Man to Redskin: Changing Anglo-American Perceptions of the American Indian." *The American Historical Review* 87, no. 4 (1982): 917-953.

"From White Man to Redskin: Changing Anglo-American Perceptions of the American Indian." *The American Historical Review* 87, no. 4 (1982): 917-953.

Vecsey, Christopher and William A Starna, ed. *Iroquois Land Claims*. Syracuse: Syracuse University Press, 1988.

Verhoeven, Sam Howe. "2 Mohawks Killed in Feud over Reservation Gambling." *The New York Times*, May 2, 1990, B5.

"Indian Reservation Sealed Off after 2 Killings." *The New York Times*, May 3, 1990, B1.

"Mohawk Reserve Quiet as Officials Meet." *The New York Times*, May 4, 1990, B2.

"Mohawk Reserve Quiet as Officials Meet AEC." *New York Times*, May 4, 1990, B2.

"Mohawks Ask Cuomo to Join a Peace Effort." *New York Times*, April 28, 1990, 27.

"Standoff Ends, but Not Mohawk Defiance." *The New York Times*, April 14, 1990, 25.

"Whose Law Applies When Lawlessness Rules on Indian Land?" *New York Times*, May 6, 1990, 4.

Wallace, Paul A. W. *Conrad Weiser, 1696-1760, Friend of Colonist and Mohawk*. New York: Russell & Russell, 1971.

White Roots of Peace: The Iroquois Book of Life. Santa Fe, N.M.: Clear Light Publishers, 1994.

"Warrior's Words Call for Execution." *Indian Times: A Voice from the Eastern Door*, June 15, 1990.

Watson, Laurie. "Iroquois Confederacy to Meet over Warrior Society." *United Press International*, August 24, 1990.

Wells, Paul. "Khnawake Reserve: Talks on Self Government." *The Ottawa Citizen*, December 14, 1991, A3.

What Is the Boundary Waters Treaty? International Joint Commission, January 29, 2007. Accessed January 31, 2007. Internet. Available from http://www.ijc.org/rel/agree/water.html.

Wilson, Hugh. "Kahnawake, Que.: Cigarettes and Money." *Maclean's*, April 25, 1988, 10c.

Wire and Staff, Reports. "Insurance Briefs." *Journal of Commerce*, August 3, 1990, 9A.

Wong, Tony. "Oka Violence Wrong Strategy, U.N. Forum Told." *The Toronto Star*, September 18, 1990, A10.

Wood, Chris, E. Kaye Fulton, and Hilary Mackenzie. "Gunfire and Gambling." *Maclean's*, May. 7, 1990, 22.

Zganjar, Leslie. "Indians Agree to Set Aside Differences to Bury One of Their Own." *The Associated Press*, May 7, 1990, Domestic News.

Zielbauer, Paul. "26 Are Arrested in Drug Smuggling Network Using Mohawk Reservation." *The New York Times*, June 9, 1999, B5.

Zipperer, Joanne. "Mohawk Feud Escalates; 2 Slain." *USA Today*, May 2, 1990, 3A.

www.ingramcontent.com/pod-product-compliance
Lightning Source LLC
Chambersburg PA
CBHW060108170426
43198CB00010B/818